Daily Life SERIES 16

DAILY LIFE IN THE FRENCH THEATRE
AT THE TIME OF MOLIÈRE

Daily Life SERIES

1. DAILY LIFE IN THE TIME OF HOMER
   by Emile Mireaux

2. DAILY LIFE IN FLORENCE AT THE TIME OF THE MEDICI
   by J. Lucas-Dubreton

3. DAILY LIFE IN PERU UNDER THE LAST INCAS
   Louis Baudin

4. DAILY LIFE IN CARTHAGE AT THE TIME OF HANNIBAL
   by Gilbert and Colette Charles-Picard

5. DAILY LIFE IN RUSSIA UNDER THE LAST TSAR
   by Henri Troyat

6. DAILY LIFE IN FRANCE UNDER NAPOLEON
   by Jean Robiquet

7. DAILY LIFE IN CHINA ON THE EVE OF THE MONGOL
   INVASION
   by Jacques Gernet

8. DAILY LIFE IN 18TH CENTURY ITALY
   by Maurice Vaussard

9. DAILY LIFE IN THE KINGDOM OF THE KONGO
   by Georges Balandier

10. DAILY LIFE IN COLONIAL PERU
    by Jean Descola

11. DAILY LIFE AT VERSAILLES IN THE 17TH AND
    18TH CENTURIES
    by Jacques Levron

12. DAILY LIFE IN EARLY CANADA
    by Raymond Douville and Jacques Casanova

13. DAILY LIFE IN SPAIN IN THE GOLDEN AGE
    by Marcelin Defourneaux

14. DAILY LIFE IN PAPAL ROME IN THE 18TH CENTURY
    by Maurice Andrieux

15. DAILY LIFE IN ENGLAND IN THE REIGN OF GEORGE III
    by André Parreaux

16. DAILY LIFE IN THE FRENCH THEATRE AT THE TIME OF
    MOLIÈRE
    by Georges Mongrédien

GEORGES MONGRÉDIEN

DAILY LIFE
IN THE FRENCH
THEATRE
AT THE TIME OF MOLIÈRE

Translated by Claire Eliane Engel

London
GEORGE ALLEN AND UNWIN LTD

CONTENTS

page

PART ONE: ACTORS IN SEVENTEENTH-CENTURY
       SOCIETY
1. The Church and the Theatre   13
2. Actors and Public Opinion   27

PART TWO: THE THEATRES OF PARIS
1. An Intermittent Theatre (1598–1629)   45
2. The Royal Company at the Hôtel de Bourgogne
    (1629–1680)   56
3. The King's Company at the Theatre du Marais (1634–
    1673)   73
4. The King's Company at the Palais-Royal (1658–1673) 84
5. The King's Company at the Hôtel Guénégaud (1673–
    1680)   92
6. The Comédie-Française (1680–1700)   97
7. The Italian Comedy (1600–1686)   105
8. The Birth of Opera (1669–1673)   113
9. Theatrical Performances   121
10. How the Companies Lived   138

PART THREE: THE THEATRES IN THE PROVINCES
1. Life in the Provincial Theatres   155
2. Free Companies   160
3. Patrons   175
4. The Family Life of Actors   199

INDEX   207

ILLUSTRATIONS

facing page

1. Molière in Theatrical Costume, by Eustache Lorsay   32
2. Scaramouche. Engraving of Le Blond   33
3. The Players of the Hôtel of Bourgogne   48
4. Turlupin, a Famous French Actor of the Early Seventeenth Century   49
5a. Scene from Le Bourgeois Gentilhomme (Molière)   80
5b. Venus and Mars, by Mignard   80
6. French and Italian Comedians, 1670   81
7. The Palais-Royal. Engraving of Perelle   96
8. Théâtre de L'Opéra, Burnt Down in 1763   97
9. Molière Breakfasting with Louis XIV at Versailles   128
10. Louis XIV's Fête at Versailles. First Day   129
11. Scene from L'École des Femmes (Molière)   144
12. La Fontaine, Boileau, Molière and Racine Dining   145
13. Le Malade Imaginaire Played before Louis XIV and his Court, 1676   176
14. Scene from Le Malade Imaginaire (Molière)   177
15. Molière and his Troupe, by G. Melingue   192
16. The Travelling Comedians. Engraving of Pater   193

PART ONE

ACTORS IN SEVENTEENTH-CENTURY SOCIETY

CHAPTER ONE

THE CHURCH AND THE THEATRE

Actors have always lived in a world of their own, rather different from the world at large. The reasons are several: the way, for instance, that their profession delivers them to the judgment, the abuse or the enthusiasm of the public; the prestige of the art to which they are devoted; the curiosity aroused by their rivalries and intrigues; and today, the boundless and often scandalous publicity focused on their professional and private lives.

In the seventeenth century their social position was mainly influenced by a factor which has now fortunately disappeared: the attitude towards them of the Church, an attitude which, in a Christian society, influenced public opinion heavily. It has often been said that actors were 'excommunicated': taken literally, this is untrue. For excommunication is a sanction which severs the guilty party from the communion of the Church, and it has been pronounced according to canonical rules against a hardened sinner by a member of the ecclesiastical hierarchy, a bishop, an archbishop or the Pope. The victim, after submitting to the laws of the Church, can only be pardoned by the one who has punished him. No such sentence has ever been pronounced against any actor as such.

But excommunication *de facto* could also derive from some general rule. During the seventeenth century the Church was very hard on actors. To understand this point of view, one has to go very far back into history. In ancient Greece, plays, either tragedies or comedies, were an integral part of religious ceremony. Actors were highly respected and granted high honours. It was the same in Rome at the time of Terence, Plautus and even Seneca. But under the Empire tragedy and comedy made way for pantomimes that were often obscene, exhibitions by players of low caste, excessively licentious displays by clowns and buffoons, lascivious bacchanalian dances, circus games, fights between gladiators and the degrading scenes during which Christians were thrown to the wild beasts. It is easy to understand why the Church thought it was its duty to step in and side against such ignominious spectacles. The civil powers followed suit and the actors were taxed with infamy, which was punished by Roman law. And, from our point of view, from the accession of the Emperor Constantine, the Church and the Imperial power were one.

As the Scriptures were silent on the subject, the early Fathers of the Church, St Isidorus, St Cyprian, Tertullian, St John Chrysostom were obviously obliged to formulate a doctrine and they condemned both the theatre and the actors. They attacked public shows, not only for their frivolity, their coarseness, their cruelty, but also for their idolatry, because of their emphasis on mythological subjects and the pagan gods. Moreover, for them the stage appeared as a public training in profanity, on account of its blasphemies and its parodies of the sacraments and of the Christian martyrs. The council of Elvira in 305 was the first to compel actors to renounce their profession before being received into the Christian church. Clerics were barred from public shows, and the Council of Trent confirmed that measure.

The Barbarian invasion put an end to these scandalous spectacles. Yet it was actually in the Catholic churches themselves that the theatre was reborn with the mystery plays, which were often a mixture of scenes from the Passion and the lives of saints, interspersed with indecent clowning and displays by dancers and tumblers. A number of bas-reliefs on our cathedrals survive to prove that such an unsavoury mixture did not displease our forebears. Similar shows took place, moreover, in monasteries.

In 1598 Charles VI of France sanctioned the creation of the Confraternity of the Passion to perform mysteries, and at the same time new divines like Albertus Magnus, St Thomas and St Bonaventure accepted the theatre, provided it kept within the limits of decency, and they stopped condemning the actors. St Thomas wrote that *'ludus est necessarius ad conservationem humanae vitae'* (play is necessary to the conservation of human life). He forcibly states that actors *'non sunt in statu peccati, dummodo moderate ludo utantur'*. It was the lay administration which, in accordance with the rules laid down by the early Councils, banned the performances of sacred mysteries in the sixteenth century, but allowed profane plays, provided they were 'honest and lawful'.

Early in the seventeenth century the Roman ritual of Pope Paul V appeared, which contained no condemnation in principle

14

of the stage or of actors. For a long time, moreover, the Vatican had had its own theatre. But the Gallican church was bent on maintaining the older rules, at least in certain dioceses.

A minute study of French rituals made by M. Jean Dubu enables us to see things more clearly. The Orléans ritual (1642) simply excluded actors from holy orders. The Roman ritual had denied communion, the right to stand as godparents, and to Christian burial, to *concubinarii*, *foeneratores* (usurers), *magi*, *sortilegi*, *blasphemi*. A few rituals, among which was Gondi's for the diocese of Paris, slyly added *comoedi*. But there was no question of excommunication, since the ritual very definitely stated: '*nisi de eorum poenitentia et emendatione constet, et publico scandalo prius satisfecerint*'. The parish priest was sole judge of the sinner's repentance.

It was the publication of the *Actae Ecclesiae Mediolanensis* by Cardinal Federico Borromeo, Archbishop of Milan and St Carlo Borromeo's cousin, which marked a return to older rules. In 1664 was published the *Traité contre les danses et les comédies* (A treatise against the use of dances and comedies), a translation of St Carlo Borromeo's work, dedicated to the Princess de Conti, whose husband was soon to be found among those who opposed the theatre. This translation had distorted the author's ideas. It appeared as a polemical work, placing the saint in opposition to the Bishop of Geneva, St Francis de Sales, who was favourable to dancing and acting. Through a blatant interpolation, what St Carlo Borromeo had written against dancing was applied also to comedies; moreover, he had only condemned them on Sundays and feast days. Hence developed a kind of rivalry between bishops, some of them siding with the indulgent St Thomas Aquinas and others with the strict St Carlo Borromeo.

Several bishops imitated the Archbishop of Paris by inserting in their rituals the exclusion against actors. Nicholas Pavillon, Bishop of Aleth and a member of the Company of the Holy Sacrament, inserted a general condemnation of the theatre as 'an opportunity for immediate sin' and denied the Eucharist to actors, clowns and mountebanks. His ritual was placed on the index by Rome but was revived the following year with the approval of twenty-six French bishops who had adopted the same attitude. But other bishops refused to insert this clause: actors are not mentioned in the rituals of Reims (1677), Langres (1679), Périgueux (1680), Coutances (1682), Amiens (1687), Agen (1688)

15

and Chartres (1689). It can be seen that such a condemnation was far from general in France. On the other hand, the Metz ritual, much later (1713), was very hard on those who '*spectaculis quibuslicet quovis modo inserviunt, sive in scena, sive alio quovis modo*'. Consequently, not only were actors excluded from sacraments, but also all those who had anything to do with the stage: stage hands, decorators, dressers, wig-makers, composers and even bill-stickers!

Linked with this attitude, taken by some prelates, a quarrel concerning the theatre, which led to violent polemics, promoted and encouraged by Jansenists and the Company of the Holy Sacrament and supported by Protestants, raged through the greater part of the seventeenth century. We shall later record its various episodes, but we may emphasize here in passing that it was only through a faulty interpretation of the texts that one could apply to the plays of Corneille, Racine and Molière and to the actors of the Hôtel de Bourgogne or of the Palais-Royal the old canons against the gladiators and saturnalian mountebanks.

However a large number of bishops kept in their rituals the condemnation of actors and other public sinners. Faced with this condemnation in principle, we must now consider what was, in practice, the attitude of the Church towards actors.

After the dramatic works of Théophile de Viau, Mairet, du Ryer, Scudéry and Rotrou were published, which truly represented a literary renaissance in the theatre, leading in 1636 to the triumph of *Le Cid* and continuing without interruption until about 1680, the theatre was now a social fact and a fashion, thanks to public enthusiasm. It was patronized by the highest authorities. Cardinal de Richelieu had an enthusiasm for the drama and built a *théâtre* in the Palais Cardinal in 1630, where *Mirame* was performed, together with plays written by the five dramatists who were in his pay. It was the Cardinal who started the quarrel which raged about *Le Cid* by submitting Corneille's play to the judgment of the French Academy. After him Cardinal Mazarin—another prince of the Church—introduced Italian opera to France at considerable cost in production and machinery. Later, the young Louis XIV, who was a keen enthusiast for plays and ballets, in which he even danced himself, maintained several companies of actors. At the court theatre no one was shocked to see a bench reserved for the bishops, on which Bossuet himself was not afraid to take a seat. Princes and wealthy commoners invited the King's actors to their houses to give greater lustre to the entertainment they offered their guests. The audience would queue up at the gates of the Hôtel de Bourgogne, the Théâtre du Marais or the Palais-Royal.

Futhermore, the civil powers also took part in the 'rehabilitation' of the actors, who in the eyes of the public were now accepted as genuine artists, with nothing in common with the low clowns of the beginning of the century, and newspapers never failed to mention their successes. So Richelieu, as early as 1641, made Louis XIII sign a declaration according to which the actors were forbidden, under pain of dismissal, fine or exile, to 'represent any dishonest episode or to use lascivious words, or phrases *à double entendre*, liable to offend public decency'. Together with the renaissance of dramatic literature already mentioned, there was an effort to cleanse the theatre and make it more 'honest', so that a constantly growing public could be present without fear of being shocked by indecent words or gestures.

This royal declaration of April 16, 1641, registered by the Paris parliament, affirmed the dignity of the theatrical profession under the above-mentioned conditions: 'If actors so conduct the action on the stage that it is completely free from impurity, we desire that their activities, which can innocently divert our people from various nefarious occupations, shall not bring them any blame nor mar their reputation in public life: this we do, so that their lawful desire to avoid the reproaches hitherto lavished on them, provide them with a desire to keep within the terms of their duty in public performances, together with the dread of unavoidable penalties should they ignore this present declaration.' In consideration of which, the actor Molière could maintain his official duties as Upholsterer Royal, the director of the Hôtel de Bourgogne, Floridor, was allowed to prove his nobility, and Lulli was granted letters of nobility. Moreover, after 1680 the Dauphine herself supervised the internal affairs of the Comédie Française, engaging new actors, deciding the percentage they were entitled to, and casting parts.

It is easy to see why, with such an attitude on the part of the authorities, so far removed from the prejudices of the Church against actors, the Church had for a time to draw in its claws and tolerate what it could not prevent. Louis XIV, founder of the Royal Academy of Dancing and Music, stood as godfather to

Molière's first-born, with Madame [Henriette d'Angleterre] as god-mother; also for a son of Domenico Biancolelli, the Arlechino of the Italian company, and for a son of Lulli, who was the creator of French opera.

Even pious Anne of Austria saw no reason why she should not show a keen interest in plays, either French or Italian. When the curé of St Germain l'Auxerrois[1] reproached her for this, she decided to consult the Sorbonne. Over the signature of ten doctors, the answer was that, 'admitting that nothing was said which might cause a scandal or was contrary to morality, plays were a matter of indifference, and could be listened to without scruple; this because the attitude of the Church had much diminished from that apostolic severity which the early Christians observed in the early centuries'.

Besides, if a few actors were living dissolute lives which shocked some people, many lived 'in Christian fashion', as Chapuzeau emphasized. He cited Molière at the head of his list. He added: 'An honest man is an honest man everywhere.'

Consequently, there is no reason to be surprised if during the whole period the Church, in spite of *antiquiores canones*, refrained from worrying the actors, who were enjoying such manifold and high patronage and were acclaimed by the public everywhere. When rituals were too strict, they were simply ignored.

It was sometimes possible to observe a real understanding between actors and members of the clergy. For instance, in 1660, to celebrate the Peace of the Pyrenees, the actors of the Hôtel de Bourgogne had a mass sung at St Sauveur and, when the religious ceremony was over, the journalist Lovret tells us that:

> *Le curé, prêtres et vicaires,*
> *Chantres, comédiens et moi,*
> *Criâmes tous: Vive le roi!*
> *La troupe des chantres ensuite,*
> *Dans un cabaret fur conduite*
> *Où messieurs les musiciens*
> *Par l'ordre des comédiens,*
> *Furent pur achever la fête,*
> *Traités à pistole par tête,*
> *Où l'on but assez pur trois jours.*[2]

[1] The parish church of the Louvre.

[2] The vicar, priests and curates, precentors, actors and I shouted together: 'Long live the King!' And then the choristers were taken to a tavern where, on

18

There was peace between priests and actors.

On examining the parish archives of any diocese, ample proof can be found that, not only did itinerant players, according to the hazards of their wanderings, have no difficulty in getting their children christened, with members of the company standing as godparents, but they also had no trouble about marrying in church, and they were granted Christian burial. The whole company signed the certificate, so that the curé could not pretend ignorance of the matter. Very often, the profession of player of the bridal couple or of the deceased was actually mentioned in the certificate. At most, some timid curés replaced the mention of *comédien du roi* by the vaguer phrase of *officier du roi*. An interesting instance is the baptism of the Beauvals' son, which took place in Rennes on July 3, 1667: the godfather was a priest and the godmother an actress, Philandre's own wife. Moreover, the clergy never regarded the tax which they levied for the poor on the dour-money as unholy.

It is interesting to note that, while the Church was, on the whole, fairly broad-minded, provincial Parliaments were stricter and even more hostile towards actors. The Parliament of Britanny drove strolling companies away from Rennes in 1606 and 1619. On the other hand, at Dijon in 1667, we find the contrary: the Parliament of Burgundy defended a company of players against the Mayor and the Intendant, who both wanted to drive them off. But this was the Prince de Condé's troop, and he was Governor of Dijon.

The one notable incident which took place at that time between the Church and the players was when Molière died. It is well known that the director of the Palais-Royal died in his house in the rue de Richelieu on February 17, 1673, at about ten in the evening, having had the greatest difficulty in completing the fourth performance of the *Malade Imaginaire* in the presence of his wife, Armande Béjart and Baron, together with two nuns. It was certainly not Molière's fault that he could not make his confession and voice the traditional renunciation of his play-acting profession. His wife stated this in the application she sent the next day to the Archbishop of Paris, adding that the dying man wanted

'to show that he repented and to die a good Christian, insisting that a priest should be fetched in order that he might receive the

the instructions of the players, they were treated to a feast at a *pistoles* apiece, so that they drank enough for three days.

Sacrament, and he several times sent his valet and his maid to St Eustache, his parish church, where they saw MM. Lenfant and Lechat, the two priests on duty, who several times refused to come, which compelled M. Jean Aubry to go himself to get one to come, and he got the so-called Paysant out of bed, who was also one of the priests on duty. All those comings and goings had taken above an hour and a half, and during that time M. Molière had died; M. Paysant arrived when he had just breathed his last. And as the said M. Molière had died without having received the sacrament of confession, and as he had just been acting in a play, the curé of St Eustache refused burial . . .'

What can we think of those two priests, called to the bedside of a man, dying but ready to repent, who had gone through the Easter ceremonies the year before, and they had refused? Was that Christian charity? However, Baron called on Louis XIV, who condescended to tell the Archbishop to settle the matter so as to avoid scandal. So the Archbishop allowed

'the curé of St Eustache to bury the body of the deceased Molière in the parish cemetery, on condition, nevertheless, that this should be without display, with only two priests present, and not in daylight, and that no ceremony shall be performed either in St Eustache or elsewhere, not even in a monastery chapel, and that this our permission shall not interfere with the rules of the ritual of our church, which we require to be observed both in the letter and the spirit'.

Thus, the author of *Le Misanthrope*, whose body had been covered with the pall of office of the Upholsterers' Guild, was buried by candlelight, almost secretly, at night and without music, at the foot of the cross in the Cemetery of St Joseph in the rue Montmartre. No member either of his family or of his company was asked to sign the death certificate in the parish register. In the days that followed a number of satirical epigrams were hurled at Molière's memory, regarded as a miscreant and an atheist. We must add that it was more as the author of *Tartuffe* or *Dom Juan* than as an actor that he had drawn to himself the wrath of the Church.

This famous incident may now be regarded as a portent of a profound change in the attitude of the Church. The whole general climate was going to change, too. The days when Louis XIV was staging stuttering pageants, plays and ballets for Mlle de la

Vallière or Mme de Montespan were over. From 1680 the King had fallen under the sway of the austere Mme de Maintenon, who thought it was her personal duty to lead the King back to God. Louis XIV practically ceased to attend plays, even those performed at court. Deeply involved in the quarrel of the stage, which we will discuss later, the clergy were ready to fight hard against the theatre; they were to revive the strict rules of the rituals against the actors which, for about half a century, in spite of the insistence of Jansenists and divines, they had thought better forgotten. The period of religious toleration was over.

The curé of St Sulpice preached against the theatre and its actors and received this firm rejoinder from Brécourt:

> *Pasteur qui nous damnez par vos sermons austères,*
> *Le sage dit qu'il est des moments pour prier,*
> *Qu'il est des temps pour rire et d'autres pour pleurer:*
> *Pourquoi nous imposer des règles si sévères?*
>
> *En vain vous nous prêchez des maximes contraires,*
> *Sur le théâtre on peut quelques fois folatre;*
> *Dans l'église on ne doit que gémir, qu'adorer;*
> *L'un est le lieu des ris et l'autre des mystères.*
>
> *Cependant chaque jour près d'un sacré pilier,*
> *On bouffonne, on cajole, on fait notre métier;*
> *Abolissez plutôt ce sacrilège exemple.*
>
> *Le Sauveur qui jadis reprima le pêchè*
> *N'empêcha pas les jeux au milieu du marché;*
> *Il ne chassa que ceux qui profanaient le Temple.*[1]

From that time on, parish priests received orders to be drastic and to compel dying actors to hand them a written renunciation of their profession before giving them the Sacrament.

[1] Pastors, who damn us in your austere sermons, think that a wise man said that there was a time to pray, a time to laugh and others to weep: why do you force such harsh rules upon us? It is useless to preach contrary texts; it is lawful sometimes to be gay on the stage. In church, we are there but to wail and adore; the one is a place for laughter, the other for mysteries. Yet, each day, near a sacred pillar, people used to laugh, caress and imitate our profession: it would be better for you to abolish this sacrilegious example. When the Saviour, in days of old, fought against sin he did not ban games on the market place: he merely drove out those who soiled the Temple.

For instance, Mlle Dupin of the Théâtre Guénégaud was a god-mother at St Jacques-du-Haut-Pas but thought it wise to hide from the curé the fact that she was an actress. Warned doubtless by some charitable soul, he wrote her these severe words:

'I cannot hide from you the deep sorrow I felt in God's name and from the bottom of my soul at the surprise I received the day before yesterday, when you concealed your profession from me when you came to present a child for baptism. I must confess that your atti-tude and your dress gave me some inkling of it, but the dread of conceiving false suspicions, and the attention you seemed to give to all that was taking place, prevented me from speaking to you. I did not want to risk being mistaken by an aspect which a per-verted age has made practically common to all women. The Church which excommunicates all those who, like you, step on the stage to act such strange characters, and deprives them, as unworthy, of the communion of the body of Jesus-Christ and all his gifts to his true children, has ruled against accepting as godparents persons of your calling. . . . I merely wish that such an opportunity may turn your thoughts on yourself and I hope it may please God to make you see in the sentence passed by the Church on your profession and your person the image of that which God will make irrevocable if you do not leave that profession and be converted.'

The actress' rejoinder was not without wit:

'As the interests of God have made you speak, do not take it amiss, monsieur, if it makes me answer and that I tell you that I am sorry for your sake if you must believe that your service is only half-hearted; had it been more ardent you would have taken the trouble to call on me to convince me, and though you may think that I am much attached to the devil, you have nothing to fear. The grace that is so strong within you would have allowed you to drive him away without the help of a stole or of holy water. What do you hope to achieve by your letter? You serve neither God nor your resentment; you do not serve God because this note is not per-suasive enough to convert me, and your resentment cannot alter the fact that the child has been baptized. So far, I had believed that only prudent persons, carefully weighing their actions, were received into the Church of God; but for a pastor with so many sheep to care for, you seem to be very hasty. . . . Until now I have lived among so many errors that I did not notice those of my profession. Perhaps you were created to make me aware of them, and your Christian zeal may not be destroyed by this encounter.'

And she signed herself: 'I am she who, despite your poor opinion, renounces the Devil, and not your very humble servant, Louise Jacob du Pin.'

In 1685, Brécourt, one of Molière's former colleagues, was about to die. The curé of St Sulpice, Claude Bottu de la Barmondière, compelled him to sign the following declaration in the presence of three priests:

'In the presence of M. Claude Bottu de la Barmondière, priest, doctor in theology at the Sorbonne, curé of the church and parish of St Sulpice, Paris, and of the witnesses named hereunder, Guillaume Marcoureau de Brécourt has acknowledged that, having hitherto been an actor, he renounces this profession entirely and promises with a true and sincere heart never to step on the stage again, even if he recovers his full health.'

Brécourt signed it and died in the arms of the Apostolic and Catholic Church, after an adventurous and far from edifying life.

Two years later, Rosimond died almost suddenly, and the curé of St Sulpice made the greatest difficulty about burying him 'and only did so because a priest assured him that in his confession he had promised to renounce the stage'. 'The burial took place at night, without a cross, without a pall, without holy water or candles, just with two priests in hats and cassocks.' And yet it seems that Rosimond had published a *Life of the Saints for all the days of the year*. In the same period, the Bishop of Séez refused Church burial to a 'clown' who had died at Alençon on August 6, 1680. Ten years later, the greatest difficulty was experienced in making the illustrious Champmeslée sign the usual declaration; she died 'in a fair state of mind, but above all very sorry to die', were the cruel words of Racine, who had been her lover. Again, in the eighteenth century Adrienne Lecouvreur was buried by the police at night, without a coffin, in a hole on the bank of the Seine.

Yet many actors, like Madeleine Béjart, included in their wills, not only legacies for the poor, but also pious gifts and they paid for masses for their souls. Moreover, companies of players not only paid a tax for the benefit of the poor, but made regular gifts to various Paris convents, as witness La Grange's accounts. Applications have even been found from various Franciscan and

Augustinian monasteries near the Comédie, humbly requesting the actor to be placed on the list of their charities, promising in return that they would pray to the Lord even more ardently for the prosperity of their very dear company.

In the same period, while fighting hard against Caffaro, who was a defender of the stage, Bossuet attacked the actors themselves in his *Maximes et Réflexions sur la Comédie*. Remembering probably the pamphlet published thirty years earlier by the curé Roullé, who had already condemned the author of *Tartuffe* to Hell, 'a fiend in the flesh and dressed like a man', Bossuet also attacked Molière with the famous curse: 'Woe to you who laugh, for you will weep!'

In his letter to Caffaro, Bossuet voiced this solemn condemnation of actresses:

'You say, Father, that in the confessions you have heard, you have never been able to detect this alleged malignity of the stage, nor the crimes it is supposed to have caused. Apparently, you don't think of those committed by actresses or singers, nor of the scandals of their lovers. Is it nothing to dedicate Christian girls to public unchastity, in a manner even more dangerous than in places I dare not name? What mother, I do not say Christian, but just averagely honest, would not prefer to see her daughter in her grave than on the stage? Has she been brought up so tenderly and with so much care for this opprobrium? Has she been kept night and day under her wings, so to speak, to be delivered thus to the public? Who does not look upon these unhappy Christian girls, if they still are, in a profession so contrary to their baptismal vows—who, as I have said, does not look upon them as slaves exposed for sale, in whom modesty has been extinguished, if only by the many eyes cast upon them and the looks they themselves return, those whose sex meant them for modesty and whose natural weakness intended them for the safety of a well-directed home?'

At this time, too, Racine, in his will, repented for 'the scandals of his past life' and forbade his son to visit the theatre. In all the churches of Paris, preachers echoed Bossuet's words. A grave threat hung over the stage. On December 23, 1694, the Palatine Princess wrote:

'We narrowly escaped having no more plays. To please the King, the Sorbonne sought to forbid them, but the Archbishop of Paris and Père la Chaise must have told him that it would be too dangerous to forbid respectable entertainment, as this would drive young people into various abominable vices. . . . As for myself, so long as they are not forbidden, I shall attend them. . . . About a fortnight ago there was a sermon against plays, and it was said that "they kindled the passions". The King turned to me and said: "He does not preach against me, as I do not go to the theatre any more, but against all of you who like it and go there." I answered: "Though I like plays and see them, M. d'Agen (Mascarron) does not preach at me, as he speaks against those who allow their passions to be kindled by plays: I don't. A play merely amuses me, and there is nothing wrong with it." The King made no reply.'

Each Sunday, in the pulpit, the curés of Paris reminded their congregations of the condemnation of actors and of the rules in the rituals. Actors were sometimes publicly refused the sacraments. Feeling that their profession was gravely threatened and, in some cases, that their own consciences were threatened also, appeal was made to the Pope himself, on his jubilee in 1696, against a form of persecution that was quite unknown in any other European country. Innocent XII referred the matter to the Council. But the Council prudently refrained from giving a definite answer, knowing quite well that the Gallican Church did not recognize the orders of Rome on matters of internal discipline, and that the French bishops would have resisted the Pope's orders. The Council sent the plaintiffs back to local jurisdiction, merely adding that all actors were not excommunicated: only those who acted in disreputable displays.

But the Gallican clergy, for once in agreement with the Jansenists and the busy bigots of the Company of the Holy Sacrament, seeking to defend public morality, refused to enter into such distinctions and maintained its general condemnation of the theatre and consequently of actors. Forgetting scholastic theologians who had accepted the religious dramas of the Middle Ages, they clung to the Church Fathers who in early Christian times had censored the scandalous and licentious shows to which our classical dramatic literature bore no resemblance whatever.

One can see how far things had gone since the time of Richelieu, Mazarin and the youthful King. It was the Palatine Princess, whose coarse frankness verged on cynicism, who provided the last words for this chapter. In a letter dated November 2, 1702, she wrote: 'As

25

bad luck would have it for the poor actors, the King will see no more plays. As long as he attended them it was not a sin. It was so little a sin that bishops came daily; there was a bench for them and it was always full. M. de Meaux [Bossuet] was there constantly. Now, as the King goes no more, it has become a sin.'

CHAPTER TWO

ACTORS AND PUBLIC OPINION

After defining the attitude of the Church towards actors and demonstrating its evolution through the century, we have now to see how the public reacted. Between 1600 and 1700 the attitude of the public differed greatly from that of the Church, but for completely different reasons, the main ones being the progress of dramatic literature itself and the growing perfection of dramatic technique.

Early in the century, before there were permanent companies in Paris, the theatre enjoyed practically no consideration whatever. Strolling players stayed in Paris for a few weeks and acted either at the Hôtel de Bourgogne, or on tennis courts, or even in the courtyards of inns. Actors were impoverished creatures, clad in rags, using rudimentary and ugly sets. The head of the company took money at the door while another actor passed around the city, trying to assemble an audience with the help of a drum.

The repertoire consisted mainly of popular but rather vulgar farces, staging Gros Guillaume covered with flour or Turlupin in his famous broad-brimmed hat; there were prologues and fantastic speeches gibbered by Bruscambille. According to Tallemant des Réaux, most actors at that time were 'thieves' and the few women on the stage 'were sluts shared in common by the actors and even by the actors of companies they did not belong to'. There was nothing attractive in all this either from the moral or the aesthetic point of view. Early in the century, a good actor, Valleran le Conte, had made an attempt to change the situation. He fought desperately to make a success of Alexander Hardy's productions; Hardy, a prolific writer, is reputed to have written some 600 plays! Valleran le Conte fought hard for several years, as Hardy's tragedies, tragi-comedies and comedies should, according to him, replace Jodelle or Garnier's threadbare repertoire. He failed, was ruined, and in 1612 had to seek his fortune abroad.

The stage at the Hôtel de Bourgogne remained the home of

farce, and the best-known performers were Gaultier-Garguilles, Turlupin and Gros-Guillaume. Their shows were not very different from those with which mountebanks and tumblers like Tabarin, Mondor or Baron de Grattelard used to amuse passers-by on the Pont Neuf, before selling them their miraculous salves and ointments. A number of texts from this period have been preserved, popular farces or songs which do not lack verve but are almost all disconcertingly coarse, the more so as the acting certainly underlined the innuendo heavily.

Such spectacles could appeal only to a very low public. The nobility attended only court ballets; the bourgeois did not patronize the Hôtel de Bourgogne. The pit was filled with prentices, soldiers, pages, hooligans and students, as well as pickpockets, making a very picturesque audience, no doubt, but one without culture or finesse, which came only for fun. They were undisciplined and noisy, continuously interrupting and cat-calling to the actors. They often fought among themselves. No respectable woman would have dared to step into such a den.

It is obvious that such shows did not attract public sympathy to the actors who gave them. Besides, they were completely ignored by good society, either the nobility or the bourgeoisie.

Yet things did undergo a swift and complete change. This was due to the sudden arrival of a new generation of dramatic writers after 1625: the generation of Rotrou, Mairet, Scudéry, du Ryen, Triston, Mareschal and, above all others, Corneille. They provided the stage with numerous tragedies, tragi-comedies and comedies, some of which, like Mairet's *Sophonisbe* and Tristan's *Mariamne*, achieved a great and well-deserved success. It was a full pre-classical period, with works of a high literary quality. The institution of the 'three unities' helped playwrights to concentrate the action of their plays in time and space.

Those poets were helped by a new generation of cultivated actors, men who were fond of good speech. Bellerose managed the Hôtel de Bourgogne company, and Montdory that of the Théâtre du Marais, where he displayed the youthful Corneille to the Parisians. By that time Richelieu had built the Palais-Royal theatre to stage *Mirame*. This was also the time when the upper class, the nobility first, and then the bourgeoisie learned good manners and acquired a taste for literature in the Marquise de Rambouillet's salon and in the various ladies' societies which blossomed everywhere in Paris. Corneille read *Polyeucte* to guests at the Hôtel de Rambouillet, and Mairet's *Virginie* had already been acted there.

The theatre was getting purer, from a literary and from a moral point of view. Tragedy made the audience familiar with noble sentiments, comedy criticized morals and habits, stripped of the vulgarity and coarseness of farce. The royal declaration of 1641 had officially rehabilitated actors. Low-class audiences were thrown back upon the mountebanks of the Place Dauphine or the St Laurent fair.

Of course, a few members of the clergy were strongly opposed to the stage. In 1632, J. P. Camus could still write: 'It is not without reason that in Italy, in France and almost everywhere else [which was not true], actors and comedians are deemed infamous; even the law regards them so, for very obvious reasons.' André Rivet, a Protestant pastor, echoed him in his *Instruction chrétienne touchant les spectacles publics*, in which he even criticized plays derived from the Scriptures, because 'it is not seemly that saints should be represented by infamous men'. But priests and pastors were now preaching in the wilderness. The public had taken to the theatre, liked its actors and did not follow their detractors. They preferred those who, like Scudéry in his *Apologie du Théâtre* (1639), rightly stressed the fact that the motives which had influenced the Fathers of the Church no longer existed. In the Jesuits' colleges, where the sons of the bourgeoisie were taught, plays were performed by the pupils. Even Balzac, in a private letter, praised Mondory because 'he had cleansed the stage of any amount of rubbish and had reconciled voluptuousness and virtue'. By slow progression, and still retaining some of its former audacity, the theatre had become the pastime of the refined society which lived in the new district of the Marais, and found in it an innocent, proper pleasure. Specialists like La Mesnerais in his *Poétique*, or Sarasin in his *Discours sur la Tragédie*, opened a public debate which was to continue in Corneille's *Discours* and the Abbé d'Aubignac's *Dissertations*. In Corneille's *Galerie du Palais* (1663), the bookseller states that 'plays are very fashionable now'.

Women did much to encourage the fashion, for there was now no reason why they should refrain from the theatre, as their modesty could not be offended. Besides, they could use their vizard to hide their blushing faces if the author made use of too daring a word. As early as 1630, Camus, Bishop of Belley, wrote: 'Our most refined ladies make no difficulty about being present in places

29

where tragedies are performed.' Mairet added in his *Galanteries du duc d'Ossone* (1636): 'The most honest women are now present at the Hôtel du Bourgogne with as little scruple or scandal as at the Luxembourg.' In a popular farce, *L'Apologie de Guillot-Gorju* (1634), the author write that 'ladies who attend it are so coy that all that Gros-Guillaume can do is to make them laugh'. We may rest assured that it was thanks to them that 'all Paris looks on Chimène with Rodrigue's eyes', when Richelieu, jealous of Corneille's triumph, tried to have *Le Cid* censored by the French Academy.

Corneille's heroic theatre, which did much to bring about that change, had a huge influence on the female public, passionately fond of grandeur and glory. The Grande Mademoiselle, the Duchesse de Chevreuse, the Duchesse de Longueville, the heroines of the Fronde, were the spiritual daughters of Corneille and they found kindred souls in Chimène, Camille or Emilie. Many years later, in Racine's triumphant hours, Mme de Sévigné could write: 'Long live our dear Corneille!'

Even the Queen set an example: an engraving by Van Lochom shows her attending a play, together with Louis XIII and Gaston d'Orléans. She agreed to have *Polyeucte* dedicated to her, and also *La Mort de Mithridate* by La Calprenède. Shortly after Louis XIII's death, she returned to the theatre. Mme de Motteville is very definite about this: 'She went to the play, half-hidden behind one of us whom she made sit beside her on the balcony, not wanting, during her period of mourning, openly to take the seat she was entitled to at other times. This diversion did not displease her.' Later, it was the same pious Queen whom Molière, persecuted by bigots, asked for help, inscribing the *Critique de l'école des femmes* to her.

Very naturally, the actors who had brought about its success made much out of this general craze for the theatre, both on the stage and in books. They did not scorn good door-money and they loved being applauded. The public had started to know, appreciate and even to love them. Paying no attention to the sermons, they bestowed interest and friendship on the actors. Montdory, Bellerose, Mlle de Beauchâteau and Mlle de Villiers were the constant subject of conversation in fashionable circles, where their talent, their elocution, their staging, their costumes and their sets were discussed. At last they were emerging from the darkness into which coarse plays had relegated them. Even the very conformist *Gazette,* published by Théophraste Renaudot, contributed to the praise of the stage: 'Now that all that could offend delicate ears has been banished from the stage, play-going is one of the most innocent and most pleasant pastimes in the good city of Paris.' He was merely voicing the unanimous opinion of the spectators who queued at the doors of the Hôtel de Bourgogne or the Théâtre du Marais. It should be mentioned that, at the time of the Fronde, a little later, a hint of the earlier coarseness stole back into plays and poetry.

We have ample proof of the new favour that was bestowed upon well-known actors.

Suddenly there appeared two short plays called the *Comédie des Comédiens,* staging the life of actors themselves, as Molière did later in *L'Impromptu de Versailles.* We should note in passing that this is the first instance of rival plays by rival companies; there were many examples later.

The first, by Gougenot (1633), brings in Bellerose, Beauchâteau and his wife, Gautier-Garguille, Turlupin, Mlle Valliot and Mlle Beaupré; the other, by Scudéry (1635), makes use of the Marais company with Montdory under the name of Blandimare, and ends with a pastoral by Scudéry himself. It must be admitted that they are both very dull and, apart from eulogies, offer no interesting information about the actors themselves. It is uncertain, moreover, if they were even performed. The one detail to note is not in the text; it is the engraved frontispiece of Scudéry's play, which represents the theatre entrance with its porter and drummer. But a more interesting detail is the fact that these two short plays were actually printed, whether acted or not. If booksellers displayed them to their customers, it was because they reckoned on their curiosity concerning their favourite actors, whom they now knew by their names, whose talent they discussed and whose rivalries and intrigues they delighted to hear about. The actors were fashionable as well as the theatre.

In *L'Illusion Comique* (1635), Corneille stressed this craze for the stage, so beneficial to authors and actors:

> *A présent le théâtre*
> *Est à un point si haut que chacun l'idolâtre,*
> *Et ce que votre temps voyait avec mépris,*
> *Est aujourd'hui l'amour de tous les bons esprits,*
> *L'entretien de Paris, le soin de nos provinces,*
> *Le divertisement le plus doux de nos princes,*

Les délices du peuple et le plaisir des grands.
Il tient le premier rang parmi les passe-temps
Et ceux dont nous voyons la sagesse profonde
Par leurs illustres soins conserver tout le monde,
Trouver dans les douceurs d'un spectacle si beau
De quoi se délasser d'un si pesant fardeau.
Même notre grand roi, ce foudre de la guerre,
Dont le nom se fait craindre aux deux bouts de la terre,
Le front ceint de lauriers, daigne bien, quelques fois
Prêter l'oeil et l'oreille au théâtre françois.[1]

For his part, Tristan, in his *Lyre* (1641), an ode to an actress, emphasized this renaissance which was bringing glory to authors, readers and spectators alike:

Fuis-tu cette profession
Comme suspecte d'infamie?
Aujourd'hui c'est une action
Dont la gloire se rend amie.

Cette crainte est le sentiment
D'une raison qui n'est pas saine,
Depuis que notre grand Armand
Daigne prendre soin de la scène.

Dis-moi, n'a-t-on pas nettoyé
Le cothurne de tous ses vices,
Depuis qu'on le voit employé
Dans ces innocentes délices?

Aujourd'hui qu'on l'a su purger
De ses matières de scandale,
Il peut être vu sans danger
De ceux qu'portent la sandale.

[1] 'Today the theatre has reached such a point that everyone raves about it, and what was despised in your time is now revered by every man of sound mind; it is the common subject of conversation in Paris, the entertainment of the provinces, the favourite pastime of our princes, the people's delight and the nobility's amusement. It stands first among entertainments and those whose deep wisdom is busy preserving the world from mishap find in the charm of such delightful spectacles a rest from their heavy burden. Our great King, this war-lord whose name is dreaded from one end of the earth to the other, his brow crowned with laurels, condescends sometimes to listen to and to look at the beauties of the French stage.'

1. Molière in Theatrical Costume, by Eustache Lorsay

Scaramouche
Scaramouche est Inimitable
Au Theatre comme a la Table

Le Blond ex Auec Pruilege

2. Scaramouche. Engraving of Le Blond

Son beau lustre n'est plus termi
D'une libertine pensée;
On y voit le crime puni
Et la vertu récompensée—[2]

When Desmarets de St Sorlin in his *Visionnaires* (1634) put a number of rather strange women upon the stage, whom Molière remembered when writing *Les femmes savantes,* he did not forget to have a stage-struck girl among them.

The theatre was now a social fact, and the remarkable achievements of French dramatic literature, now submissive to the famous 'three unities', was to make it even more striking. Neither sermons nor theories could oppose it. The public ignored them and went to the theatre.

Yet, laymen and clerics continued to issue polemics for and against the stage; their controversy continued throughout the century; public opinion was fascinated and its curiosity was tickled. As a matter of course, the actors were involved in the discussion which put them and their profession in the limelight.

It all began in 1637 with the quarrel about *Le Cid.* Jealous of Corneille's laurels, Cardinal de Richelieu, who prided himself on being a specialist of the stage and who controlled and paid a team of five authors who worked for him, decided to submit *Le Cid* to the judgment of the Academy he had just created to rule over literature. Corneille's rivals, Mairet, Claveret, and others stepped in; Corneille replied and undertook his own defence. A public discussion and much pamphleteering encouraged theatre addicts into taking sides. With great caution, the Academy, through young Chapelain's pen, brought out a small booklet entitled *Les Sentiments de l'Académie sur la tragi-comédie du Cid,* in which praise and criticism were adroitly counter-balanced.

Two years later (1639), Scudéry answered in his *Apologie du Théâtre* to Pastor Rivet's *Instruction chrétienne touchant les spectacles.* A few years later still, the Abbé d'Aubignac, who had created a small and extremely active academy, deeply interested in all that was new, wrote at Richelieu's command a *Pratique du Théâtre*

---

[2] Do you shun this profession, thinking it is taxed with infamy? Nowadays, it is an action to which glory is friendly. This dread comes from a wrong idea, as now our great Armand [Richelieu] condescends to get interested in the theatre. Tell me, has not the profession of acting been cleansed of all its vices, as it is now able to provide such an innocent delight? As all that could have shocked spectators has been eradicated, it can be seen without danger by those who walk in sandals [monks]. Its beautiful resplendence is no longer tainted by libertine thoughts; crime is always punished and virtue rewarded.

C

which appeared only in 1657. Very much in favour of the stage, this book was the first study of dramatic technique and the laws of the theatre. It enjoyed a great and lasting success. It expressed the general attitude of scholars to this controversial problem.

But the narrow-minded had not abandoned the fight. The Company of the Holy Sacrament continued its campaign against the stage; from his parish of St Sulpice, M. Olier harried the actors.

Before coming to Paris, one of his priests, Jean du Ferrier, had already fought against the actors of Narbonne where, as soon as a company of strolling players arrived, he had stopped all preaching and the exposition of the Sacrament. The public was horrified and threatened the players, who had to flee. When he arrived in the parish of St Sulpice he was more than ready to support M. Olier's efforts. In his *Mémoires* he recorded a very significant episode. A company of actors, protected by the Duc d'Orléans, had settled at the Foire St Germain, quite close to the church of St Sulpice. One of the actors was taken seriously ill and called on a priest of St Sulpice, who referred the matter to M. du Ferrier:

'I told the priest who told me of the state he was in to absolve him if he had repented, but to deny him communion, which he did. The man became worse and his companions, seeing him very low, came at night with several candles asking that the Holy Sacrament should be carried to him. I went to speak to them, but as they were comedians and mountebanks, deprived of piety or culture, all I said against their profession, instead of persuading them, merely angered them. Finally, I flatly refused to confess the dying man. Some of them abused me, others threatened me, and most of them flattered me to try and win me over.'

M. du Ferrier did not give in. The leader of the troop came to see him, and it was the priest who was victorious, converting him and making him abandon his profession!

The end of the tale throws a clear light on his sentiments:

'I cannot say how astonished I am to see priests silly enough—not to say sacrilegious—to hear actors and gypsies in confession. One might say the same of fiddlers and those who play at dances: how is it possible to forgive the vicars-general who should at once punish and dismiss cowardly confessors who have given the Sacrament to dogs and pigs?'

34

M. du Ferrier did not mince words.

The Jansenists approved; Nicole published his *Traité de la Comédie* with a sweeping condemnation of the theatre as a whole —even decent plays—because they speak always 'the language of passion', which would arouse lust, pride, ambition and selfishness. In his *Lettres sur l'hérésie imaginaire* (1664) he wrote: 'A novelist and writer for the stage are public poisoners, not of the bodies, but of the souls of the faithful, who should look upon themselves as guilty of an infinite number of spiritual murders.' The scathing way in which Racine replied to Nicole is well known: he had escaped from Port-Royal to join the enemy and had been formally renounced by his devoted aunt, Mother Agnes de Ste Thècle, who refused to see him again as long as he frequented 'people whose name is abominable to all persons of piety'.

Even a well-balanced man like Godeau, who had been Julie d'Angennes' 'dwarf' before becoming Bishop of Vence, while admitting that all licentiousness had been banished from the theatre, still wrote in 1662 about the morality the stage claimed to teach:

> *Mais en cette leçon si trompeuse et si vaine,*
> *Le profit est douteux et la perte certaine;*
> *Le remède y plaît moins que ne fait le poison.*
>
> *Elle peut réformer un esprit idolâtre,*
> *Mais, pour changer leurs moeurs et régler leur raison*
> *Les chrétiens ont l'Eglise et non pas le théâtre.*[3]

While adversaries and supporters argued in public, incidents in the theatre itself continued to inflame feelings. Molière's success with the *Précieuses ridicules* had aroused the fury of the Hôtel de Bourgogne company, and they set poor Somaize against him. A few years later, Molière triumphed again with *l'Ecole des femmes* at the Palais Royal. Rival actors sided with bigots who were denouncing Arnolph's 'sermon' as blasphemy. They accepted plays against Molière: Boursault's *Portrait du peintre*, Donneau de Visé's *Zélinde ou la Vengeance des Marquis*. Then Molière retaliated with *La Critique de l'école des femmes* and *L'Impromptu de Versailles*, into which he put caricatures of the 'great stars' of the

---

[3] Yet this vain, deceitful lesson ends in doubtful profit and obvious damnation. The remedy is less attractive than its poison. It can reform an idolatrous spirit, but to change their morals and rule their reason Christians must go to church and not to the theatre.

Hôtel de Bourgogne, and the public hooted with laughter. Then came another rejoinder from Montfleury's son, *L'Impromptu de l'Hôtel de Condé*. The Théâtre du Marais, which had kept out of the fray, took this opportunity to put Molière on the stage in Chevalier's *Amours de Calotin*. Thus all the theatres in Paris were swayed to and fro by the quarrel: those who were for and those who were against Molière argued and fought. There had never been such rivalry on the French stage. The public was delighted and took sides.

Two years later there was an even more lively episode with *Tartuffe*, which was an answer to the bigots who had publicly criticized *L'Ecole des femmes*. Even before the first night, the Company of the Holy Sacrament, which was well informed, had already started proceedings to have the play banned. While still unfinished, it was acted at Versailles during the great fêtes of the spring of 1664. After this first and solitary performance, the King prohibited the play from being acted in public. It took five years for Molière and his friends to secure the resurrection of *Tartuffe*. The Gazette, which usually avoided speaking of Molière, nevertheless mentioned the banning of a play, 'which abuses religion and may have very dangerous results'.

Meanwhile, the subject was discussed everywhere. Roullé recommended that 'the most outrageous godless libertine who ever lived' be burned at the stake; this would be merely a first taste of hellfire. Molière protested in a first letter to the King who, at that time, was firmly protecting him, but he had to submit to the King's will. The Company of the Holy Sacrament stopped any mention of *Tartuffe*, even invidious ones, thinking that 'it was better to forget it than to attack it, lest the author should defend it'. Yet Molière could give private performances of his play in noblemen's castles: le Raincy, Villers-Cotterêts, and Chantilly. He did not mince words when replaying to his professed enemies of the 'Cabale des Dévôts' in the fifth act of *Dom Juan*. This started a new scandal and the play had to be withdrawn. It led to harsh *Observation* by a M. de Rochemont, who may have been the Jansenist, Barbier d'Aucour. Going beyond the play, d'Aucour attacked the actor and the man:

'We must admit that Molière personally is an accomplished Tartuffe, and the perfect hypocrite, and that he resembles those actors mentioned by Seneca who in his time corrupted public morality and, pretending to chastise vices, skilfully instilled them into the public mind; this philosopher calls those people State pests and sentences them to exile and punishment. If comedy is meant to correct men while entertaining them, Molière wants to ruin them through laughter . . . his Agnes' malicious simplicity has corrupted more virgins than the most licentious books. His *Cocu Imaginaire* is a trick to create real ones; and more wives have been debauched while attending his school than in days of old when attending the school of that philosopher who was driven from Athens, boasting that no one who had come to him walked out chaste.'

That is what Port-Royal thought of Molière, who carried on his shoulders, as Abel Lefranc pointed out, 'all the burdens of the fight'. This attack provoked several answers, and Molière was probably not a stranger to them.

Various critics think with good reasons that Molière gave his Dom Juan—an atheist, a libertine and finally a hypocrite—various aspects of the Prince de Conti's character. The younger brother of the Prince de Condé, he had protected Molière and his company some ten years earlier, when he was the governor of Languedoc and was leading there a fairly riotous life. A spectacular conversion led him to forsake the theatre, and made him side with the strictest members of the Company of the Holy Sacrament.

Soon after his death his *Traité de la Comédie selon la Tradition de l'Eglise* was published (1666). After a long list of condemnations of the stage by early Fathers of the Church, the author, mentioning Molière by name, used practically all Nicole's arguments and passed a general sentence against all plays without distinction, including religious tragedies: 'Between comedies, the aim of which is to arouse passions, and the Christian religion, the aim of which is to silence, calm and destroy them as far as possible in this world, opposition is complete.'

The Abbé d'Aubignac, who was a specialist in contemporary drama, answered with a *Dissertation sur la Condamnation des Théâtres*. It was followed by a new answer by J. de Voisin, who had been one of the Prince de Conti's associates and possibly the real author of the treatise published under the prince's name. In 1671 he brought out a *Défense du traité de Mgr le prince de Conti*. On the other hand, the worldly Abbé de Pure wrote an apology of the stage in his *Idée des spectacles anciens et modernes*.

Shortly after Molière's death, Samuel Chappuzeau, a converted protestant who wrote about many things, including the theatre, published his *Théâtre français*, possibly at La Grange's suggestion. The book is most useful, full of information about the life of strolling companies and Paris theatres. Chappuzeau was an optimist who thought that all was for the best in the theatre, provided his own plays were performed. With excessive artlessness, he praised actors without reserve and swore to their perfect morals, piety, their regular attendance at church ceremonies and their respect for Lent, during which they ceased acting. He stressed the fact that none of them had ever been convicted under the law, which was true. For him the stage was now cleansed of all dirty jokes and improper thoughts. Consequently, it is an anachronism and a wilfully false interpretation of old texts to apply to the theatre of Molière and contemporary tragedies the threats uttered by former Fathers of the Church. His straight answers to Conti and the Abbé de Voisin put things right. The adversaries of the contemporary stage were wrong 'in confusing the comedies with all the shows of Antiquity and in refusing to see any difference. There is nothing cruel in comedy like the displays of the gladiators.'

As the years passed, the public debate continued on the religious, moral or literary level, between partisans and enemies of the stage, leading to impassioned discussions between those who read all those controversial works. The success of the opera, a new and gorgeous kind of spectacle which was to contribute largely to the decline of tragedy, is proof of the lasting favour of the public for the theatre in all its forms.

The quarrel flared up again at the end of the century with the celebrated Caffaro-Bossuet controversy; the former, an obscure Italian monk, had published in 1694 a new edition of Boursault's plays, preceded by a copious *Lettre d'un théologien illustre*, which took up once more all the arguments already widely developed in favour of the stage. Caffaro agreed that the ideas of the early Fathers of the Church could not be applied to the literary and morally expurgated contemporary drama. This was the first time that a churchman publicly wrote such words: a deserter was siding with those who defended the stage.

Bossuet believed it was his duty to intervene. In a private letter to Caffaro, he directly attacked Molière's memory:

'We shall therefore have to accept as honest the impieties and infamies with which Molière's comedies are filled, or else you do not include among contemporary plays those of an author who has

38

just died, which still fill the theatres with the grossest innuendoes which have ever polluted Christian ears. Do not compel me to repeat this; just consider whether you can dare to uphold before Heaven those plays in which virtue and piety are always ridiculed, corruption always defended and made pleasant, modesty always offended or always in danger of violation, by the worst outrages. I refer to the most shameless expressions, to which only the thinnest veils are given. . . .

'At least, if it is God's will, you will eventually banish from among Christians the prostitution and adultery which fill Italian comedies even at a time when you believe that the stage has been so cleansed, and which are still only too clearly seen in Molière's plays. You will reprove the discourses of that rigorous censor of the great canons and the expressions of our *précieuses*, who meanwhile openly advocate the advantages of infamous tolerance by husbands, and suggest to their wives shameful means of revenge upon their jealousy.'

In conclusion, Bossuet asked Caffaro to return to a deeper understanding of the requirements of the Christian Church, adding that, if necessary, he would speak as a bishop. Faced with such a blast, Caffaro bent very low, assuring Bossuet that he had never read Molière's comedies, disavowing and disowning his imprudent *Lettre*.

Shortly afterwards, Bossuet took up the same theme in his *Maximes et rèflexions sur la comédie*. Then Laurent Pégurier, following Bossuet, resumed the criticism of *Tartuffe* and *Dom Juan* in his *Réfutation des sentiments relâchés d'un nouveau théologien touchant la comédie*, as did Le Brun in his *Discours sur la comédie*. It was always the author of *Tartuffe* and *Dom Juan* who served as target to the censors of the theatre, and whose sudden and well-deserved death remained a threat and a warning to his kind. Pierre Coustel used the same language in his *Sentiments de l'Eglise et des Sts Pères pour servir de décision sur la comédie et les comédiens*, and also L. Soucanye in his Latin epistle *In pestem theatralem*, the title of which is clear enough.

The contrary thesis was taken up by Gacon in his *Poète sans fard*, and even Leibnitz answered all these theologians with these simple lines:

> *Sévères directeurs des hommes,*
> *Savez-vous qu'au siècle où nous sommes,*

> *Un Molière édifie autant que vos leçons?*
> *Le vice bien raillé n'est pas sans pénitence.*
> *Il faut, pour réformer la France,*
> *La comédie ou les dragons.*[4]

While so many booklets and pamphlets were being issued for or against the theatre, the success of the Paris theatre continued. At the end of the century, while the works of Corneille, Racine and Molière were daily performed at the Comédie Française, and those of Lulli at the Opera, a new generation of dramatists was emerging. It is a fact that tragedies were becoming impoverished, but Regnard, Dufresne, Baron and Dancourt, though lacking Molière's strength, were maintaining the reputation of comedy—comedy that was even freer in its literary expression than what had been written by the author of *Le misanthrope*.

The successes of Baron or Champmeslé echoed those of Floridor, Molière or Mlle du Parc a generation earlier. The public did not discard its favourite actors, and did not listen to the abuse of them by theologians and moralists.

At the end of the century, many actors were men of solid culture and perfect taste. Baron bequeathed to his heirs a library of 4,000 volumes and a fine collection of prints and paintings. The theatre remained very popular, which accounted for the flourishing financial condition of the actors and their consequent social respectability. La Bruyère mentioned the fact with some asperity: 'The actor, as reclining in his coach, splashes mud on the face of Corneille, who passes on foot.' The moralist, a keen observer of contemporary society, stressed the contradiction between its attitude and the moral position of those who attempted to rule it: 'Actors were deemed infamous by the Romans and were highly respected by the Greeks: how about ourselves? We think like the Romans and live with them like the Greeks.' And again: 'Could anything be stranger? A crowd of Christians gathers to applaud a company of reprobates, excommunicated merely because they provide pleasure. It seems to me that one should either close the theatres or be less severe on the actors.'

All this uncontrolled emotion, all these spoken and written attacks upon the stage and upon actors, failed to rid the spectators

---

[4] You harsh censors of men, do you realize that nowadays a Molière is as edifying as your lessons? Vice, when well laughed at, is not without penitence. To reform France, you need either comedies or dragoons.

of their enthusiasm, of their need for this means of escape, that helps a man to bear or to forget his cares, and may sometimes help in the fight against vice, or at least to laugh at it. The actions of hostile moralists and old-fashioned theologians ended in complete failure, which Antoine Arnold admitted bitterly on May 16, 1694, in the midst of the Caffaro-Bossuet affair: 'The Prince de Conti and M. Nicole have wasted their time in their written attacks on comedy; everyone goes to see it as before.' The accounts of the Comédie Française are extant and prove that he was right.

PART TWO

THE THEATRES OF PARIS

CHAPTER ONE

AN INTERMITTENT THEATRE
(1598–1629)

The history of the Paris stage in the seventeenth century provides
a first surprise in the fact that, in the first thirty years, during which
one of the most striking dramatic literatures in the world was born,
Paris had no permanent theatre. The capital city was on the level
of any provincial town, the inhabitants of which were only provided with theatrical performances when a strolling company
stopped there for a few days in the course of its wanderings.

Provincial companies would some times halt in Paris for a few
performances; yet, to settle there, they had to face difficulties they
did not meet in the provinces. The proprietors of the Hôtel de
Bourgogne, the Confrères de la Passion, held a monopoly of spectacles in Paris, according to privileges which had been granted
them by Charles VI and renewed by all his successors. The company
could hire out the Hôtel de Bourgogne; then there was no trouble.
But some companies, which were undoubtedly afraid that they
could not fill the Hôtel de Bourgogne, preferred acting in the courtyards of inns during spring and summer, and in one of the numerous Paris tennis courts in winter. In those long, narrow quadrangu-
lar halls, where the players were sheltered from wind and rain,
carpenters could erect a rough stage quickly and cheaply and
bring in benches for the audience to sit on. But permission from the
Confrères de la Passion was required, and they granted it, or rather
sold it, for an *écu* a day. Of course, strolling companies, especially
when they had failed to draw a big audience, often forgot to pay.
Being very careful of their profits, the Confrères de la Passion sued
them regularly before the Châtelet court and were frequently
successful. But some of these lawsuits lasted for months and often
ended in a deal.

The short-lived companies that entertained Paris audiences were
fairly numerous and some returned regularly. All we know about
their activities comes from the documents signed when they rented
the Hôtel de Bourgogne and from their company deeds, which are

quite silent about their activities. They are incomplete, too, because of the partial destruction of the notaries' archives. But the arrival of a considerable number of foreign companies between 1598 and 1629 can be noted: Englishmen in May 1598; Italians in April 1599, February 1600, December 1603, February 1608, October 1613, June 1614, May to July 1621 and October to November 1621; and Spaniards in April 1625. Several French companies alternated with them, among them the Prince of Orange's comedians, who came every summer from 1622 on. Those *bandes*, as they were termed, stayed usually for only a short time, from two to four weeks, sometimes a little longer, but very seldom for three months.

It should be said that all these companies were constantly being disbanded, reorganized, amalgamated and separated, and were constantly signing on new actors to replace those who had gone. The total impression is one of a rather unstable theatre, constantly on the move, a condition very detrimental to serious work and to the production of a coherent programme. Everything was probably improvised with very little money, dull and rudimentary sets, and costumes which, according to Tallement des Réaux, had been bought second-hand in a rag-shop. We know very little about their choice of plays. Besides farces, which were very popular, it is likely that they still made use of the old Renaissance tragedies and comedies, which we know were still performed in the provinces.

Of the twenty or thirty companies whose arrival in Paris has been recorded, though we know nothing of their activities, there are at least two we know a little better, each of which, in its own speciality, seems to have been much better than its rivals. They are the Valleran le Conte Company and that of Robert Guérin, nicknamed Gros-Guillaume.

Valleran le Conte was doubtless a great actor, very fond of literature and drama, greatly gifted and full of courage. Hardly anything was known about him before Mme Deierkauf-Holsboex published the results of her researches into the archives. She has done much to enrich our knowledge of the history of the stage in the seventeenth century.

Like all his fellow-actors, Valleran le Conte started with strolling companies: he was in Bordeaux in 1592, in Rouen, in Frankfurt and Strasbourg in 1593. His social rank was much higher than that of most of his colleagues since, as servant of the bedchamber of the Duc de Nemours, he discharged the offices of *maître voyeur juré* for the King in Nemours and collector-general of taxes for Verneuil-sur-Oise, two fairly respectable offices; the modest salary they brought him probably enabled him to carry on his true profession, that of actor.

He arrived in Paris in March 1598, after the disturbances of the Ligue, at the head of a threadbare company; but he was provided with a paid poet, none less than Alexandre Hardy, whose new plays they had performed in the provinces. Valleran was an innovator, seeking to discard circumscribed routines and the old-fashioned repertoire. In order to launch Hardy's tragedies and comedies in Paris, he joined forces with another company, that of Adrien Talmy, 'to act and live together like colleagues, in all honour, respect, faithfulness and friendship'. According to a custom of the time, the head of the company had to provide costumes and stage properties. For the two companies, Valleran bought seven theatrical dresses in a second-hand shop, 'five of cloth of silver and cloth of gold, one in blue damask and one of shot silk'. We do not know where the new company performed, but it was short-lived, since Talmy and his actors soon resumed their freedom. Valleran then joined forces with another company, led by Benoît Petit, who had settled at the Hôtel de Bourgogne. They decided to act there on alternate weeks and, if necessary, to borrow each other's players. Petit was to pay the rent and Valleran to provide the costumes. As early as January 1599, Valleran was already acting Hardy's plays, as well as a farce. From a painter he ordered the sets and fittings he required, representing 'cities, castles, rocks, woods, bowers and lawns'. This first spell in Paris lasted for over a year, with breaks of course, for at least one Italian company is known to have acted at the Hôtel de Bourgogne in the same year.

Now, even at that early stage, Valleran ran into severe financial trouble, a proof that the Paris audience, mostly of the lower classes at that time, was not ready to swallow the new literary plays he was trying to press on them. They wanted to keep to the traditional farces, which were good enough to make them laugh and were not above their intellectual level.

So Valleran, having acted too often to empty theatres—'they' hadn't come, as Louis Jouvet used to say—found himself unable to pay the 200 *écus au soleil* he owed his dressmaker for the costumes he had bought. Providential help came from an admirer who offered him 'a black velvet cloak heavily embroidered and lined

47

with orange satin', which was accepted by the dressmaker; but the scene-painter had still to be paid. Valleran was compelled to sell his office of *maître voyeur juré* of Nemours for 450 livres. He repaid old debts to some of his companions by mortgaging the door-money of the next day. He was really at his wits' end. By ill chance an Italian company had just arrived in Paris and was attracting everybody, for the public was fond of the *lazzi* of the *commedia dell'arte*, while Valleran continued to play to empty halls. He thought of a last trick: to associate with the Italians who had greater luck. He succeeded in convincing them and with them gave a few bilingual performances. But the Italians realized they had made a fool's bargain and they dropped Valleran. He made a new attempt in a courtyard in the rue Le Coq, which was a complete failure. His first Paris season led him nowhere; leaving the stage of the Hôtel de Bourgogne to Gros-Guillaume, he left Paris with his companions and his poet Alexandre Hardy. For five years he toured the provinces, seeking there the laurels which Paris had denied him. Nothing whatever is known about his itinerary.

Early in 1606 he was again in Paris, where with great courage he was going to try again. It is possible that he had had better luck in the provinces and was arriving with a rather heavier purse. If that is true, his prosperity was ephemeral despite a first-class recruit in the person of Hugues Guéru, the well-known clown Gaultier-Garguilles, and a new repertoire of 'comedies, tragi-comedies and other entertainments', all by the tireless Hardy. He soon faced the same difficulties as six years earlier. The heavy frosts of the winter of 1607–8 had helped not a little to empty the Hôtel de Bourgogne. Unable to pay the rent, Valleran's companions left once more to try their luck in the provinces.

Three years later, in September 1609, they were back in Paris with a few young actors, among whom were Pierre le Messier, known as Bellerose, the future manager of the Royal company, his sister Judith, and Jeanne Crevé, who became the mother of André Baron. Valleran had assumed the task of 'showing, teaching and making them learn under him the art and skill of performing all tragi-comedies, comedies, pastorals, and other entertainments'. Later, another beginner was to be seen at his side: Guillaume des Gilberts who, when his time came, led the Théâtre du Marais company to success under his stage name of Montdory. These apprentices, as in other professions, were taken *au pair*, unpaid but fed and clad. This was how actors learnt their trade at that time.

48

3. The Players of the Hôtel of Bourgogne

Turlupin.

4. Turlupin, a Famous French Actor of the Early Seventeenth Century

The process soon disappeared—about 1620 in fact; later, apprentices gave way to the actors' children, who learnt their trade by their parents' side on the stage of the strolling companies.

Bad luck struck again: Valleran happened to be in Paris when a rival company came, acting at the Hôtel d'Argent under Mathieu Le Febvre, called Laporte. The two principals, realizing that there was no room for two companies in Paris, instead of fighting each other, decided to unite. So together they hired the Hôtel de Bourgogne in the spring of 1610. They also performed in Senlis and Orléans. The murder of Henry IV probably had unfortunate effects on performances. The amalgamation of the two groups, planned to last three years, scarcely lasted one. By the end of the year, Mathieu Laporte retired from the stage. Ten years later, he would be 'rehabilitated' by royal patents, but his company had drifted apart. Valleran alone remained in Paris with his faithful companions all through 1611. He continued his courageous struggle against an audience which did not care for Hardy. To make some money, he had to sub-let the boxes and the amphitheatre, only keeping the receipts from the pit. To pay a dressmaker who was threatening to sue him, he had to borrow money from his landlord in the rue de la Truanderie, so that he could recover his stage costumes, which had been distrained. The same generous landlord lent him money to bury his sister. The dire straits in which Valleran found himself, heavily in debt and driven to his last shifts, can clearly be seen. The rats were leaving the sinking ship: several of his actors left him, unable to pay the whole of their forfeit money under their contract. Even the helpful landlord was getting restless, and he had a notary draw up a list of the sums owed him by Valleran: 1266 *livres tournois*.

Yet he did not give up the struggle. He reorganized his company and again rented the Hôtel de Bourgogne for six months, paying 1,650 livres. Alexandre Hardy remained faithful to him and even turned actor to reduce expenses.

Alas, bad luck continued to dog them. The public would not come. At his wits' end, Valleran thought of new means to survive. Another Italian company, led by Jean-Paul Alfieri, had just arrived: an unforeseen and formidable occurrence. Valleran contacted them and the two groups got together to exploit the hall in common. Each group would act a play in its own language. Valleran was hoping that the Italian comedies would help the French tragedies. But he was unable to pay the rent at the agreed

D

date, and the Confrères de la Passion seized the box which contained the door-money of both groups. Valleran lost his last penny. This was total ruin.

Valleran realized that Paris was not for him. His company disintegrated, but he organized another in which Montdory took part as a beginner on half-pay. The company can be traced in Leyden and at the Hague in 1613, but after that Valleran le Conte disappeared. No one knows when and where this great actor died.

If we have recorded Valleran le Conte's brief, restless and unhappy Paris career in some detail, it is because first of all it shows, at the very beginning of modern stage history, a moving example of genuine dedication to the theatre. The man who well deserves to be called Valorous Valleran seems to us, after three centuries, to be an ancestor of the modern managers of experimental companies, devoted to the true theatre. His history reveals a man of tenacious will, a pioneer who meant to free the public and himself of an old out-worn repertoire and substitute a new one, purged of the vulgarities and buffoonery of the farces, of high literary quality, full of human passion, of true and noble sentiment. The fact that he failed proved nothing against him, but it testifies to the unpreparedness of his public, which could not understand his message. The artistic dream which prompted his action and kept his faith alive through so many trials was a beautiful one: what he wanted to put into the Hôtel de Bourgogne— without, it is understood, being fully aware of it—was a genuinely classical theatre, the very one which was to triumph some twenty years later.

When Valleran had gone, a new company quickly came to the fore. Most of its members, as well as its leader, were Valleran's former companions. The leader was Robert Guérin, better known by his stage name of Gros-Guillaume. This company had first acted in Toulouse, where, incidentally, the parliament had sentenced five of its members to banishment, though they later received a royal pardon. They arrived in Paris in the autumn of 1615, led by François Vautrel. They acted at the Hôtel de Bourgogne all through 1616, probably in 1617, certainly in 1618 and 1619, and in 1621 at the Hôtel d'Argent, where they were sentenced to pay three écus a day to the Confrères de la Passion, then back at the Hôtel de Bourgogne in 1622-3, 1624-5, 1626, 1627-8, and 1629.

After 1616, Gros-Guillaume directed the company, forming, with his two inseparable companions, Gaultier-Garguilles and

Turlupin, the most hilarious trio of clowns who ever delighted the pit. Of course, they were not bothered by the highly artistic pre-occupations of Valleran le Conte. But as master clowns they gave the Paris audience all the side-splitting farces they loved. Thus they succeeded where Valleran failed. They became popular types, adored by the crowd. There were countless engraved portraits of them. They acted masked or with their faces covered with flour.

Robert Guérin's company already proclaimed its primacy over all other companies at the Hôtel de Bourgogne. Here is the contemptuous way in which Bruscambille, in one of his prologues, referred to his rivals:

'Is there anything in the world comic actors don't know, apart from sloth? I don't include, of course, a heap of little mountebanks who usurp the title of comedians and who have less learning than the yellow, red or white ribbons tied to their moustaches or their wrists, woven with I don't know which repulsive hair stolen from the dirty comb of some village barmaid. On the contrary, I mean those who represent in their actions the pure and true microcosm of comic nature. Let us go back to them, and leave those chameleons who feed on nothing but wind and smoke.'

And that is how members of Gros-Guillaume's company referred to 'Roscius' abortions'.

Let us follow the three clowns on to the stage. The performance began with one of Bruscambilles' funny *prologues* or *paradoxes* which he acted 'behind his huge spectacles'. His rambling text resembled the rigmaroles spoken on the Pont Neuf by Tabarin and Mondor. The clown dealt with anything and everything with a sense of fun and a verbal superabundance that made the audience roar. Then the farce began, and the trio kept the puns and the *lazzi* going prolifically, Italian fashion. This was half-way between a play and a circus show.

Gros-Guillaume acted either male or female parts. His belly alone was something to look at; he secured it with two belts, one above and one below. Sauval wrote that his 'talk was coarse and, to get into the right mood, he had to get drunk first with his boon companion the cobbler'. Yet his fun was irresistible. 'He said every-thing naïvely', wrote Tallemant, 'and he had such a funny face that no one could refrain from laughing at the sight of it.'

Gaultier-Garguilles, who had married Mondor's niece and was Tabarin's friend, was tall, gaunt and clad entirely in black.

51

Sauval described Valleran's former companion thus: 'Every part of his body obeyed him, in such a way that he looked like a puppet. He had a lean body, with long, thin, straight shanks, and a large face; he never played without a mask, and had a long pointed beard, a flat black skull-cap, black slippers, sleeves of red Frisian, black Frisian doublet and hose; he always took the part of an old man.' We still possess the love songs he wrote: they are free and bawdy, always dealing with a well-known theme; yet, in spite of their coarseness, they are not without wit. The pages and the valets loved them.

As for Turlupin, he was the replica of Brighella in the Italian comedies, with his broad-brimmed hat, his short doublet, his wide striped multi-coloured trousers, his wooden sword thrust into his belt. He acted especially the parts of swaggering, greedy and cowardly valets, like the Italian *zanni*. His countryman and friend, the poet Auvray, described Turlupin's ideal in life:

> *Fi d'amour, vive la cuisine,*
> *Vive les pots, vive les plats,*
> *Andouilles, gogues, cervelas,*
> *Vive la chair, vive la soupe,*
> *Et vive l'amour quand je soupe,*
> *Car vivre toujours sans souci*
> *Avoir le ventre bien farci*
> *De salmigondis, de salades,*
> *De jambons et de carbonnades,*
> *Et voire sec comme un lapin*
> *Sont les amours de Turlupin.*[1]

He lived a regular, or even bourgeois life. He did not want his wife to go on the stage; in spite of his immoderate taste for food, he had a subtle mind and his *lazzi* made the crowd shout with laughter. Sauval's conclusion was: 'No man composed, acted or carried on a farce better than Turlupin; his repartees were full of fun, fire and sense; in a word he lacked nothing but a little simplicity, and yet everybody confesses that nothing like him had ever been seen.'

Such was the unforgettable trio who for twenty years delighted

[1] 'Fie upon love! Long live cooking! Long live pots and dishes, chitterlings, sausages and saveloy! Long live meat! Long live soup, and long live love when I sit down at supper! For a life deprived of worries, a belly well-filled with salmagundy, salads, ham and grills and copious drink are the kind of love Turlupin delights in.'

the Paris audience. We retain only the titles of some of their farces, probably made out of old, often-used material, *La Malle de Gaultier, Le Cadet du Champagne, Tire la corde, j'ai la carpe* and *La Farce du Mari*: they were never printed. Were they even put into writing? Possibly not. It is likely that some of our clowns, like their Italian counterparts, acted *all'improviso*, embroidering the bare canvas with the highly coloured elaborations of the free imagination. What is certain is the fact that there were many vulgarities and improper situations. But the audience would not have stood for a performance without a farce. 'If a comedy was not flavoured with that kind of accessory,' wrote Guillot-Gorju, 'it would have been meat without sauce and a Gros-Guillaume without his flour.'

These clowns also acted comedies but, to avoid confusion, they did so under another name, so that, with their real names as well, they had three names in all. Robert Guérin, Hugues Guéru and Henri Legrand were therefore Gross-Guillaume, Gaultier-Garguilles and Turlupin in farces, and La Fleur, Fléchelle and Belleville in comedy.

Another pupil of Valleran le Conte, who had probably followed him in Holland, soon joined Gros-Guillaume's company. This was Pierre le Messier, who was to succeed Gros-Guillaume in managing the company and became illustrious in Paris under the name of Bellerose. In 1620 he was in Marseilles with a company whose paid poet was the same Hardy who once provided Valleran with plays. They both arrived in Paris in 1622; a few years later, Beauchâteau joined them; together with Bellerose, protected by farces which assured the company's success, they did much to thrust upon the public a wholly new set of tragedies, comedies and pastorals written notably by Hardy, Mairet and Rotrou. The renaissance of the stage which Valleran had failed to achieve was now about to succeed.

It was facilitated by the presence in the company of good actresses who drew the bourgeois and aristocratic audience to the Hôtel de Bourgogne. Italian companies had employed actresses for a long time. But the appearance of women on the French stage was much delayed; they did not take part in farces, and female roles were acted by boys.

The first woman of whom we know anything certain was also one of Valleran's former pupils, Rachel Trepeau, whose presence in his 1607 company is proved; she reappeared in Gros-Guillaume's

53

in 1616. We know nothing more about her, but in her we have to recognize the ancestress of all French actresses. At the same period, Marie Venier, Mathieu Laporte's wife, was also acting at the Hôtel de Bourgogne, from which she retired in 1610, tamely ending her life as a lawyer's wife. Her sister, Colombe Venier, who was one of a strolling company, married Fleury Jacob, Montfleury's father.

After 1625 Charles Le Noir, the head of the Prince of Orange's company, which alternated with Pierre Guérin's royal company at the Hôtel de Bourgogne, was accompanied by his wife, Françoise Mestivier. A contemporary praised 'her sweet little manners and her gaiety which endeared her to everybody'. Tallemant des Réaux is a little more informative: 'This Le Noir woman was the loveliest little person to be found. The Comte de Belin, who had Mairet at his beck and call, had plays written on condition that she should be the leading lady, for he was in love with her, and the company benefited thereby.' There were many other actresses at that time who had powerful protectors. The one who admired Mme le Noir so much, Belin, is well known as a generous patron of the stage. Scarron praised him in his *Roman comique* under the name of Marquis d'Orsé. It is possible that Mme le Noir acted in Racan's *Bergeries*, in Théophile de Viau's too famous *Pyrame et Thisbé*, and in some of Rotrou's plays. It is certain that she acted in Mairet's early plays, *Chryséide et Arimant* and *Sylvie et Sylvanire*. She later made a fine career for herself at the Théâtre du Marais.

The King's Comedians (the company assumed this impressive title even though it received no royal subsidy yet) with a good supply of clowns, actors and actresses, easily succeeded in holding a leading position in Paris among the various companies performing there. This success provoked the ambitious to settle permanently in the Hôtel de Bourgogne and to drive away all their rivals. According to the diary of Doctor Héroard, Louis XIII was filled with admiration of the King's Comedians from childhood on. One of their supporters, who had his say at court, probably spoke for them to the sovereign, possibly through Cardinal de Richelieu, who was all his life a keen play-goer. Finally, the Royal Council decided on December 29, 1629, to bestow the Hôtel de Bourgogne upon the company of the King's Comedians, led by Robert Guérin, for three years at a yearly rent of 2,400 livres, reduced by mutual consent to 2,000 in 1639, but brought back to its original figure in 1647. The Châtelet, regarding the King's decision as a concession exclusive to Bellerose's company, forbade him to sub-let the theatre. The Confrères were only entitled to dispose of 'the Masters' box'. That decision put an end to the innumerable lawsuits between the Confrères de la Passion and other comedians; it marked the final and exclusive installation of the King's Players in the theatre in the rue Mauconseil. They played there for three years. They were successful. Their repertoire grew richer with each season and was often changed. The Royal Company of the Hôtel de Bourgogne was born.

CHAPTER TWO

THE ROYAL COMPANY AT THE HÔTEL DE BOURGOGNE (1629–1680)

If Paris, so far, had never enjoyed a permanent company, it did possess, apart from the tennis courts where some performances took place, a real theatre, the Hôtel de Bourgogne. This stood at the junction of the rue Mauconseil and the rue Française in the Halles district, in the parish of St Eustache, where the rue Etienne Marcel now lies. The old Jean-sans-Peur tower still stands and round it a school has been built: this is all that remains of the former Hôtel de Bourgogne.

It has already been said that the Confrères de la Passion owned 'the house known as the Hôtel de Bourgogne'. This association had been formed at the end of the fourteenth century to perform mystery plays in churches or their precincts. They usually performed their plays at St Maur, near Vincennes. Charles VI, by an ordinance of 1402, made them into a dramatic guild. They then moved to the Trinity Hospital, and in 1539 to the Hôtel de Flandres, near the Porte Coquillère; this was demolished, together with the Hôtel de Bourgogne, which had belonged to Charles the Bold, on the orders of Francis I. The guild bought part of the ground and built a theatre there in 1548. Excluding all others, Parliament allowed them to perform their morality plays on condition that they were 'honest, lawful and not religious'.

In 1588, the *Remontrances très humbles au roi de France et de Pologne* (Henri III) already hinted at the scandalous performances 'in a muddy pit, Satan's abode, known as the Hôtel de Bourgogne', where shameless farces were mixed with holy mysteries.

The performance of mystery plays or biblical scenes, forbidden in Paris in 1588 and again ten years later, survived in the provinces for a long time.

Thus the Confrères held a monopoly of dramatic performances in Paris, a considerable advantage, a privilege of which they had no intention of allowing themselves to be deprived. But their old repertoire, decried by new dramatists who had their own plays performed in colleges, had driven the public away. Knowing the value of their privilege, they decided to end their own shows and merely to exploit their theatre. We have seen how they rented their hall to various companies, and how they hounded out the rest, who acted on tennis courts or in private houses, by demanding a rent of three écus a day. In order to make their rights clear, they also demanded a box, 'the Masters' box', made noticeable by its bars, and another box for the King of Fools, the short-lived Shrove Tuesday sovereign. On either side were two rows of boxes, one above the other, above a pit where the lowly audience stood. At the back of the hall were benches in the form of an amphitheatre. The stage was narrow and from the boxes it could only be seen sideways.

In that unique Parisian theatre Robert Guérin's company settled in December 1629: it consisted of what remained of Valleran le Conte's. They had great difficulty, for they had to fight against other companies which were spied upon and held to ransom by the Confrères. But it had been acting in Paris, off and on, since 1612. Against the others it could boast of its seniority and greater regularity. And it had already assumed the title of 'King's Company'.

Yet it was not on friendly terms with the Confrères de la Passion who owned the building. As soon as he arrived in Paris in 1612, Robert Guérin had applied for the withdrawal of their ruinous privilege, which now had no justification because so many French as well as foreign companies were touring the kingdom. But the King, who had been attracted to their plays since childhood, maintained the Confrères' privilege. When in 1622 their rivals, the Prince of Orange's comedians, settled in the Hôtel de Bourgogne, Robert Guérin had to make do with the Hôtel d'Argent and, as usual, was forced by the Châtelet to pay the Confrères their usual tax.

Thenceforward, Robert Guérin, helped by Bellerose, fought on two fronts: against the Prince of Orange's company which he wanted to get rid of, and against the Confrères to deprive them of their property. In 1625 they tried to have Charles le Noir's lease annulled, and to act in a building near the Hôtel de Bourgogne in order to snatch away his public. Once more the *lieutenant civil* stepped in, confirmed Le Noir's lease and sent the King's Comedians back to a building in the rue St Antoine. Two years later the same thing happened with the same result. In 1629, back in the rue

Mauconseil, they renewed their attack on the Confrères, paying their rent only when a writ was served, and they fought a long legal battle against them until the time when the King, possibly under Richelieu's inducement, put them into the Hôtel de Bourgogne for three years, a length of time hitherto quite unprecedented. They pretended to understand that this royal grant meant that the Confrères had been dispossessed, which would mean for them a free royal concession and the saving of 2,400 livres a year in rent.

Having come across 'friends powerful enough to help them with the King', they applied to him direct. In their letter they began by abusing the Confrères, whose profession 'compelled most of them to earn a scanty living with their own hands, as a result of which they cannot have much honour and civility, as Aristotle says, and so are unable to fulfil honourable public offices and unworthy of the title of bourgeois, since the Greeks used to put their slaves and artisans side by side'. After this base and baseless libel, the actors put their request to the King:

'Their present claims, Sire, are exactly those which were moved some time ago at your Council between our actors and the so-called Masters of the Confrèrie de la Passion, when Your Majesty thought fit to give the Hôtel de Bourgogne to the former for three years only, provisionally and at the charge stated by the writ, until a decision on the principal subject is reached, and that is what your players are applying for today.'

The King's privy council merely requested the Confrères to produce their title-deeds, which was not difficult. And to justify their rights they published these deeds, together with the royal ordinances which from 1402 to 1612 granted them a monopoly—now disputed—over all spectacles in Paris. The actors had no choice but to agree. They understood at last that it would be better to live in peace with their proprietors. Consequently, in 1632 they renewed their lease for three years and they accepted a clause according to which they desisted from any legal action against the Confrères. Yet relations between the parties did not improve; in 1638 the Confrères had to distrain the furniture of Bellerose and his companions, who had refused to pay their rent; they wished to make alterations to the auditorium, to which the Confrères were opposed, requesting Parliament to prevent Bellerose from 'pulling the Hôtel de Bourgogne to the ground'. It was not until 1677 that they were dispossessed of the Hôtel by the King to the benefit of

58

the recently created General Hospital, to which the Royal Company had hitherto to pay the rent.

The Robert Guérin-Bellerose company which settled in the rue Mauconseil in 1629 was now known as the Royal Company. Indeed, shortly afterwards the company received a grant of 12,000 livres a year, double what was given later to the Marais and the Palais Royal, as if to testify to its pre-eminence. Proud of the King's and the Minister's protection, the company brandished its title of 'the only Royal Company': the other companies which the King later subsidized were simply 'the King's companies'. The Hôtel de Bourgogne alone was allowed to use red posters. Guérin's and Bellerose's actors and their successors were called by the public the 'Great Comedians', to distinguish them from all others. The company always claimed its primacy thereafter, and fought constantly against its most dangerous rivals, the Marais and the Palais-Royal. It stuck to the rue Mauconseil until 1680, when the Comédie Française was inaugurated.

Although the company continued under the direction of Gros-Guillaume, Bellerose played an increasingly important role. When he joined the company he brought with him from Marseilles his salaried poet, old Alexandre Hardy, who was turning out tragedies, comedies and pastorals as easily as a hen lays eggs. After him, Bellerose used Rotrou. We shall see later how he was able to get all he wanted from his authors.

Yet he provided the company in this way with what it needed most: a new, high-class repertoire. It was under him that a better-educated audience began to feel attracted by the plays of Théophile de Viau, Racan, Rotrou, du Ryer, Georges de Scuédéry and Mairet, in short by what is now known in France as the pre-classical theatre. To those completely new plays were added, of course, the usual farces, in which Bellerose condescended to act, while the trio composed of Gros-Guillaume, Turlupin and Gaultier-Garguilles continued daily to delight the audience in the pit. But Gaultier-Garguilles died in 1633, Gros-Guillaume in 1634 and Turlupin three years later. This spelt the end of rollicking classical farce at the Théâtre de Bourgogne. In the framework of the classical comedies it continued only at the Théâtre du Marais, where another flour-powdered clown, Jodelet, carried on. We have to wait until Molière's return to Paris in 1658 to see it return in full vigour in the successful *Les précieuses ridicules*.

Henceforth the Hôtel de Bourgogne specialized in literary

59

drama. In his *Maison des Jeux*, Charles Sorel emphasizes this fact: 'When comedy as a pastime began to give extreme pleasure, one wished that, to make it more pleasant, actors should be provided with fine plays to act in. For a very long time their only poet had been old Hardy who, according to gossip, wrote some five or six hundred plays.'

Bellerose, who directed the company after the death of Gros-Guillaume, proved an active, enterprising manager. He led his company to triumph and struggled ceaselessly against rival companies. He had powerful friends. His company acted *Mirame* and the *Comédie des Tuileries* at the Palais Cardinal. Bellerose knew how fond of plays Cardinal de Richelieu was. He easily made the Cardinal understand that the theatre in the rue Mauconseil should be the first, if not the only one in Paris, and that the best actors should go there. That is why Renaudot, in the *Gazette* of December 15, 1634, published the fact that six new actors had been taken into the royal company. Four of them were among the best of the Théâtre du Marais: Charles le Noir and his wife, Jodelet and his brother L'Espy. At the same time, Bellerose got rid of Beauchâteau by sending him to the Marais. Jodelet and L'Espy were to go back to the Marais a few years later.

These 'royal commands' were the first examples of the intrusion of royal authority into the organization of Paris theatres; this intrusion would increase continuously until the royal monopolies over the Opéra and the Comédie Française were at last created.

Three years later other actors of the Marais joined the Hôtel de Bourgogne: André Baron and his wife, and Villiers and his wife. Mme Villiers later created the part of Chimène in *Le Cid*. Bellerose's power was rather like that of a superintendent of the stage, angling for stars from rival companies to improve his own. His master stroke occurred in 1647, when from the Marais he grabbed Floridor, who, besides his great talent, was Corneille's intimate friend, the godfather of one of Corneille's sons and the creator of his first tragedies. And Bellerose once again succeeded in effecting an important change when it was arranged that the first tragic dramatist was to have all his plays performed at the Hôtel de Bourgogne. The Marais felt this loss keenly and to keep itself in business had recourse to a new kind of performance: plays with stage effects.

Of course, when a tragedian of Floridor's standing agreed to join the Royal Company, there was no question but that he must take first place. In the interests of the company, Bellerose agreed to make the necessary sacrifice: to the newcomer he relinquished his directorship, his job as 'orator', even the wardrobe, as well as his half-share in the takings—for the large sum of 20,000 livres. But he remained with the company and his name is still mentioned in the records for 1660.

Bellerose was not content to serve the company through his own talent, and by the new recruits he brought in and the authors, such as Hardy and Rotrou, and later Corneille, who provided him with the best possible repertoire. He tried also to turn the hall of the Hôtel de Bourgogne into the most beautiful and the richest auditorium in Paris. A fire had destroyed the Marais hall in 1644 and the company had rebuilt it, with improvements of course. So Bellerose undertook to modernize the hall in the rue Mauconseil so as not to be outdone by his principal rivals.

Consequently, through a higher rent (2,400 livres instead of 2,000) and a lease of five years instead of three, the Confrères de la Passion undertook, in a legal deed, that they would 'rebuild and redecorate the boxes in accordance with the design of the Marais playhouse, bringing the stage forward into the hall, ten feet further than at present, and all this with the least possible delay, that is within four months'. The deed was signed 'in the presence and with the advice' of a King's councillor, the *maître des requêtes*, a proof of the interest of the King in the upkeep and redecoration of the theatre in which his company performed, and which he often came to see.

An estimate and a contract were found which give an idea of what was undertaken and carried out. The stage was lengthened to seven *toises* and one foot (about forty-two feet) and raised by about $6\frac{1}{2}$ feet, provided with a deal floor and separated from the auditorium by a masonry wall. Thirteen dressing-rooms were built above and below stage; the old ones, which encumbered both sides of the stage, were destroyed. Two rows of nineteen boxes, each two yards wide and furnished with a door which locked, were built for the fashionable public; the amphitheatre was made as comfortable as possible, the pit floor was reboarded and repainted. All this cost the Confrères de la Passion 3,500 livres. It was into this rebuilt, repaired and remodelled hall of the Hôtel de Bourgogne that Corneille's plays made their entry.

Bellerose led the royal company for twenty-five years, removing it from the grossnesses of the farces and endowing it with a stage worthy of the classical plays it had now to perform. What do we know of his career? Pierre le Messier had followed the fashion set by contemporary players in assuming stage names which evoked the beauties of nature and especially the flowers: Beaupré, Préfleury, Beauchamp, Beauchâteau, Champmeslé, du Parc, Floridor, Montfleury, Beauval, La Fleur, Bellefleur, Rosidor, Rosimont: a whole flower-bed is conjured up by the names of seventeenth-century actors. Le Messier himself assumed the charming and simple name of Bellerose. We know that he began as an apprentice to Valleran le Conte and that he lived the picturesque life of a strolling player before returning to Paris and joining the Royal Company. His wife, who was also one of the company, was the widow of another actor, Mathias Meslier, and the sister of Philibert Gassot, better known as du Croissy, Molière's companion.

We have seen that he was an enterprising and masterful manager, but it was actually Bellerose who welded the company together. He may not have been a great tragedian, but he was excellent in pastorals, a very fashionable kind of play. His extreme and slightly stilted refinement, his soft musical voice and his natural distinction made the *précieuses*, who loved that rather insipid sort of play, ecstatic. Robinet wrote in his gazette:

> *Dedans ses rôles de tendresse,*
> *Où chacun l'admirait sans cesse.*[1]

He also acted Corneille's young heroes when Corneille's first plays, created at the Marias, were revived in the rue Mauconseil. Yet critical spectators, like Mme de Chevreuse, who thought he had 'the most insipid face in the world', or Tallemant des Réaux, found fault with his lack of strength: 'Bellerose was a painted actor', wrote the latter, 'who looked first where to throw his hat, lest he should harm the feathers; he sometimes spoke some speeches fairly well, but he did not in the least understand what he was saying.'

On the other hand, according to the same Tallemant, Mlle Bellerose (his wife), though she was so fat 'that she looked like a tower', was nevertheless the best actress in Paris. It was she who first played Corneille's *Rodogune*; a seventeenth-century chronicle has recorded her affair with the young Benserade, who wrote his *Cléopâtre* for her. The Abbé de Rivière, Gaston d'Orléans' chaplain, was one of her lovers. The Bellerose couple, like all actors,

---

[1] 'He was constantly admired in parts in which he had to display tenderness.'

went through a difficult time during the Fronde, a troubled period during which the public deserted the theatre. According to the pamphleteers, Mlle Bellerose fell into dire straits. In a bad pun they wrote that:

> *Ne gagnant plus rien sur la Seine,*
> *Elle tragique sur le Rhin.*[2]

Her last lover was the Abbé d'Armentières who, according to Tallemant, 'was so strangely infatuated with her that after her death he kept her skull in his room for a long time'.

Besides the clowns, Bellerose's chief companion was André Boiron, called Baron, the father of the youth who was to become Molière's dearest pupil; also his wife, an actor's daughter with whom Floridor fell madly in love; and above all, Beauchâteau who, but for five years with the Marais, made all his career at the Hôtel de Bourgogne.

Beauchâteau was no genius; he was Floridor's understudy in his chief roles, like Horace or Cinna. But Boileau was probably too hard on him when, one day when he was cross, he called him an 'atrocious actor'. On the other hand, his wife was, according to Tallemant, 'an actress one could rely on', and a clever woman whom authors like Tristan or Scarron did not hesitate to consult. Molière made easy mockery of the couple when, in his *Impromptu de Versailles*, he made fun out of rival actors. He ridiculed Beauchâteau declaiming passages from the *Cid* stanzas and also his wife in the part of Camille (in *Horace*), cruelly emphasizing 'the smiling face she maintained in the greatest affliction'.

Though Mme Beauchâteau had presented her husband with three children, the couple led a very free life. Beauchâteau's affairs were well known. The author of the apocryphal *Testament de Gaultier Garguilles* wrote: 'To Beauchâteau, who never found a chastity strong enough to resist him, who is no sooner seen than loved, I bequeath the walks of my Montmartre garden, and allow him to present ladies with the flowers of the bulbs I planted, yet charging him not to be over-active and imperil his days to please them.'

It seems that his wife was equally free. She had had an affair with

[2] 'As she can no longer earn any money on the Seine, she has started trading her charms on the Rhine.' The lines only make sense when one realizes the double pun on Seine (both the river and 'stage') and Rhin (both the river and 'kidney' or, more precisely, the back view of the lady).

L'Espy, Jodelet's brother. As a joke, she once asked Jodelet what love was:

'I don't know,' Jodelet answered.

'It is a blindfolded god with a torch, a bow and arrows.'

And the clown answered: 'I see. He is a god who has an arrow which was shot by M. de l'Espy into Mlle de Beauchâteau's chamois drawers.'

There were other stars at the Hôtel de Bourgogne under Bellerose's direction. For instance, Mlle Le Noir, who acted in Mairet's first plays; but we shall find her later at the Marais with Mlle Beaupré. There was also Mme La Fleur, Gros-Guillaume's wife, who stepped upon the stage after his death, and especially Mlle Valliot, whom everyone knew as 'La Valliotte'. Her husband was also in Gros-Guillaume's company. Tallemant wrote that she was 'the best-built woman ever seen'. She was one of the first generation of actresses, having probably joined the company when she married in 1620. That is why Tallemant, some forty years later, speaks of her as 'a decrepit old hag'. His contemporaries praised her tall stature, her eyes full of fire, her refinement and grace, but no one thought of telling us what roles she performed in the plays of Hardy and Rotrou.

With Floridor as successor to Bellerose, we reach the Hôtel de Bourgogne's period of glory. Josias de Soulas, called Floridor, was no ordinary player: he was distinguished from the rest by his talent as well as by his birth. He was the son of a protestant pastor who had renounced his religion. He was *Sieur* of Primefosse and of authentic nobility. He was an officer in the Rambures regiment. The fine painting in the museum of the Comédie Française which, according to an old tradition, is his portrait, reveals a man of fine and distinguished features and a noble, powerful manner. One of his sons became vicar of Vaux-le-Pénil, near Mélun. The Duc de Saint Simon and the Comtesse de Fiesque were godparents to his third son. We are very far indeed from the beggars of the beginning of the century.

Like the rest, Floridor began as a strolling player. He was in London in 1635, in Saumur in 1638 and then he joined the Théâtre du Marais. He was the friend of Pierre Corneille, who was godfather to one of his sons, while the poet's wife, Marie Lempériere, was godmother to another. Floridor acted in Corneille's tragedies, which were the glory of the Marais theatre; they could only be revived at the Hôtel de Bourgogne after they had been printed, according to the usage of the time. As we have said, in 1647 Floridor went over to the Hôtel de Bourgogne and replaced Bellerose as director of the company.

There he met with uninterrupted success; in 1657 he revived the parts of Horace and Cinna, which he had created at the Marais, performed Corneille's *Oedipe* for the first time, and later appeared as Massinissa in Corneille's *Sophonisbe*. In Molière's company he took part in the court performances, acting before Monsieur, the King's brother, and on each of these occasions bowed most gallantly to the King and the princes. Donneau de Visé, the first dramatic critic, praised him mightily.

'He actually looks his part in all the plays he performs. The whole audience wants to see him all the time, and his gait, his air, and his motion are so easy that it is not necessary for him to speak to attract the attention of everyone. Finally, to praise him it is enough to utter his name, as it carries with it all the eulogies imaginable.'

Loret's gazette never failed to mention his success with every new part he took up.

The illustrious tragedian who acted in all Corneille's plays also had the luck to do so in all Racine's tragedies from *Alexandre* on. Later he was Pyrrhus (*Andromaque*), Nero (*Britannicus*) and finally Titus (*Bérénice*), acting with Mlle de Champmeslée. What a career for a tragedian, to spend thirty years of his life creating all the great parts in Corneille's and Racine's plays, helping himself to unforgettable triumphs! He only left the Paris stage to die in 1671, and the only funeral speech we have about him is Bussy-Rabutin's cold and cruel remark that 'It is high time Floridor left the stage!' This is the constant and typical callousness of the public when its idols grow too old.

Floridor had been unanimously admired and respected: he was a refined, well-bred man, a kind father, a scholar, as good as director and inspiration of his company as Molière was of his. He once wrote to the carpenter-poet of Nevers, Adam Billaut, about alterations that should be carried out on the stage of the Hôtel de Bourgogne: the poet refused any salary for his work and Floridor thanked him in a clever, pleasant madrigal. Molière himself held the director of the royal company in high esteem. When, in *L'Impromptu de Versailles*, he drew caricatures of the actors of the Hôtel de Bourgogne and jeered at their bombastic elocution, he carefully refrained from attacking Floridor, the best-known and the most popular member of the company.

E

Even Louis XIV, who was passionately fond of the stage and often applauded Floridor, either in the rue Mauconseil or at Versailles, 'looked kindly on him and condescended to favour him each time they met', wrote Chappuzeau. We have proof of this. Besides frequent presents, the King granted him in 1661 the privilege 'to provide all the ropes required from the Quai des Bonshommes de Chaillot to the Porte de la Conférence, in the city of Paris, with all the boats, either up or down the Seine.' Floridor owed this royal grant to an 'adviser', a captain of the Cent Suisses of the Duc d'Orléans, with whom he shared the income of the business. Two years later, Quinault and Floridor together shared the royal grant of the running of stage-coaches between Paris, Cahors and Sarlat. In 1668, when the King ordered a check of the proofs of nobility, he granted Floridor the title of squire and a year to produce his deeds of nobility, which the comedian had probably mislaid.

Such was the great actor who put all his talent to the service of classical tragedy and for twenty-five years led the Royal Company of the Hôtel de Bourgogne.

One of his colleagues, known as Montfleury, was Zacharie Jacob by birth, the son of two comedians in Valleran le Conte's company, and the father of two actresses, Mlle d'Ennebaut and Mlle Dupin, and of a son who married one of Floridor's daughters. Montfleury achieved fame in the Hôtel de Bourgogne company. Like the rest, he trained in the provinces; then Bellerose summoned him to the Hôtel de Bourgogne. Arriving in Paris in 1638, he married an actress, Jeanne de la Chappe, Pierre Rousseau's widow. The wedding took place in Richelieu's country house at Rueil, a proof that the newcomer enjoyed powerful connections.

For thirty years, together with Floridor, Montfleury served the classical theatre devotedly. He actually wrote a tragedy, *La Mort d'Asdrubal*, but this was only a versified adaptation of La Serre's prose play, *Le Sac de Carthage*. Chappuzeau recorded as something quite unusual that Montfleury acted in both tragedies and comedies. He hardly touched anything but Corneille's plays. Among other parts, he was given that of Prusias in *Nicomède*, Syphax in *Sophonisbe*, and also Seleucus in Thomas Corneille's *Antiochus*. He also acted Porus in Racine's *Alexandre* and Oreste in his *Andromaque*. According to tradition, he died of the strain of declaiming Oreste's lines in the mad scene.

For Montfleury was an actor of the old school, when the pit

delighted in bombastic elocution and loud speech. He was very stout and had a tremendous voice. His over-acting and over-shouting made him the victim of innumerable jokes. Molière mocked him cruelly in *L'Impromptu de Versailles*, where he parodied Montfleury in the part of Prusias.

Cyrano de Bergerac wrote a letter in which he made fun, rather heavily, of Montfleury's large stomach: 'I can assure you', he wrote 'that if a beating could be sent by post, you would read my letter with your shoulders; and don't be surprised by my suggestion as, your rounded surface being so great, I am convinced you are a land in which I would like to plant sticks to see what would become of them.' Edmond Rostand, in *Cyrano de Bergerac*, turned it into these lines!

> *Faudra-t-il que je fasse, ô monarque des droles,*
> *Une plantation de bois sur vos épaules?*[3]

Yet we know, thanks to Chappuzeau, that the Court, which was not interested in Cyrano de Bergerac, had considerable regard for this 'polished actor'. A good amateur, St Evremond, thought that *Andromaque* lost much with Montfleury's death.

Bellerose, Montfleury, Floridor and Hauteroche, who succeeded him as director of the company, were the 'great actors' of the seventeenth century. Of course, they had a number of worthy female colleagues who shared their success.

Loret, in his rhymed gazette, often praised the grace and feeling of Mlle des Oeillets. She was the wife of a strolling player who went first to the Marais; so did she, before joining the Hôtel de Bourgogne. She was acclaimed in the roles of Sophonisbe, Hermione and Agrippine.

Yet at that time the greatest applause was lavished on the illustrious du Parc. Marquise-Thérèse de Gorla, the daughter of an Italian mountebank who lived in Lyons, began as a dancer in her father's show. When he was passing through Lyons in 1653, Molière took her into his company and married her to one of his companions, Gros-René. Thanks to her beauty and charm, she had the extraordinary privilege of including Corneille, Molière and Racine among her admirers. She met the first in Rouen in 1658, but this young woman, who was an accomplished coquette, spurned the attentions of the grey-haired poet. He was deeply wounded and took his revenge in this delightful poem:

---

[3] 'Must I plant sticks on your shoulders, you King of scamps?'

Marquise, si mon visage
A quelques traits un peu vieux,
Souvenez-vous qu'à mon âge,
Vous ne vaudrez guère mieux.

Le temps au plus belles choses
Se plaît à faire un affront,
Et saura faner vos roses
Comme il a ridé mon front.

Le même cours des planètes
Règle nos jours et nos nuits,
On m'a vu ce que vous êtes,
Vous serez ce que je suis.

Chez cette race nouvelle
Où j'aurai quelque crédit,
Vous ne passerez pour belle
Qu'autant que je l'aurai dit.

Pensez-y, belle Marquise,
Quoiqu'un grison fasse effroi,
Il vaut bien qu'on le courtise
Quand il est fait comme moi.[4]

Molière, too, made love to Mlle du Parc, to forget the worries caused by his wife's flirtations, and it seems he was not better treated. But Racine succeeded where the others had failed.

As soon as the company reached Paris, the du Parcs went for a year to the Marais, then back to Molière. Loret wrote about Molière's *Fâcheux:*

La du Parc, cette belle actrice
Avec son port d'impératrice,

---

[4] 'Marquise, if my face displays some rather elderly features, do remember that, at my age, you won't look much better. Time enjoys insulting the loveliest things, and he will wither your roses just as he has wrinkled my brow. The course of the planets rules our days and our nights alike: once I was just like you; and you will be like me. Among some future people with whom I shall enjoy some credit, your beauty will be praised just as I have praised it. Think, lovely Marquise, that though a grey-beard may be terrifying, he deserves being courted when he is made like me.'

Soit récitant, soit en dansant,
N'a rien qui ne soit ravissant.[5]

She acted in *La Critique de l'Ecole des Femmes*, in *L'Im-promptu de Versailles*, and in *Le Mariage Forcé*; riding on a Spanish horse, she was Spring in the *Ballet des Saisons* which opened the *Plaisirs de l'île enchantée*, the magnificent display offered by the young King to Mlle de la Vallière in the gardens of Versailles; it is possible that she created the part of Elvire in Molière's *Dom Juan*, and she certainly was the first Arsinoé in *Le Misanthrope*.

Her beauty and her talent aroused Racine, who had just quarrelled with Molière about *Alexandre*. He took Mlle du Parc with him to the Hôtel de Bourgogne and shortly afterwards she became his mistress. He wrote *Andromaque* for her, for he had noticed her feeling for music and rhythm in verse, and he taught her her part line by line, stressing all the nuances and every hint and allusion. 'He made her rehearse like a school-girl', wrote Boileau.

This collaboration, as well as the idyll, did not last for long. She had borne him a daughter and some thought that they may have been secretly married. But Mlle du Parc died suddenly, in mysterious circumstances, on December 11, 1668. The Voisin, a hideous witch, accused Racine of having poisoned his mistress in order to steal her jewels, and Louvois even thought of having him arrested. Yet it is more likely that she died in childbed, possibly after an attempt at abortion. Newspapers mentioned her death and described her burial service, to which came all the French and Italian actors and the dramatic poets:

Dont l'un, le plus intéressé
Etait à-demi trépassé.[6]

Mlle du Parc had vanished when scarcely thirty-five, leaving Racine deeply distressed; her career at the Hôtel de Bourgogne had lasted just under eighteen months; she had passed like a shooting star across the painted canvas sky of the Paris stage.

Her place was taken by an illustrious tragedian, Mlle Champ-meslé. Her name was Marie Desmares, and she had begun her

[5] 'Mlle du Parc, that lovely actress, with her splendid deportment when acting or dancing, was wholly delightful.'
[6] 'One of them, the most deeply hurt, was looking half-dead.' (Racine, of course).

career in Serdin's touring company. In Rouen in 1666 she married one of her companions, Charles Chevillet, called Champmeslé, whose comedies had enjoyed some reputation, though they have sometimes been ascribed to La Fontaine. They both went into the Marais in 1668 and two years later moved to the Hôtel de Bourgogne, eighteen months after Mlle du Parc's death, and six before that of Mlle des Oeillets. From now on, Mlle Champmeslé's career was that of a great star; she certainly was the greatest tragic actress of the seventeenth century. Until the end of the century she passed from success to success at the Comédie Française. She created all the leading parts in Racine's plays, including that of *Phèdre*, which he taught her line by line, just as he had taught Mlle du Parc the lines of *Andromaque*.

For Mlle Champmeslé had not only replaced Mlle du Parc on the stage of the Hôtel de Bourgogne: she had also taken her place in Racine's heart. Truth compels us to say that, before this new affair, she had led a very gay life.

Mme de Sévigné, for a period at least, has given us plenty of information on the subject. Mlle Champmeslé had been the mistress of Mme de Sévigné's son Charles, so she playfully called her 'my daughter-in-law'. Speaking of her connection with her son, she once wrote to Mme de Grignan: 'There was also a little actress, and Despréaux and Racine with her: these suppers were delightful, or rather pretty boisterous.' But she did admire the actress. Having seen her as Roxane in *Bajazet*, she wrote: 'My daughter-in-law seemed to me the most beautiful actress I had ever seen. She is miles better than Mlle des Oeillets. . . . From close up she looks plain, but she is adorable when speaking her lines.' Mme de Sévigné, who was the elderly Corneille's faithful admirer, tells us that Racine wrote his plays for Mlle Champmeslé 'and not for the centuries to come', in which she was completely mistaken.

The affair with Charles de Sévigné was joyous but short-lived. The one with Racine was, for the poet at least, a *grande passion* which lasted until he retired from the theatre. Journalists thought it great fun:

> *Champmeslé, cet heureux mortel,*
> *Ne quittera jamais l'Hôtel:*
> *Sa femme a pris Racine-là,*
> *Alléluia!*[7]

[7] 'This blessed mortal, Champmeslé, shall never leave the Hôtel. His wife has taken root there.' There is a pun on Racine's name (*racine*=root).

Racine was succeeded by M. de Tonnerre; hence new puns:

> *A la plus tendre amour elle fut destinée*
> *Qui prit longtemps racine dans son coeur,*
> *Mais par un insigne malheur,*
> *Le tonnerre est venu qui l'a déracinée.*[8]

In 1689 she was forty-five. Mme de Sévigné wrote: 'Mlle Champ-meslé's tricks to keep all her lovers together without prejudice to the parts of Atalide, Bérénice and Phèdre, make you drive for five leagues with the greatest ease.' Ten years later, when she was at the point of death, the vicar of Auteuil had the greatest difficulty in making her sign the indispensable renunciation of her profession, 'finding herself very proud to die an actress'. Finally, she did give in. A few days after her death, Racine, who had retired from the theatre for twenty years and had gone back to the Port-Royal of his childhood, wrote to his son that Mlle Champ-meslé 'had died in a fairly good state of mind, having renounced the stage, very repentant of her past life, and above all very sorry to die'. For Racine's memory, one could wish that he had never written this heartless sentence about his former mistress who had devoted all her talent to his benefit.

If the Hôtel de Bourgogne knew no rivals in tragedy, it was not the same with comedy. It could not compete with the Palais Royal, with Molière, his company, his repertory and a long tradition of comic acting. Yet in the rue Mauconseil they always acted a comedy after a tragedy. The Hôtel therefore had a number of comedy writers, among whom was Champmeslé, while the best of them was Belleroche, better known by his real name of Raymond Poisson, the ancestor of a long line of comic actors.

He too had been a touring player for years; then, in 1659, thanks to the Colberts' protection, he became the director of a company which accompanied Louis XIV when the court moved, so that he received large royal grants. Soon afterwards he and his wife, who also acted, entered the Hôtel. A bust of him, dressed as Crispin, a role which he created, can be seen at the Scala in Milan. This type of shrewd, stammering servant, always ready to help his master in his love intrigues, for some honest reward, is found in many

---

[8] 'To the most tender love she was devoted, as it was rooted in her heart for long, but through a striking piece of ill-luck, the thunder struck and uprooted her.' Again, there is the double pun, on Tonnerre's (thunder) and Racine's (root) names.

comedies by Regnard or Le Sage, and it was created by Scarron in his *Ecolier de Salamanque*, acted in 1654 at the Théâtre du Marais. Crispin was dressed in the traditional Spanish costume: a round hat, a white ruff, a short black doublet, a broad yellow leather belt, with a large copper buckle, a black cloak and high riding boots.

Raymond Poisson's verve and high spirits made this new type popular once more; every comic author put a Crispin on the stage as, twenty years previously, they had staged a Jodelet. So did Chappuzeau, de Villiers, Donneau de Visé, Hauteroche, Champ-meslé, Montfleury *fils*, La Tuilerie, and Raymond Poisson himself, for he was also an author and his *Le Poète basque* and *Le Baron de la Crasse* were quite successful. Yet, as most of those short comedies had but one act, he called himself pleasantly 'a fifth of a playwright'. He also acted Jodelet when Scarron's old comedies were revived. Molière, though he belonged to a rival company, liked his comic style, and it is said that 'he would have given anything in the world to be as natural as this great actor'.

Raymond Poisson pursued a very fine career at the Hôtel de Bourgogne and then at the Comédie Français. A skilful and obstinate beggar, he increased his income as an actor by asking anything from his protectors at any time: the noblemen to whom he inscribed his comedies, and the King in person, whom he bored with requests in verse or madrigals, always shamelessly adding that his praises were worth a fee. Yet his wit and gaiety helped so much that his solicitations were usually well received. Raymond Poisson had something of Crispin in him. Once Louis XIV had started granting his requests, dukes and ministers had no choice but to do the same.

Those were the main stars who, for half a century, led the Hôtel de Bourgogne and taught the Paris audiences to understand and to like the classical theatre in all its pristine freshness.

The company ceased its activities in the autumn of 1680, leaving the Hôtel de Bourgogne to the Italians. In circumstances we shall describe later, it was entirely absorbed by the new Comédie Française.

CHAPTER THREE

THE KING'S COMPANY AT THE THÉÂTRE DU MARAIS (1634–1673)

In 1629, the very year in which Robert Guérin's company finally settled at the Hôtel de Bourgogne, a new touring company arrived in Paris. It came from Rouen, where its director had received from a yet unknown poet, a young lawyer, the manuscript of a comedy, *Mélite*. The author was Pierre Corneille and the manager Montdory. For fifteen years those two names were to be linked in theatrical glory.

Who was Montdory? His real name was Guillaume Desgilberts. Son of a Thiers cutler, he was one of Valleran le Conte's pupils, and is mentioned in this connection as being on half-pay, a modest position, in 1612. At one time he was a member of the Prince of Orange's company with Le Noir; but in 1624 he formed his own company together with Villiers, Beaupré and their wives. It seems that when he arrived in Paris he had joined another company where he had found his old friend Le Noir. Paris was for him the only city which could provide glory and fortune.

They settled in a tennis court in the Impasse Berthaud (now 37 rue Beaubourg) and performed *Mélite*. Corneille wrote later: 'The success was surprising. It gave standing to a new company in Paris, in spite of the talents of those who thought themselves unique [the Royal Company]: it equalled all the best that had been done so far and it made me known.' A first success that was shared by both poet and actors.

Of course, in settling into the Impasse Berthaud, neither Montdory nor Le Noir paid any attention to the Confrères de la Passion, but the Confrères took action and in accordance with their privilege demanded the rent of two écus for each of the 135 performances. As usual, the Châtelet had to be brought in to compel the actors to pay.

In 1631 Montdory's company moved into a new tennis court, Le Sphère, in the rue Vieille-du-Temple, paying a rent of twelve livres a day. As it was probably too expensive, the company moved again, this time to a gaming house called La Fontaine, in the rue Michel-le-Comte. There it doubtless drew crowds, as the local people complained of the large number of coaches and horses which blocked the narrow streets of the Marais quarter. The matter was brought before parliament, but its decision is not known. But what we do know is that early in 1634 Montdory moved once more and rented another tennis court, *Les Marais* in the rue Vieille-du-Temple (No 90), this time for five years.

It was a fine, large hall, but the rent was high and weighed heavily on the affairs of the new theatre: 3,000 livres, while that of the Hôtel de Bourgogne was between 2,000 and 2,400. But they were granted a long lease of five years, which is proof of their will to settle in Paris for good. Paris was thus to have a second stage, and the Théâtre du Marais was born. There were eight actors in the company, counting Villiers, Beaulieu, Jodelet and his brother L'Espy, and two or three actresses, two of whom were Mme Le Noir and Mme Villiers. Strangely, Montdory's wife was not an actress; he said that 'she was a witless person who sticks to the church'.

Corneille provided the new company with plays: after *Mélite*, they performed *Clitandre, La Veuve, La Galerie du Palais, La Suivante* and *La Place royale*: the public was amused by these comedies with a very definite Paris setting. Malicious critics would ask Montdory whether 'he would soon advertise the St Jean Churchyard, the Samaritaine and the Place aux Veaux'. But, sure of the protection of the Comte de Belin, who was Mme Villiers' lover, and soon after that of Richelieu himself, he paid no attention to the jeers and was glad to collect the daily increasing income. He was on the road to fortune; the public was delighted to have a choice between two theatres and two repertoires. Just like the Royal Company, that of the Marais received invitations to perform from private persons. When the Duc de la Valette was married, they performed *Mélite* at the Arsenal. Montdory and his colleagues became 'the Royal Company in the Marais'. As early as 1635 they were granted an allowance of 6,000 livres, half what the Hôtel de Bourgogne, 'the only Royal Company', received, but it was not a bad beginning.

The one-time strolling players had become an official Paris institution, stable and prosperous, protected and subsidized by the King.

Of course, the Royal Company became anxious, worried by the

success of these unexpected rivals. Bellerose did not remain inactive: he tried hard to break up the Marais theatre. A clever, resourceful, not over-scrupulous fellow, he succeeded in getting from the King an order for four of Montdory's company to join the Hôtel de Bourgogne: Le Noir and his wife, Jodelet and L'Espy. The *Gazette* added: 'The old company, with this welcome addition, brought a crowd that overflowed the Hôtel de Bourgogne on the 10th, when they performed M. de Scudéry's *Le Trompeur puni*; while Montdory, who yet did not despair of the success of his little republic, tried to repair the damage and, as in the past, we can rely on his industry.'

This paragraph should be noted: it is the oldest piece of theatrical news in the history of the French press.

Poor Montdory was at his wits' end. He had been robbed of four of his best actors out of a company of eleven. Bellerose's attack might prove fatal. Another of his actors, François Mestivier, Mme Le Noir's father, from pique, left the stage for good. The director of the Marais found himself unable to give a performance. Of course, he was not without encouragement and help. The Cardinal de Richelieu, who thought that two theatres in Paris were not too much, came to the rescue, as 'he liked Montdory very much'. He immediately granted him 500 *écus* as a private gift, and gave 300 more to the company to pay the rent. Full of gratitude, Montdory sent him a pompous ode of thanks, which comprised 210 rather flat verses. As for Corneille, who did not relish the disappearance of the theatre in which his plays had achieved such a triumph, he addressed a Latin ode to the Archbishop of Rouen into which he slipped this praise of his principal actor: 'The stage is there, the gesture and voice help us, and if the work is imperfect, Roscius makes amends. He imparts life to flat lines, his whole person contributes to the success and he also gives fire and grace to my lines.'

It was all right so far, and Montdory was taking heart again, but he had to retrieve a very difficult situation. On December 18, 1654, he produced Mairet's *Sophonisbe* 'with his old company gathered together for the last time'. With great courage he endeavoured to build a new one. With Richelieu's help, he got the King to send the Beauchâteaus from the over-full Hôtel de Bourgogne company to the Marais: two good new elements but not enough. In great haste, he signed on Pierre Regnault Petit-Jean, known as La Roque, an old companion who had left him before he came to the Marais and who would one day become the theatre's brilliant

75

manager; also André Baron Père, who was acting in Paris for the first time, and Bellemore, a comedian who specialized in braggarts' parts and could replace Jodelet. In less than a fortnight Montdory had been able to reorganize a company which was soon completed with the celebrated Beaupré. On December 31, 1634, the emergency was over and the Marais reopened its doors.

The public did not fail him, and the theatre entered upon one of its proudest and most brilliant periods. After Scudéry's *La Mort de César*, in which Montdory acted Brutus, Mairet's *Marc Antoine* and Mareschal's *Le Railleur*, the ever-faithful Corneille, who filled the Hôtel de Bourgogne with envy, gave them *Médée* and *L'Illusion Comique*, a baroque comedy on completely new lines. Then came Tristan l'Hermite's *Mariamne*, a triumph in which Montdory as Herod was unanimously praised. Corneille noted his excellent interpretation and Tallemant des Réaux wrote: 'To make people aware of his skill, he asked some intelligent people with knowledge of the stage to come and see *Mariamne* four times in succession. Each day they noticed something new; also, to be truthful, this was his masterpiece, and he was better as a hero than as a lover.' Montdory had become the best tragedian in Paris; even Bellerose had to acknowledge his great art.

Things went further in December 1636 and January 1637. Corneille, now at the height of his genius, had *Le Cid* acted at the Marais. It is well known that the play aroused Richelieu's jealousy and started a resounding quarrel in the newly created French Academy.

The pamphlets multiplied, for or against the new masterpiece: the public became excited and divided. Rodrigue's high sentiments set Paris on fire. No play had ever caused such a disturbance. It was a fight to get into the theatre. 'The crowd was so big at our door', Montdory himself wrote to Balzac, 'and our hall so small that the tiniest corners of the theatre, where the pages were usually to be found, provided the coveted seats for which holders of the Blue Ribbons[1] queued up, and the stage was usually crowded by Knights of the King's orders.'[2]

Of course, Montdory acted Rodrigue; Mlle Villiers played opposite him as Chimène. Balzac said that the tragedian, thanks to his talent, was the *Cid*'s 'second father' and that to be Montdory's friend was to be the favourite of a thousand kings. In short, the

---

[1] The insignia of the Order of the Holy Ghost.
[2] The orders of St Louis or St Michel.

same glory crowned both the author and the actor. It was of no avail that Corneille's enemies wrote venomous sentences like the following: 'The skill and talent of the actors, in their perfect acting and for their ability to make it worthy of praise by unexpected tricks which M. Montdory understands just as well as he does his own profession, have been the *Cid*'s richest ornament, and the main cause of its false reputation.' The public, in its enthusiasm, made no difference between the poet and the actor.

Alas, so many efforts, in spite of their triumphal reward, had prematurely exhausted Montdory, who was hardly above forty when, in August 1637, while voicing Herod's imprecations with great zest, he forced his voice and had an apoplectic fit. Montdory was paralysed and his career cut short. In spite of a courageous but unsuccessful attempt to come back at Carnival 1638, he had to abandon acting for good. Richelieu smoothed his retirement by making him a grant of 2,000 livres.

The theatre is a continuous struggle: as on the battlefield, when the leader is killed, another must step out of the ranks and take his place. It was Villiers who, with his companions' agreement, was henceforth to manage the Marais company. He renewed the lease for five years. To replace Le Noir, who died shortly after Montdory's retirement, de Villiers was lucky enough to engage a young actor, Floridor, an excellent tragedian who was to take the lead in Corneille's new tragedies. For *Horace, Cinna, Polyeucte, La Mort de Pompée* and *Le Menteur* enabled the Marais to pursue a brilliant career, the prestige of which would certainly eclipse that of the rival company at the Hôtel de Bourgogne for several years. Shortly after André Baron's marriage, his wife, nicknamed 'La Baronne', who was also a former pupil of Valleran le Conte, joined the Marais theatre, to which Jodelet and L'Espy had returned. The company now had thirteen members and was in a position to perform the whole repertoire, old and new.

And yet, as it was too successful, the company referred to as 'the little players', as distinct from the 'great players' of the Hôtel de Bourgogne, again aroused Bellerose's greed; for he was at this moment deprived of first-rate actors and saw the prestige of his theatre eclipsed by that of the Marais. As in 1634, he went straight to the King and had no difficulty in obtaining the transfer to the rue Mauconseil of six actors, Villiers, Baron and Beauchâteau and their wives. Once more the Marais company was broken up, deprived of its manager and reduced to five actors and two actresses.

Floridor picked up the sceptre which had fallen from the hands of Villiers. With great difficulty he increased the number of his companions, adding a few secondary recruits. Yet he did not lose faith in the future. If Bellerose had deprived him of his best people, he still held a trump card, Corneille, who was faithful to the Marais throughout its vicissitudes, and whose intimate friend he soon became. A new blow, for which fate was responsible this time, suddenly destroyed all Floridor's hopes. On January 15, 1644, a fire destroyed the theatre, all the wooden structures of which were reduced to ashes. This disaster overwhelmed the actors, who lost all their scenery and all their costumes, their only wealth; it also overwhelmed the owners of the tennis courts, who held the company responsible and considered suing it. Such is the tale told by Mme Deierkauf-Holsboer in her excellent *Histoire du Théâtre du Marais*, so full of unpublished documents. Mutual friends stepped in, trying to find some means to reach an understanding suitable to the two parties equally, and they succeeded on March 31.

The proprietors agreed not to ask a rent until the auditorium had been rebuilt but, being granted a new five years' lease, the comedians had to pay 10,500 livres *tournois*—some 50,000 new francs—to rebuild all the destroyed buildings, the hall and the secondary structures. A large part of their savings—for they had earned good money for some years—went into it. Floridor hurried the workers as much as possible; each day he was on the site, harassing them all. In less than ten months a new hall, finer and larger than before, was erected, with two superimposed rows of eighteen boxes each, with room for the gods on top, a large amphitheatre at the back of the hall, a stage twice as large as the earlier one, and on a slanting floor, so that the pit was able to have a better view of the actors, and ten comfortable dressing-rooms, an unheard-of luxury. The auditorium was about thirty-eight metres long, which was more than the usual tennis court. It could hold some 1,500 people.

In October 1644 the Théâtre du Marais reopened with *La Suite du Menteur* and *Rodogune*. For lovers of comedy, Scarron and d'Ouville wrote a set of *Jodelet* in which the famous clown triumphed. Thanks to Floridor's energy and to the players' sacrifices, the situation that had been so seriously affected by the fire was quickly retrieved.

The Théâtre du Marais seemed to be on its way to a new era of prosperity when a further misfortune occurred. Early in 1647, as we have already mentioned, Floridor went over to the Hôtel de

Bourgogne. He did not desert his theatre, as it was thought at first; it was by royal command that he did so, but it was achieved by Bellerose who was still jealous of the achievements of the Marais. The Marais hall lost not only its manager and best actor, but also his wife, who followed him to the rue Mauconseil and, worst of all, Corneille's new plays. *Héraclitus* was performed at the Hôtel de Bourgogne. That was utter ruin for the Marais, and this time it was tragedy. Bellerose had succeeded: he had crushed the rival stage which was making a greater success of its business than was his own.

The 'little players', defeated by the 'great' ones, were once more in despair; so were the proprietors of the theatre who were in urgent need of their rent, as the buildings were mortgaged. Once more, the company tried to fill the gaps. Floridor himself provided them with a good strolling player, Philandre, who later became manager of the Prince de Condé's company. Philandre bought Floridor's share for 550 livres; with him came Nicolas Biet de Beauchamp and his wife. The proprietors, who were afraid of losing everything, became conciliatory and gave the actors a new three-year lease for a rent of 2,400 livres, a reduction of 600.

Under the direction of Philibert Robin and, soon after, of La Rocque, the Marais weathered the gale and survived. But the actors well knew that, without Floridor and without Corneille's repertoire, they could not hold out against the Hôtel de Bourgogne, which remained henceforth the temple of the Tragic Muse, to which Racine, in his turn, brought his plays.

So they had to find something else to act; of course, they continued to perform tragedies—those by du Ryer, Gillet de la Tessonnerie, Thomas Corneille—but also some comedies in which Jodelet was still supreme. But they were now making efforts to produce plays 'with effects', that is to say, with plenty of spectacle, music, singing and dancing, with the help of complicated sets and machinery, like those used by Torelli when Mazarin brought Italian operas—Sacrati's *Finta Pazza* and Rossi's *Orfeo*—to the Palais Royal. They hired Denis Buffequin, a well-known painter, stage-designer and scene-shifter.

All this involved them in heavy expenses, but they were determined to make any necessary sacrifice. The whole of mythology was going to pass across the Marais stage with Chapoton's *Circé* and *La Descente d'Orphée aux Enfers*, Boyer's *Ulysse dans l'île de Circé*, *Andromède et Persée* by an unknown author and Rotrou's

79

Naissance d'Hercule, to say nothing of Corneille's *Andromède*. The public welcomed this gorgeous display of scenery and costumes, arias and new dances, all the gods of Olympus flying across the stage on cleverly contrived machinery, dryads, mermaids and nereids swimming in their watery element, heaven and hell revealed, abductions, incantations, supernatural apparitions, ships on tempestuous seas, and simulated fires. In a word, prosperity returned and the Marais, with this new genre, had found its faithful audience once more. In 1649, the trouble brought about by the Fronde interrupted that success. Parisians, starved and besieged, lost their taste for the theatre. The Marais remained closed for many months and Philandre went back to the provinces.

When it reopened, the Marais lived mostly on revivals of old plays, especially those by the Corneille brothers and Scarron. Nothing new was created in the years 1653 and 1654. The theatre was only half-alive and no longer had the full houses of the past. The public now favoured the Hôtel de Bourgogne, where Floridor was enjoying a success. The Marais company kept its proprietors waiting for their rent, which was of bad omen. Financial difficulties worsened, both for the proprietors and the actors, sharing in the same downfall. Mme Beaupré lent the former the large sum of 10,000 livres to enable them to repay their own creditors. On the other hand, the actors sold the fittings of the theatre, the scenery and the machinery to their proprietors. Day by day the Marais declined. It even closed for some time in 1654 and the actors tried to make money in the provinces, at Nantes.

The company which had resisted the Hôtel de Bourgogne for so long was on the downward road. A few actors left the sinking ship. Mme Beaupré agreed to pay the rent, at a reduction from 2,400 to 2,000 livres. Her husband assumed the management of a company reorganized with second-rate actors. For a revival of *Andromède* they again hired Buffequin as stage-designer. Corneille had for a while deserted the stage, and it was his brother Thomas, with Boisrobert and Quinault, who now provided the company with comedies and tragedies. Under La Rocque's lead, the company, once more reorganized with Jodelet, L'Espy, La Fleur, Chevalier and Hauteroche, started again with great courage. In 1656, *Timocrate*, by the younger Corneille, was acted before the King with unparalleled success: there were ninety-two performances. But it was a short-lived triumph since at Easter 1657 the theatre closed again, this time for two whole years. The company left

5a. Scene from
*Le Bourgeois
Gentilhomme*
(Molière)

b. Venus and Mars by
Mignard. These are said to be
portraits of Molière and
Madeliene Béjart when young
and acting together in the
south of France.
(Aix Museum)

Le Foyer du Théâtre-Français.

JANET LANGE

Paris for Rouen, where it had already acted during the Fronde. Madeleine Béjart was there with Molière, on their way back to Paris, and she thought for a while of moving into the Théâtre du Marais but abandoned the idea, faced with promises that led her to hope for a triumphal home-coming, to the Louvre, the King's palace.

In 1659 La Rocque reorganized his company once more: Jodelet and L'Espy went over to Molière in the Palais Royal; Mme Beaupré retired. The manager engaged Mlle des Oeillets, Hubert Etiennette and Catherine des Urlis, both du Parcs who left soon afterwards to go back to Molière, Chevalier, Brécourt (two author-actors) and La Thorillière. Fully resolved to hold his position between the Hôtel de Bourgogne and the Palais Royal, he signed a new lease of three years, renewed in 1663, for a rent of 2,200 livres. But the Troche family, who had owned the Marais for over fifty years, had sold the theatre to Pierre Aubert, King's councillor, for 63,000 livres, which enabled them to repay the heavy mortgage on the buildings.

Once more on a firm footing, the Marais stepped into a new and prosperous era; together with revivals of the older plays, plays with stage effects again attracted a big audience. The company once again called upon the indispensable Denis Buffequin; he became its general designer and started preparing a masterpiece, *La Toison d'Or*, which was created at Neubourg, the Marquis de Sourdéac's chateau, and revived on the stage in the rue Vieille du Temple. This new play, written for the King's wedding and put to music by d'Assoucy, was the elder Corneille's striking return to the stage, where he had known his first successes. The players spent a great deal of money to give this new show all the splendour it needed. For his effects, Buffequin was given 1,200 livres 'just for the trouble he took', plus twenty-two more livres for each performance. The Marquis de Sourdéac lent the sets which had been used at Neubourg.

For this exceptional occasion, which was to become a date of significance in the history of the stage of the seventeenth century, the Marais put up the price of seats: half a louis in the pit, a louis in the amphitheatre, eight louis for a box. But the Parisians paid without turning a hair, being sure the show was worth every penny. It was a triumph. Several later revivals of the *Toison d'Or* repaid the original expenses and finally brought prosperity to the Marais, after so many forced interruptions of its activities and hard

F

times. In January 1662 the King in person came to two perform-ances running and gave the company 2,000 livres.

For months *La Toison d'Or* alternated with Chapoton's *La Descente d'Orphèe aux Enfers*. It was to the rue Vieille du Temple, and not to the rue Mauconseil, that Corneille brought his *Sertorius*, produced at great expense and acted by Mlle des Oeillets. The old theatre was thriving, but again the Hôtel de Bourgogne tried to behead it, carrying away its first actress, Mlle des Oeillets, while Molière robbed it of Brécourt and La Thorillière. Commercial competition, together with quarrels we shall mention later, was fierce between theatres which stole each other's best actors: the Great Comedians had their own admirers and tried to make sure of plays likely to have a long run. The Hôtel de Bourgogne and the Palais Royal revived *Sertorius* because it was printed.

Once more, the Marais held out. It engaged Varlet, known as Verneuil, La Grange's brother, his wife Marie Vallée, Rosidor and a little later Beauval, d'Ennebaut, Champmeslé and their wives, and Rosimond, who had acted in the provinces. The theatre thrived once more. A new and spectacular piece, *Les Amours de Jupiter et de Sémélé* by the Abbé Boyer, with a score by Louis de Mollier, achieved a tremendous success and was a forerunner of Lulli's operas. The King attended the first performance; Buffequin's effects were staggering. Like *La Toison d'Or*, it was often revived. In the summer the company went back to Rouen on tour.

The Marais met with another piece of good luck in a clever writer, Donneau de Visé, always ready to grasp the latest news and the latest fashion, producing *Le Mercure galant* a few years later. He also provided the company with spectacular mythological plays. Coming shortly after Boyer's *Fête de Vénus* (1668), a pastoral written to celebrate the King's victories, and inscribed to the Duchesse d'Orléans[3], Donneau de Visé produced at the Marais *Les Amours de Venus et d'Adonis* (1669), which most successfully held the stage for three months. It was Mlle Champmeslé who acted Venus. During the next season, the same tireless playwright pro-duced *Les Amours du Soleil:* thirteen different scenes with twenty-four flying machines. All Olympus was there, brought back to life by Buffequin, the specialist in elaborate effects. De Visé exploited the same idea in *Le Mariage de Bacchus et d'Ariane* (1967), which

[3] Princess Henrietta-Anne, 'Minette'.

continued for three months and was revived fifteen years later by the Comédie Française.

With the new speciality it had created, the Marais achieved tremendous success; through many tribulations it still survived and the company shared in the very substantial receipts. The good days had returned.

But a last and fatal stroke was dealt. It did not come from its tireless rival, the Hôtel de Bourgogne, but from the sly intrigues of Baptiste the Florentine, better known as Lulli, who had just founded the Opéra. This dangerous man, who had written a beautiful score for Molière's *Le Bourgeois Gentilhomme*, literally hypnotized the King, who took all he said for granted, enjoyed nothing but the Opéra and abandoned Molière, whom he had protected for so long. Lulli managed not only to secure from the King the exclusive right to produce operas throughout France, but he also obtained letters patent by which any company but his own was forbidden to use more than six singers and twelve musicians. At one stroke the King had killed the ballet-comedies of the Palais Royal and the Marais plays with stage effects.

Corneille flew in vain to the rescue of the Marais with *Pulchérie*, to try, as he wrote, 'to bring some life into a desert . . . where no one cared to remember that there is such a thing as a theatre'. Nor could Boursault's last play, *Germanicus*, save the dying Marais.

On February 3, 1673, La Rocque was still able to get his company to sign a deed of association: it had been increased by the coming of d'Estriché, Armande Bojart's future husband, and Mlle Goyot, as if everything could still be saved. A fortnight later, Molière, the manager of the Palais-Royal company, died, leaving it shattered. It was obvious that the whole Paris theatre needed reorganization. The authorities moved in and in June the Marais and the Palais-Royal merged to create, in circumstances we shall describe later, a new company, the Royal Company of the Hôtel Guénégaud.

For forty years, the Marais had courageously served the French stage with its tragedies, comedies, pastorals and spectaculars. With its obstinate and tireless activity it had served great authors, but its greatest glory derived from the fact that, from *Mélite* to *Pulchérie*, it had been Corneille's own theatre.

CHAPTER FOUR

THE KING'S COMPANY AT THE PALAIS-ROYAL (1658–1673)

In 1643, a young man whose Christian name was Jean-Baptiste walked out of his father Jean Poquelin's upholstery shop to try his luck as a strolling player. He was inspired by an obvious vocation, but also by his love for an actress who soon became his mistress, Madeleine Béjart, a beautiful red-haired girl who was four years his senior. This was Molière's beginning.

They both collected a few convenient companions and created a company which, with the enthusiasm of very young people, they called the *Illustre théâtre*. There was an attorney's clerk, a writing master, a bookseller, the daughter of a carpenter and Madeleine's brother and sister. Altogether they were ten; the oldest was twenty-seven and the youngest sixteen. Apart from Madeleine Béjart, none had ever set foot on the stage. The contract of association was signed on June 30, 1643; as provisional manager, Madeleine Béjart had a right to choose her own parts.

The company rented the Mestayers tennis court in the rue Mazarine; the rent was 1,900 livres, payable monthly and in advance. The owner was a careful man who demanded a guarantee from Marie Hervé, the Béjarts' mother. They engaged a dancer and four musicians for three years, as if they were certain of their success. When the hall and its secondary buildings had been organized and decorated, the theatre opened on January 1, 1644, a fortnight before the Marais fire, which certainly was an advantage to these beginners. Gaston d'Orléans, who had been contacted by Tristan l'Hermite, granted his protection to these enterprising young people, but did not open his purse. The *Illustre théâtre*, full of noble ambitions, was keenest on tragedies, mostly those of the younger Corneille; they also acted Magon's *Artaxerxes*, du Ryer's *Scévole*, Tristan's *Mort de Crispe* and *Mort de Sénèque*, Nicolas Desfontaine's *Perside*. But expenses were high and takings rather few, since it was difficult for an inexperienced company to rival the Hôtel de Bourgogne or the Marais, the more so in the parish of

St Sulpice, which was under the sway of the actors' worst enemy, M. Olier.

But the rent, the authors and the costumes had to be paid. Without cash, these young people got into the dangerous habit of borrowing money. One of the King's stewards, Louis Baudot lent them 1,100 livres; three months later, they borrowed 2,000 from François Pommier, who was acting for Louis Baudot, mortgaging their future returns, the theatre buildings, their sets and their own personal properties. Mme Hervé stood surety for the share of her two daughters and those of Molière.

It was impossible to stay in the rue Mazarine, where they were acting to empty seats. Perhaps the public was averse to crossing the Seine to see a play? All right. They tried again on the right bank. They renounced the lease of the *Mestayers* tennis court and rented for three years, at the exorbitant price of 2,400 livres, another court, the *Croix Noire*, on the Quai des Célestins, the present No 32. They had to face further expenditure in organizing, upholstering and furnishing the new stage. François Pommier undertook everything: the *Illustre théâtre* had lost all its initiative and depended upon him. Creditors and tradesmen sued. Molière, at the end of his resources, borrowed 291 livres from a shopkeeper and gave her gold and silver embroidered ribbon by way of security.

On August 2, 1645, Fausser, a tallow-chandler, for a debt of 142 livres, which Molière contested, had him arrested and imprisoned in the Châtelet. The police officer released him on bail, but before he could be released another creditor, a linen merchant named Debourg, kept him in prison for a debt of 155 livres. The theatre closed and the company broke up. Molière and Madeleine Béjart borrowed 522 more livres from a merchant, Antoinette Simony, pawning all their belongings, including their theatre wardrobe, their main working asset. These poor rags were auctioned. With what was left of the company they retired to the provinces.

Accepted by Charles Dufreny, the director of the Duc d'Epernon's company, they travelled to Nantes, Bordeaux and the south-west of France. For thirteen years, completely forgotten in Paris, they lived the picturesque life of Scarron's heroes in the *Roman comique*. Molière learned his trade during this long tour.

Then, one day, the company whose manager he had soon become came back from Rouen to Paris. It had been enlarged by Du Parc,

La Brie and their wives, but Molière was not to enter the capital without having made sure of a few things. Through helpful friends he had been granted the protection of Philippe d'Orléans, the King's brother, and he opened up in the hall of the *Gardes du Louvre*, in the presence of the King, on October 24, 1658. The whole company of the Hôtel de Bourgogne was there to watch how those new rivals would be received, as the King was interested in them. Molière acted *Nicomède*, then in a brief, well-constructed speech, he asked permission of his royal spectator to perform for him one of those little comedies 'with which he had entertained the provinces'. This was *Le Docteur amoureux*.

Farces had been quite forgotten in Paris by that time. The King and his courtiers were good enough to roar with laughter: Molière had done the trick. He was to remain in Paris and share with the Italians, led by Scaramouche, the Théâtre du Petit Bourbon, which was situated more or less where the Louvre Colonnade now stands. It was a fine hall, described by Sauval as follows: '. . . the highest and longest in the kingdom. It is eighteen paces broad and thirty-five *toises* [seventy metres] long, and the roof is so well contrived that it seems as high as St Germain or St Eustache.' It was the hall where court ballets were danced.

Molière opened on November 2nd with *L'Etourdi* and *Le Dépit amoureux*, two comedies which had been created in the provinces, and with no more delay he started work. By Easter 1659 he had recruited two of the best comic actors of the Marais, Jodelet and L'Espy, and he was on the look-out for a new farce subject from the everyday life of Paris. On November 18, 1659, after *Cinna*, he gave the first performance of the *Les Précieuses Ridicules*. The Marquise de Rambouillet and her friends were seated in the front boxes. It was a triumph. At one stroke Molière had conquered the Paris public, giving them an opportunity to laugh, which they had not enjoyed for a long time. He was solidly established in the capital from now on; it now boasted not two, but three theatres. Shortly afterwards, *Le Cocu Imaginaire* was as successful as *Les Précieuses*.

The Hôtel de Bourgogne was becoming anxious, and commissioned Somaize to write *Les Véritables Précieuses*. An unscrupulous bookseller, Jean Ribou, published a pirated edition of the *Les Précieuses ridicules*. Molière was accused of having lifted his play from an Italian comedy by the Abbé de Pure. An unsigned, pirated edition of *Le Cocu Imaginaire* came out and Molière had it suppressed, but someone else produced an imitation, *La Cocue imaginaire*. In short, Molière was in the midst of a literary fight that was carefully stirred up by the Hôtel de Bourgogne. Newspapers, which could not but mention the success of the plays, ignored the author's name. But the King marked his satisfaction by a gift of 500 livres; he promised his protection to the newcomer and invited him to perform at Vincennes.

Molière had been in Paris for a year and had known nothing but success when a tragedy happened. 'Without warning', M. de Ratabon, Superintendant of the King's Buildings, had the Petit Bourbon pulled down to enlarge the Louvre. 'M. de Ratabon's evil intentions were clear', writes the faithful La Grange. At Monsieur's request, the King gave Molière's company the old Palais Royal theatre, built by Richelieu and almost derelict. M. de Ratabon had to restore it at the King's expense. All through his career Molière would have an advantage over the two other Paris companies: he would have no rent to pay. The repairs were quickly completed. The interruption had been fairly brief: only three months. During that time the company had performed in the Louvre and in private houses.

But the Hôtel de Bourgogne profited by this wonderful opportunity by trying to disorganize Molière's company, as it had disorganized the Théâtre de Marais so often before. Here is what La Grange recorded:

'The Company, tossed by all those gales, had also to resist the division which the players of the Hôtel de Bourgogne and of the Marais were trying to bring among them, through various offers to draw them into this or that group. But Monsieur's company kept together; all the actors loved M. de Molière, their director, who besides his great merit and skill had such courtesy and engaging manners that they all promised to stay with him whatever proposals were made to them and whatever the benefits that could be found elsewhere. Because of this it was rumoured that the company was held together and had settled at the Palais Royal by the King's and Monsieur's protection.'

The leader's greatest reward was this friendship between himself and his companions, who for fifteen years rallied together in the face of every new threat.

The Palais-Royal opened on January 20, 1661. We do not intend to tell the history of the twelve years during which Molière maintained his illustrious struggle with *L'Ecole des Femmes*,

Tartuffe and *Dom Juan*, in the course of a brilliant and oft-told career. It is more interesting to penetrate into the inner life of the company. First of all let us not forget that Molière was simultaneously its manager, orator and producer, and he revealed himself among his companions in *L'Impromptu de Versailles*. And he was also the main provider of plays. Corneille and Racine were acted at the Hôtel de Bourgogne; he could only revive their plays. He could only dispose of second-rate tragedians, like Boyer and La Calprenède, and comedians like Gilbert, de Visé and Chappuzeau. If the Palais-Royal had become the temple of comedy, it was because the company lived on Molière's own plays: he wrote thirty-three of them, of which, for various reasons, about ten can be regarded as masterpieces, while several deal with contemporary problems. Add to them revivals of plays produced elsewhere, Molière, during his fifteen years in Paris, produced ninety-five plays, of which he wrote thirty-one, or two plays every year. What modern manager could rival such a production?

That Molière achieved so swift a success in Paris is because he revived the farce, which had been forgotten for some twenty-five years; he mixed farces with the comedies of manners or with ballet-comedies, or even with grand comedy. The result was such scenes as that of Oronte in *Le Misanthrope*, Orgon hidden under the table in *Tartuffe*, the quarrel between Vadius and Trissottin in *Les Femmes savantes*, Sosie's entire part in *Amphytrion*. One of his last plays, written after the great masterpieces, was another farce, *Les Fourberies de Scypin*. Molière also caught his public by the roots which his plays drove into everyday life. For those romantic comedies by Scarron, Boisrobert or Thomas Corneille, in a timeless, stereotyped style borrowed from the Italians and the Spaniards, he substituted a new comedy in which he broached the problems of the time. *Les Précieuses Ridicules* was virtually a revue, while *Les Fâcheux* was a succession of sketches; *L'Ecole des Femmes* dealt with the burning problem of the education of women, which was resumed in *Les Femmes Savantes*. *La Critique de l'Ecole des Femmes* and *L'Impromptu de Versailles* were works of literary polemics, in which he attacked his rivals, whether authors or actors. *L'Amour Médecin* was a caricature of the court doctors; *Tartuffe* and *Dom Juan* broached the fundamental problem of religion and broke into the general theatrical quarrel to which we have already alluded. *Monsieur de Pourceaugnac, La Comtesse d'Escarbagnas* and *Georges Dandin* made fun of provincial noble-men, at whom it was usual to laugh at court, as other comedies of the time reveal. *Le Bourgeois gentilhomme* concerns the growing importance of the bourgeoisie whom Louis XIV had raised to top positions in the State, a fact which turned his century into 'a long reign of a vile bourgeoisie', to quote Saint Simon. Even the Turkish ballet had its source in the recent visit of an ambassador from the Sultan. *Le Malade imaginaire,* his last attack upon the pseudo-science of the doctors, becomes a modernist philosophy in favour of the 'discoveries of the age', that of the circulation of the blood, still denied by official medicine.

In each comedy the spectator could find again the people of his own age, and the quarrels, great or small, that divided them. This attracted him much more than the time-honoured episodes of romantic comedies, like abductions or disguises. Thus he could pleasurably seek in Molière's plays what others could not provide.

His contemporaries tell us that he was strongly built but that overwork harassed all his life: his terrible struggles against rival companies and bigots, his worries as manager—'There are no stranger animals to instruct than actors'—his matrimonial crises (since he, a passionate and jealous man, had married the frivolous and flirtatious Armande Béjart), the constant demands of the King which could not be ignored, his work as an actor and his difficulties with Lulli. All this overwork, without respite, soon ruined his health, so that he died at fifty-one, a few hours after leaving the stage.

An important part of his dramatic activity was devoted to court festivities, for which he created the new genre of ballet-comedy, seen for the first time at Fouquet's palace at Vaux-le-Vicomte, with *Les Fâcheux, Les Plaisirs de l'Ile Enchantée, Le Grand divertisse-ment de Versailles,* and at the festivities given at St Germain, Fontainebleau and Chambord, in which every possible show was staged. Molière was sometimes asked to take part concurrently and sometimes simultaneously with the Hôtel de Bourgogne company. It was a great honour for him and excellent publicity, from which he derived great profit for his company. As early as 1665, Louis XIV became the patron of the Palais Royal, which became the 'royal company' like the Marais. The company drew an allowance of 6,000 livres, which was soon raised to 7,000, as compared with the 12,000 granted to the 'King's own company', which thus retained its nominal pre-eminence. But Molière's repertoire was better

89

suited to court festivities than that of the Hôtel de Bourgogne, which consisted mainly of tragedies.

La Princesse d'Elide, l'Amour médecin, Le Sicilien, Les Amants magnifiques and even *La Pastorale comique* and farces interspersed with musical interludes, like *Monsieur de Pourceaugnac* or *Le Bourgeois Gentilhomme*, pleased courtiers more than austere tragedies and were more in harmony with courtly entertainments. The extraordinary thing is not the fact that the man who wrote *Le Misanthrope* could also write *Mélicerte*, but that the author of *Mélicerte* found time to write *Le Misanthrope*.

Those visits to court provided the company with a very handsome income; the King was generous and, apart from substantial gratuities, the actors were freely entertained during their stay in the royal palaces. They were free of all expense. The Palais-Royal company, as we shall see later, earned plenty of money. *Les Plaisirs de l'Ile Enchantée* brought them 4,000 livres and *La Princesse d'Elide* produced for its author 2,000.

This favourable situation helped greatly to keep the company together. In fifteen years there was but one defection: Mlle du Parc, whose excuse was her love for Racine, who took her to the Hôtel de Bourgogne. The friendship between the members of the company was forged during the provincial years when Madeleine Béjart, a level-headed woman, was manager. When Molière had married Armande Béjart, of whom it is still not known for sure whether she was Madeleine's daughter, as their contemporaries said, or her sister, five members of the Béjart family were members of the company, which was rather like a family enterprise.

The result was that Molière, as a comic playwright, wrote for his companions and for himself. The lawyer Guéret very rightly said: 'He certainly thinks of them all when writing.' And similarly Perrault: 'He has also the gift of casting his actors so well and training them so cleverly that they look less like actors in a play than like the very people they represent.' De Visé wrote about *l'Ecole des femmes*: 'No comedy has ever been acted with so much talent; each actor knows how many steps he must take and how often he can ogle.' Besides being an excellent comic actor who had learned from the Italians how to give an expression to his face and his entire body, Molière was also a first-rate producer.

It was he who, by his comic grimaces, made the audience roar with laughter when he played Sganarelle; in *Les Précieuses ridicules* he planned a part that admirably suited Jodelet, the leading comic actor in France; he wrote the part of Cathos for Catherine de Brie and that of Madelon for Madeleine Béjart. La Flèche hobbled because Louis Béjart also hobbled, and Gros-René was rotund because so was du Parc. The 'devilish face' of the notary in *L'Ecole des femmes* was that of de Brie; Zerbinette's and Nicole's laughter was that of gay Mlle Beauval. The gay humour of Marinette or Dorine belonged to Madeleine Béjart, Célimène's cruel coquetry came from his wife, and Harpagon's cough was his own. He wrote for himself the parts of Orgon, Alceste and Argan.[1] La Grange testifies that he sometimes put on the stage 'his own family affairs and the things that happened in his home'.

Consequently, Molière's companions had parts written for them which perfectly fitted their persons and their natures. It was a factor of success not to be found in the other companies.

The public's faithfulness and the King's effective help—at the time when *Tartuffe* was in difficulties, for instance—kept the Palais Royal to the fore among the Paris theatres. But in 1672 luck turned against Molière, who was already dangerously ill. Madeleine Béjart died, his life-long friend and first inspirer. The King abondoned him to give all his support to Lulli, as has been explained already. His last play, *Le Malade imaginaire*, meant for a court performance as the prologue shows, had to be staged in Paris. Thus it was in a sort of disgrace that Molière died on February 17, 1673, and the story of the Palais-Royal ended with him.

[1] In *Tartuffe*, *Le Misanthrope* and *Le Malade imaginaire*.

CHAPTER FIVE

THE KING'S COMPANY AT THE HÔTEL GUÉNÉGAUD (1673–1680)

When Molière died his widow and his companions at once made known their intention to continue. Three days after his semi-clandestine burial, the Palais-Royal reopened on February 24th and revived *Le Misanthrope* and on March 3rd *Le Malade imaginaire* with La Thorillière in Molière's part. On March 5th Monsieur with Madame[1] and their retinue came to the performance, to affirm publicly their support for the company. Helped by Armande Béjart, who was to defend her husband's memory and repertoire for twenty years, La Grange undertook the management of the theatre, whose orator he had been for several years. But the absence of Molière, who had been the life and soul of his company, was cruelly felt; the leader was no longer there to impose his will. On the other hand, the Hôtel de Bourgogne, as usual, was about to profit by the occasion in order to dismantle the company which had been its dangerous rival. It summoned Baron, La Thorillière and the Beauvals. After the Easter recess the theatre could not continue. On April 28th the King gave the Palais-Royal to his beloved Lulli, whose privilege, incidentally, forbade him to revive Molière's musical ballet-comedies. Armande Béjart compelled him to repay a loan of 11,000 livres, already three years old.

La Grange made tremendous efforts to complete the company, taking in du Croisy's fifteen-year-old daughter, and on May 3rd succeeded in robbing the Marais of one of its best actors, Rosimont, whom he signed on for six years. The Marais, which was disintegrating, tried to pull itself together; the company was re-engaged for four years. Looking for a new hall in which to continue its performances, Molière's company made contact with the Marquis de Sourdéac, the man who had had *La Toison d'Or* performed at Neubourg, and his partner Champeron. They jointly owned

[1] The second Madame, the Palatine Princess.

a hall, built in 1670, in the tennis court at the sign of *La Bouteille*, rue Guénégaud, which belonged to the Laffemas family; they had staged operas there, but Lulli's recent privilege had reduced them to silence.

For 30,000 livres, of which 14,000 had to be paid at once, Sourdéac and Champeron ceded their lease, 'the theatre, orchestra, machinery, winches, ropes, paint and generally all that was connected with and useful in a playhouse for its performance', which completed the equipment La Grange had brought from the Palais-Royal. The 14,000 livres were borrowed from André Boudet, Molière's brother-in-law, and each proprietor received a share, instead of the 16,000 livres which remained owing. As we shall see, this was the origin of endless difficulties. The yearly rent was 2,400 livres. A month later a royal decree, countersigned by La Reynie, authoritatively ordered the Marais to be closed and allowed the Palais-Royal company to move with all its equipment into the Hôtel Guénégaud.

From that day on there were but two theatrical companies in Paris, the Hôtel de Bourgogne and the Hôtel Guénégaud. But two actresses from the Marais, Catherine des Urlis and Marie Vallée, demanded the execution of the last deed of association of the Marais and the condemnation of each their former colleagues to a fine of 2,000 livres for breach of contract. In fact, nine of them, whose cases were to be taken up by Colbert on the King's instruction, had hurried to join La Grange at the Hôtel Guénégaud: La Rocque, Verneuil, Dauvilliers and his wife, Guérin d'Estriché, Dupin and his wife, Guyot and Auzillons. It was the final amalgamation of the two companies with nine actors from the Marais and ten from the Palais-Royal, dividing $15\frac{1}{2}$ shares, according to Colbert's calculation, who very fairly granted $7\frac{3}{4}$ shares to each former company, not counting the shares given to Sourdéac and Champeron. The amalgamated companies put their scenery into a common pool.

On July 9, 1673, the new 'King's Company of the Hôtel Guénégaud', no longer subsidized by the King, opened with *Tartuffe*, an obvious act of homage to Molière's memory. Throughout the first month they acted nothing but Molière's comedies. It was a means of affirming publicly the primacy of the former Palais-Royal company in the new organization.

However, *Le Mercure Galant* advertised new and attractive programmes:

'The late M. Molière's company, having selected the best members in the Marais company, has built a new one, one of the largest and best ever seen. As it is now able to entertain His Majesty, the King has granted it the honour to be known as his company. The numerous audiences that have honoured it with their presence since it has returned to the stage have loudly stated that comedy cannot be acted with greater perfection. That is why it has attracted practically all the authors, whose plays will shine this winter in their theatre.'

This was excellent publicity. But let us not forget that *Le Mercure Galant* was edited by de Visé and Thomas Corneille, whose plays were performed at the Palais-Royal and the Marais, and who meant to continue at the Hôtel in the rue Guénégaud. And that is exactly what happened. The two clever journalists had carefully prepared the ground. When you want to be praised, it is safer to blow your own trumpet.

Despite public favour and the unfailing collaboration of 'all the good authors', the new theatre thrived mostly on Molière's plays. Yet, at least so far as royal favour went, it no longer took first place. It was very seldom summoned to perform at court. The Hôtel de Bourgogne was pre-eminent again as the 'only royal company', the more so as it could now itself revive Molière's comedies, except for *Le Malade imaginaire*, which had not yet been printed.

As it owned the old machinery of the Marais, the Hôtel Guénégaud also revived the tradition of plays with stage effects. *Circé*, by Donneau de Visé and Thomas Corneille, was a great success and was unexpectedly worth two shares to its authors instead of one. The new company also followed another inherited tradition, rivalling the all-powerful Hôtel de Bourgogne. In opposition to Racine's *Iphigénie*, it offered an *Iphigenia* by Leclerc and Coras, and Pradon's *Phèdre* in opposition to Racine's play of the same name. The result was a violent quarrel. Thomas Corneille not only provided the company with comedies, but with Armande Béjart's agreement he undertook to write a version in verse of Molière's *Dom Juan* which had not yet been printed and had not been put on the bill for twelve years. It was carefully toned down. This new *Dom Juan* started a new career which lasted until the middle of the nineteenth century. Finally, as good journalists always on the lookout for news, de Visé and Thomas Corneille exploited the Poison Affair and the execution of the sinister Voisin in the form of a comedy called *La Devineresse* (1680) which attracted the whole of Paris, passionately interested in that fantastic succession of crimes. The play was performed forty-seven times in succession and brought some 6,000 livres to its authors, thanks to the clever publicity of *Le Mercure Galant*.

In 1679 the Hôtel Guénégaud had a great stroke of luck; Mlle de Champmeslé, the leading tragedienne of her time, left the Hôtel de Bourgogne and with her great talent and fame brought all Racine's plays to the Guénégaud company. The Champmeslés were not asked to pay their part of the company's debts and they were anually given 1,000 livres in addition to their shares. It can be seen how much the company valued these new recruits. For the seven years of its life, the new theatre was prosperous and met with frequent successes.

Unfortunately, the actors had to argue money matters with the Marquis de Sourdéac and his associate Champeron for years. It should be remembered that in an earlier transaction each had been granted a share in the door money. This partnership of non-actors in a company of players was a blunder worsened by the two men's bad faith. Champeron tried to have his brother put in control of receipts. The company was suspicious and refused. To revenge themselves on their associates, the brothers sided with four of the actors, Dauvilliers, Dupont and their wives, who opposed the performance of *Circé*, on the grounds of its excessive cost. Performances were stopped. The company sacked the four agitators for breach of contract, a decision which was upheld by the Châtelet. Mlle de Brie sided with them and refused to act. Together with her husband, she joined the four rebels.

The company then turned against those really responsible for the little plot, Sourdéac and Champeron, and produced a request to have them expelled from the society against payment of the 16,000 livres owed them. The court of justice gave its decision for the actors, but Sourdéac and Champeron had the theatre's machinery dismantled. A compromise was found. The expelled actors were taken back and *Circé* could be acted.

But two years later the incorrigible *machinistes*, as La Grande called them, made trouble again, and questioned the accounts of the company. A new lawsuit began which lasted five years, longer than the Théâtre Guénégaud itself. The company expelled them, changing their shares into life annuities of 500 livres. After a long

95

discussion, Parliament came out in favour of the players, under-lining the bad faith of their adversaries, who were ordered to pay the costs.

The inner life of the Théâtre Guénégaud was not a peaceful one and the actors, knowing they were in their right, fought hard for their profits. La Grande's celebrated register, which records all these episodes, also proves that the theatre earned plenty of money. It was in the very middle of a successful period that it disappeared on the occasion of the 1680 reunion.

7. The Palais-Royal. Engraving of Perelle

THÉÂTRE DE L'OPÉRA. — Salle du Palais-Royal (ancienne salle de Molière), incendiée le 6 avril 1763.

8. Théâtre de l'Opéra, Burnt Down in 1763

CHAPTER SIX

THE COMÉDIE-FRANÇAISE (1680–1700)

The amalgamation of the Palais-Royal and Marais companies in 1673 marked a new step by the authorities to interfere with the theatre. Colbert's centralizing policy applied not only to the administrative and economic life of the kingdom: with the foundation of the various academies, it had already extended to the intellectual field. The stage had already felt its effects. The opera monopoly granted to Lulli was a portent of something similar for comedy. Indeed, in 1680 the King decided to amalgamate the Hôtel de Bourgogne and the Hôtel Guénégaud into one company, upon which the royal administration could make its authority felt more easily. Thus was the Comédie-Française born, and was to remain for a long time the only Paris theatre of comedy.

On August 18, 1680, the Duc de Créqui, First Gentleman of the Bedchamber, sent out the royal order for the amalgamation of the two theatres. The new company now numbered twenty-seven actors, fifteen men and twelve women, with twenty-one-and-a-quarter shares between them, a further half-share being retained by the King to dispose of as he wished. Several actors had been dismissed or given reduced salaries, such as du Croisy who, after his protest, was taken back on half-pay only, and Mlle La Grange, reduced to a quarter-share, though with an annual guarantee of 2,000 livres, and Guérin, Mlle Molière's husband, whose share was returned to him, but who had to pay a pension of 1,000 livres.

On the other hand the actors had to pay, besides the pensions to their colleagues who had retired, an annual indemnity of 800 livres to the Italians who went to act in the Hôtel de Bourgogne, which was now empty; its rent was greater than that of the Hôtel Guénégaud. Thus did the King's authority intrude upon the administration of the acting community itself.

But he maintained the payment of 12,000 livres which he had formerly given to the Hôtel de Bourgogne.

No company had ever been so numerous in its personnel, which

G

led to a small revolution in theatrical life. Formerly, there were only three performances a week. After 1680 there was one each day, which substantially increased the actor's annual salary. The company was also able to give on the same day one performance in the town and another at court.

The amalgamation order was published on August 22nd and on the 26th the Comédie-Française gave its first performance at the Hôtel Guénégaud: *Phèdre* with Mlle Champmeslé, and a comedy. The amalgamation created serious difficulties between those who had claim to the leading roles. It was accepted that Corneille, Racine and Quinault would attend to the casting of the roles in their own tragedies. As for Molière's comedies, the Duc d'Aumont handed out the main parts between Rosimont, Brécourt and Raisin. Other authors had their plays cast by the First Gentleman of the Bedchamber. The Comédiens-Français were becoming officers of the realm, under the orders of the King. This new system of monopoly, coming after that of the privilege, cost them most of their liberty. A *Lettre de Cachet* signed by the King on October 21st ratified the change. On the other hand, the comedians signed a new act of association, 'at His Majesty's pleasure', to regulate the life annuities of those who had retired on pension.

The Comédie-Française continued to live on its classical repertoire, but it should be recalled that when it started its new life tragedy was on the decline. Neither Boyer, nor Pradon, nor Campistron, nor La Grange-Chancel could bear comparison with Corneille or Racine. As for comedy, the situation was rather different. Of course, there had been no successor to Molière of the same scale, but the new generation of comedy authors, such as Boyer, Dufresny, Regnard, Lesage and a few others of smaller account, were extremely successful and amused the spectators with lighter plays of sometimes doubtful morals, but full of ingenious situations, and plenty of fun and wit.

We have already seen that the First Gentlemen of the King's Bedchamber had their say in the administration of the Comédie-Française, but those high and powerful persons did not act of their own free will. They were themselves under a higher authority, that of the Dauphine, Anne Christine-Victoire of Bavaria, Monseigneur's wife, who had been made the Superintendant-General of the French and Italian theatres. She acted in the name of the King and the Dauphin.

As early as 1684 she was organizing a new division of the shares among actors and deciding who should retire. She fixed the number of shares at twenty-three, and this remained effective until the Revolution. She cast plays according to all sorts of influences, dismissed most talented actors like Baron or Raisin, and so persecuted Dauvilliers, whose ugliness shocked her, that he went mad and died in the lunatic asylum of Charenton; she compelled the restive players to perform Campistron's *Arminius* and was the supreme organizer of court performances. All the decisions of the general assembly of actors had to be approved by the Dauphine, especially the 'rules of entrance', drawn up in 1688 and revised in 1697, which was the list of the lucky persons who could enter the theatre without paying. Everyone had to submit to the Dauphine's orders, and the actors were only entitled to one complimentary ticket for two people on every other day; it was a double ticket, one part to be sent to the admission desk, the other given to the usherette. On first nights authors were entitled to four tickets for five-act plays, or two for the shorter ones. The only persons allowed free entry were the civil and police lieutenants, the King's attorney, the district commissaires, the authors, former and pensioned members of the company, a few persons who had rendered services to the company, such as their notaries, the masters of the revels, Procope (as a neighbour), Blancolelli, the director of the Italian company, the actors' parents, wives, husbands and children (so far as there were seats available) and a few other privileged people, whose seats in boxes, the amphitheatre or the pit were carefully regulated. Very strict written orders were given to the usherettes: for one thing, they had to provide foot-warmers without asking for tips. The rules settled the time when plays began (five o'clock) and players who were late were fined.

The players were truly strait-jacketed. But they did not complain for, on the whole, all those rules protected them against all those abuses from which they had suffered so long. Besides, now that they had no rivals and could act daily, their yearly share was almost doubled. The Comédie-Française had retained La Grange as its administrator, he had managed Molière's business so well. The company was financially prosperous and everybody was delighted.

Unfortunately, the company was compelled to move to other quarters. They were still acting in the Hôtel Guénégaud when, in 1687, the Collège des Quatre-nations, endowed by Mazarin, was opened in the palace built by Le Vau and d'Orbay, now the

Palais de l'Institut. We have seen that at that time the quarrel between the church and the stage was at its height. Could one have a theatre within a stone's throw of a religious college, dependent upon the doctors of the Sorbonne?

By that time the King was no longer interested in the theatre, and in June 1687 he ordered the players to get out and 'find somewhere else' before October. It was like a bolt from the blue; the royal order was easy to give but much more difficult to carry out. In one of the Comédie's registers La Grange wrote:

'On June 20, 1687, M. de la Reynie, the Police lieutenant, summoned the company and read the King's orders, which he had received from M. de Louvois, according to which we had to leave the Hôtel Guénégaud within three months and settle elsewhere. Whereupon we decided to go to the King and M. de Louvois to explain our plight and the serious damage we should suffer by this change. . . . Monseigneur told us that the orders could not be changed; we must look around for another place to act in, and any protection we might need would be granted us.'

The 'protection' the wretched comedians were granted was rather strange.

The company held a meeting and faced the situation. There could be no question that the only French comedy company could move into a tennis court, as it had done earlier in the century. A real theatre had to be built, which meant considerable expense and long delay. In order to face the situation, the first financial measures were taken: 66 livres a day—2,400 livres a year—were deducted from receipts before paying what was due to shareholders. The royal grant was set aside and 4,000 livres added to it, which made a reserve fund of 40,000 livres. Then began a search for a new site. The Hôtel de Sourdis, where 21 rue de l'Arbre Sec now stands, was for sale for 60,000 livres.

The King gave his consent; the architect d'Orbay drew up a plan; the sale was concluded. But the curé of St Germain l'Auxerrois did not like the Comédie-Française next door to his church and he complained to the King, who withdrew his permission 'for special reasons'. Racine, who was hostile to the theatre from the time he had retired, wrote to Boileau on August 8th: 'It is marvellous to hear how priests shout wherever the comedians go. The Curé of St Germain l'Auxerrois has already succeeded in preventing them from going to the Hôtel de Sourdis, because from their theatre one would have heard the organs at full blast, and from the church one would have heard the violins.'

The players had to look elsewhere; they selected the Hôtel de Nemours, rue de Savoie (now 6 rue de Séguier). Plans were drawn up and taken to Louvois, who showed them to the King. Louis gave his consent. This time the cost was 84,000 livres. But the Hôtel de Nemours was very near the monastery of the Grands Augustins, which had been on the quai since the thirteenth century. The curé of St André des Arts, warned by some members of his parish, opposed the players' plans. The latter sent a delegation to Versailles and had a meeting with the curé at Louvois' house. The King was still favourable: could the problem be solved? No! A few days later the company heard that new representations had been made to the King to which he had listened. They sent a new letter to Louvois and La Reynie, carefully explaining that on the bank of the Seine and at the very end of the parish they could cause no trouble at all. Besides, wherever they might go they had to be within some parish, as the King wanted them to be in Paris.

Racine, who followed the matter very closely, was delighted with the new obstacles which the players faced each day. He made fun of them, though he was the author of *Phèdre*, still a very successful play, and his humour sounds a bit unpleasant today.

'Now they are in the rue de Savoie, in the parish of St André', he wrote. 'The vicar has hurried to the King to represent to him that there is hardly anything but inns and drinking houses in his parish; if players should move in, his church will be empty. The Grands Augustins also went to the King with Father Lambrochons to make the speech. It is said that the players told His Majesty that those Grands Augustins, who would not have them as neighbours, are very regular spectators of the comedies, and that they even wanted to sell to the company some houses they own in the rue d'Anjou to build a theatre, and that the deed would have been drawn, were the place a little more convenient. M. Louvois ordered M. de la Chapelle to send him a map of the place they want to build in, and they are waiting for his decision. Yet the alarm in the district has been great; all the bourgeois have had their streets blocked by carriages. M. Billard, who lives opposite the pit door, protests the loudest, and when he was told that he was very well placed to go and amuse himself, he answered tragically: "I don't want to amuse myself".'

Louvois, busy with war preparations, was only too glad to pass the muddle over to Seignelay, Colbert's son. Louis XIV once more abandoned the comedians, despite the intervention of the Dauphin and Dauphine, who were less influential than Mme de Maintenon. They were forbidden to settle in the rue de Savoie.

The actors were in despair. Boileau wrote to Racine:

'If there is any misfortune one takes pleasure in, in my view it is that of the comedians. If they continue to be treated in this way, they will have to settle between La Vilette and the Port St Martin [that is, Monfaucon: the refuse depository of Paris], and I still don't know whether they will get into trouble or not with the vicar of St Laurent.' A few days later he added, with a most unpleasant lack of tact: 'Though you told me in a very pitiful way about the comedians' bad luck, I couldn't refrain from laughing. But tell me, Sir, if they go and dwell where I said, do you think they will drink the local wine? It might not be a bad penance to suggest to M. de Champmeslé, for all the bottles of Champagne he has drunk, and you know at whose expense. . . .'[1]

Tirelessly, the actors tried to find some place where they might be allowed to settle in peace. They considered a house near the Croix du Trahoir, which belonged to Blainville, another of Colbert's sons. Once more, d'Orbay made a plan. The King seemed to be in favour of the new idea and again asked La Reynie's advice: it was refused.

Would the Hôtel de Sens or the Hôten de Lyon, rue St André des Arts, do? No, the King would rather the Hôtel de Lussan, rue des Petits-Champs (today, rue Croix des Petits-Champs), near the Place des Victoires. It was auctioned on November 15th and the actors bought it for 100,000 livres, a huge price. But at last it was done and d'Orbay could start planning his theatre at last.

Alas! the vicar of St Eustache also opposed the presence of actors in his parish. He complained to the King, who went back on his word once more, withdrew his permission and sent the poor people to the Hôtel d'Auch, rue Montorgueil. It was a populous district with narrow streets, many cul-de-sacs, few exits and, to make things worse, bestrode several parishes. Besides, architects told them they could not build anything convenient within a stone's throw of the Hôtel de Bourgogne. 'We would have been ruined had we settled

[1] Champmeslé's wife had been Racine's mistress. Boileau implies that the bottles were drunk at Racine's expense.

in that district,' wrote La Grange. This time the refusal came from the players. They started off on two new plans, either the Hôtel de Colbert de Baulévrier (a relative of the minister), next door to the Hôtel de Lussan, or the Etoile tennis court in the rue des Fossés St Germain des Prés, near the Porte de Buci. The latter was quite near the Hotel Guénégaud and far from any church, and the vicar of St Sulpice had no reason to oppose the players, as they were already living in his parish. This last argument probably did the trick and, 'after plenty of difficulties from Mgr. de Seignelay', the King agreed at last, bored as he was by this endless affair. A decision of the Conseil d'Etat settled the matter on March 1, 1688.

After eight months of tribulations, disappointments and royal promises continuously betrayed, the Comédiens-Français finally found refuge from the storm. The Etoile tennis court (now 14 rue de l'Ancienne Comédie) cost them 62,614 livres. It was pulled down at once and the plans of the new building entrusted to François d'Orbay, le Vau's collaborator, assisted by the well-known Vigarini, 'superviser of the machinery, royal theatres, ballets and festivities', the experienced technician of the great Versailles festivities.

Meanwhile, the Paris vicars were fighting a rearguard battle against the players. The curé of St Sulpice complained that the temporary altar erected for some feast was right beside the tennis court. The company pacified him by paying part of the cost of the altar. The curé of St Paul tried to buy the land secretly, and the curé of St Germain tried to put pressure on the owner's son-in-law. But to no avail. This time the decision had been taken.

D'Orbay worked with incredible speed. On May 16, 1688, the plans were finished and accepted by the comedians. The sculptor Le Hongre decorated the front with a statue of Minerva with helmet and spear, which still stands above the royal coat of arms. The painter Bologne undertook the ceiling, where an allegorical decoration depicted Truth, surrounded by Tragedy, Comedy, Poetry and Eloquence; a second group represented the vices, Vanity, Avarice and Lechery.

In less than a year all was ready. The comedians had now a fine, elliptical hall in the Italian style, the first to be built in France, with remarkably good acoustics. It had been richly decorated with paintings and sculptures and provided with twenty-four chandeliers. The boxes were comfortable, the pit very large. At that time it was the finest auditorium in Europe. It had cost 200,000 livres and the players would be in debt for a long time to pay for it. But the Comédie-Française stayed there for almost a century. To his credit, François d'Orbay refused any salary and returned to Mlle Molière the purse of eighty louis d'or which the company wanted to give him. He said that he merely wanted to help his actor friends, 'and it would be an insult to make him a present'.

The new theatre opened up on April 18, 1689, with Mme Champmeslé in *Phèdre* and *Le Médecin malgré lui*, to show that Molière was still present in spirit. The company had never stopped acting during the two years of its tribulations and it continued its brilliant career, right opposite the famous Café Procope, attracting a large audience. It had been a bad spell for the actors and they were in debt for a long time, but receipts were increasing. Their prestige in Paris grew and extended to the provinces as well as abroad. Here is a little-known proof: in a contract drawn up by an itinerant company managed by Volledieu, signed in Mons in 1696, there is the following clause: 'Moreover, it is understood that, should there be any dispute between the above-mentioned associates, rather than go to the city judge, they should refer the discussion to the Paris comedians.'

This undisputed prestige of the Comédie-Française, though the theatre still had to face many difficulties, especially during the Revolution, was to endure until our own day.

CHAPTER SEVEN

THE ITALIAN COMEDY (1600–1686)

Long before the establishment of the various French companies of which we have just told the story, Italian companies had arrived in Paris. Two Florentine queens were responsible for this, Catherine and Marie de Medici. According to Brantôme, Catherine de Medici took great pleasure in the farces of 'Zanni and the pantaloons, and laughed heartily, as she loved a good joke and a risky word, and was of a hearty nature.' All through the seventeenth century, Italian comedy played a great part in the amusements of Paris.

It was a very original kind of play, quite different from French comedy. The companies consisted of conventional, immutable characters, Leander, Isabella, Mezzetino, the Matamore, the Doctor, Pantaloon, Scapino, Arlecchino, etc., who acted mostly in *commedia dell'arte*: unwritten plays, built on a scanty outline, on which the actors improvised according to their wit and imagination. Their texts were full of coarse jokes, political satires, parodies, skits against the police, the law, and the Academy, which made the pit laugh and worried the authorities. The actors were remarkable performers—musicians, mimics, acrobats, buffoons, dancers, singers and experienced producers of any comic action, all at the same time. They were very free with jokes, puns, *lazzi* and 'gags'. They expressed themselves not only by their voices; their entire bodies took part in the top-speed dramatic action from their facial expressions to their grotesque postures. All this was very necessary since in Paris they were acting to a low-class public, most of which knew no word of their language. It was only by the full use of mime—attitudes, gesture and motion—that they could convey clearly the meaning of a text which was fairly simple and without mystery.

The leading historian of the Italian theatre, Gherardi, wrote in 1695:

'By the term "a good Italian actor" was meant a man with brains, who acted more with his imagination than his memory, who improvised as he went along, who knew how to help those on the stage with him, that is, who was able to blend his action and words with those of his comrade so well that he entered at once into everything and into all the movements required of him by the other.'

During the whole of his Paris career, either at the Petit-Bourbon or the Palais-Royal, Molière shared his theatre with them. The two companies were on friendly terms. There were even Franco-Italian marriages, and Molière, who was an excellent comic actor, owed them much. His enemies and rivals thought they were insulting him when they called him the heir of such clowns and the pupil of Scaramouche, but Molière knew that, if the Italians were so very successful, it was because they were possessed by their love of the theatre and that, so far as comic plays were concerned, they were unequalled. Palaprat, one of their great friends, wrote later about the hilarious meals he ate with them and he added: 'Molière was often our guest, but not so often as we wished, and Mlle Molière came even less often.'

The first Italians came to France in the reign of Charles IX. A company led by Albert Ganasse acted at Blois and at Paris at Henri de Navarre's wedding, three days before the St Bartholomew's Eve. In 1577, the Gelosi, whom Henri III had seen in Venice on his return from Poland, and who usually acted at the Court of Vienna, came to Blois for the Etats Généraux. In May they acted in Paris in the Bourbon hall. Parliament was shocked by these public profane displays, but the King protected them. Another Italian company acted at the Hôtel de Bourgogne in 1583 and the next year the Comici Confederati took their turn. The Gelosi came back in 1588; between 1600 and 1604, the company, led by Francesco Andreini, a renowned Capitano, and Isabella of Padova, rented the Hôtel de Bourgogne on various occasions. In 1608 came the Accesi, the company which belonged to the Duke of Mantua, whose wife was Marie de Medici's sister. They acted at the Hôtel de Bourbon, the Hôtel de Bourgogne and Fontainebleau, where the little Dauphin saw them for the first time.

After two years of subtle negotiations with the Duke of Mantua, Marie de Medici succeeded in having them back in Paris in October 1613, paying all their travel expenses. The company was managed by Tristano Martinelli, who proudly signed himself *Dominus arlechinorum*. This illustrious Arlecchino addressed the Queen in his letters as '*ma commère*' and called her '*regina gallina*' and 'Queen of half the bridge of Avignon'.[1] He was on most friendly terms with the sovereigns whom he amused. The Queen gave him a 'welcome few people can credit'. He was most successful in Lyons, as well as at the Louvre and Fontainebleau.

Tristano Martinelli was a witty and cultured man. He wrote the following amusing letter to the Queen:

'Within a few days, my wife will be delivered of a child whose godfather must be the King and whose godmother shall be the Queen of Spain. Both want to bring them in person to the font. If it is a boy, the King wants to keep him; if it is a daughter, the little Queen wants her and, anyhow, my wife wants it for herself, so that I am greatly embarrassed how to please them all. To make things easy, I thought of giving my wife two more children and handing them over one by one as one does with kittens, as it seems that Arlechino's children are kittens to give away.'

Marie de Medici was bountiful with her 'compère'; he received a beautiful gold chain, 500 ducats, 15 ducats a month for his wife's expenses, and 200 ducats a month for his company. On September 10, 1613, she invited Malherbe, the poet, to come to meet them at the Louvre. The poet, who was always bad-tempered, was not pleased:

'Arlequin is certainly not so good as he was, nor is Petrolin. The former is fifty-six years old and the latter eighty-seven. One is not fit for the theatre at such ages. It requires a lively temper and an adventurous mind, not found in such old frames. They perform a comedy which they call *Due Simili*, which is Plautus' *Menaechmi*. I do not know whether the sauce was rotten or my taste bad, but I came out with no other pleasure than the pride of having been summoned there by the Queen. God willing, we shall see more of it and judge more leisurely.'

The Queen, the court and the young King were less harsh; in two months they saw thirty-nine Italian performances at Fontainebleau. On November 24, 1613, they opened up at the Hôtel de Bourgogne, where, according to Malherbe, who was still cross, 'they were neither good nor bad'. Yet they filled the theatre until July, when they went back to Mantua.

The company led by Gianbattista Andreini replaced them. Andreini acted Lelio and wrote comedies as well as sacred poems.

---

[1] Avignon belonged to the Pope, so that the bridge was only half French.

From 1618 to 1625 they acted for several seasons in Paris. Louis
XIII saw them twenty-three times at the Hôtel de Bourbon in
January and February 1621. They earned plenty of money. But
Arlecchino got into trouble with his companions and wanted to
leave them and retire after having been on the stage for forty years.
Marie de Medici and Anne of Austria spoke in his favour to the
Duke of Mantua. Arlecchino eventually left the company, but the
old actor was found with the *Fèdeli* in Venice for Carnival in 1623,
in Padua and in Verona. The imp of the theatre does not easily
renounce those on whom he has cast a spell.

Andreini's company remained in Paris; as soon as he came back
from the Midi, where he was making war upon the Protestants,
Louis XIII attended sixteen more Italian performances early in
1622.

After having been abroad for a year, the Mantua company came
back to Paris in 1623; it was still led by Andreini and his wife
Florinda. They acted in public in 1624 and 1625, but the company
was soon dissolved, for war had begun and the Duke of Mantua,
attacked by the Duke of Savoy in league with the Spaniards, had
other concerns than comedies.

For twenty-five years the Italians, led by Andreini and then his
son, were the dangerous rivals of the French actors of the Hôtel de
Bourgogne. Charles Sorel, the author of *Francion*, preferred them
to their French rivals and bore witness to their success:

'What leads us to think that their plays are better than our farces
is simply the charm of a foreign language and the naive and
ridiculous actions of their characters who indeed are more clever
at finding what can make us laugh than the actors of any other
nation; but when they try to perform a serious play, they cannot
refrain from introducing their comic tricks, which are too natural
to them for abstention. As they do a great deal of gesturing and
convey much by action, even those who do not understand their
language make out something of the story: that is the reason why
so many people in Paris delight in them.'

Paris was not deprived of those masters of fun and laughter for
long. In 1639 a company led by Tiberio Fiorelli, better known
as Scaramuccio, arrived. Its members were Giacomo Torelli,
Domenico Locatelli (known as Trivelin), and the well-known
Arlecchino, Domenico Biancolelli. They acted *a Finta Pazza* at
the Petit Bourbon in 1645, but performances were stopped by the

Fronde. They came back soon and afterwards settled at the Petit-Bourbon in 1653, which they were to share with Molière's company five years later. That is where they created the *Convive de Pierre*, translated from the Spanish by Giliberti. It was the first of a long list of plays about Don Giovanni. The journalist Loret praised their gorgeous productions which:

> *Font voir de telles raretés*
> *Par le moyen de la machine*
> *Que de Paris jusqu'à la Chine*
> *On ne peut rien voir maintenant*
> *Si pompeux et si surprenant,*
> *Des ballets au nombre de quatre,*
> *Douze changements de théâtre,*
> *Des hydres, dragons et démons,*
> *Des mers, des forêts et des monts,*
> *Des décorations brillantes,*
> *Des musiques plus que charmantes,*
> *De superbes habillements . . .*
> *La grâce et les traits enchanteurs*
> *Des actrices et des acteurs,*
> *Flattant les yeux et les oreilles,*
> *Ne font que le quart des merveilles*
> *(Et j'en jure, foi de mortel!)*
> *Que l'on voit au susdit hôtel.*[2]

Henceforward, their shows were part of everyday theatrical life in Paris. They followed Molière to the Palais-Royal and, after his death, they accompanied his company to the Hôtel Guénégaud. French and Italian actors went on playing on alternate days, sharing the rent, each company retaining its own sets and properties. When the Comédie-Française was created, they moved into the now empty Hôtel de Bourgogne, where they performed every night, like their French colleagues. They were 'the only Italian company maintained by His Majesty', who made them a grant of

[2] 'They display so many rarities through their use of machinery that from Paris to China you cannot see anything more staggering or stupendous: four ballets at the same time, twelve different sets, sea-monsters, dragons, and sprites, the sea, mountains and forests, glittering decorations, delightful music and splendid costumes. . . . The grace and the delightful features of the actors and actresses, who charm eyes and ears, make but a quarter of the wonders you gaze at in this house—and that I can bear witness to.'

15,000 livres, a higher sum than he granted to the Comédiens-Français (12,000).

They might have continued on these friendly terms with their French colleagues, had they not wilfully spoilt them by acting plays with certain scenes in French, which was unfair. The French Comedians complained.

Baron for the French company, and Domenico Biancolelli for the Italians, brought their suit to the King in person. Baron spoke for his company. When it came to the wily Italian to speak, he addressed Louis XIV, saying:

'In which language does Your Majesty wish me to speak?'

'Speak as you wish,' answered the King.

'Then I have won my suit,' answered Biancolelli. 'That is exactly what we are asking for!'

It is said that the King laughed and declared that he would abide by that decision.

Things returned to normal and the Italians continued a long and happy career at the Hôtel de Bourgogne. Nolant de Fatouville, Regnard and Dufresny wrote many comedies for them. All would have been well if in these last years of the seventeenth century they had not made the great mistake of excessive language which was their habit. As early as 1689, Aurelio had been expelled for his unguarded remarks about Louis XIV's hostile attitude towards the Pope. A little later, on January 8, 1696, the Minister Pontchartrain wrote to La Reynie:

'As the King has been told that the Italian players perform indecent plays and use improper language in their comedies, His Majesty has sent word through M. de la Trémoille, forbidding such things in the future, and has also ordered me to write to you that his wish is that you summon them and explain that, should they assume indecent postures or use objectionable words, His Majesty will break them and send them back to Italy. In fact he desires that you send each day to the comedy someone reliable to report on what takes place, so that at their first offence you close the theatre.'

The warning was clear and the threat precise. One would have thought that the Italians would have taken it to heart and acted accordingly. But they thought themselves above punishment. Their satirical gusto knew no limits. The next year, they announced *La Fausse Prude*, a comedy written by Fatouville on the basis of a Dutch pamphlet against Mme de Maintenon. No one was misled. This time they had gone too far; the scandal was one which touched the King himself. This was too much. Here is what St Simon wrote:

'The King drove the Italian players away at top speed and would not have any more. So long as they had merely spilled smutty remarks and even blasphemies upon the stage no one did anything but laugh, but they staged a play entitled *La Fausse prude* in which it was easy to recognize Mme de Maintenon. Everybody hastened to see it, but after three or four performances, which they gave in quick succession, as they were making plenty of money, they were ordered to close their theatre and leave France within a month. There was a big scandal, and if the players lost their establishment through their daring and thoughtlessness, the woman who had them driven away gained little, on account of the liberty with which this stupid episode was discussed.'

This was the end of the Italians and it was their own fault entirely. They never returned during the King's lifetime. It was the Regent who summoned Riccoboni—called Lelio—back in 1716. The new Italian plays, with Marivaux and Favart, were the origin of French Comic Opera.

To complete this survey of Paris spectacles, we must briefly mention the existence of a very popular sort of entertainment, that which took place at fairs. There were two big fairs in Paris each year, one in the spring at St Germain-des-Prés, the other in summer at St Laurent. Among booths and displays of all sorts, many spectacles were produced: short scenes acted in the style of Tabarin or Mondor, acrobats, tight-rope dancers, automatons, exhibitions of giants, dwarfs, strange or trained animals, puppets or waxworks. These popular displays delighted the idlers, and they were meant to attract and amuse customers. They were a great asset to those large gatherings of buyers, idlers, sightseers and seekers after picturesque scenes. They had something in common with the circuses of today.

It seems to have been as late as 1678 when the first real travelling theatre was opened at the St Germain fair by a certain Alard. The actors were mostly tumblers and acrobats. The same year at the St Laurent fair, the 'Royal Company of Pygmees' produced opera-acting puppets, but Lulli, always intractable and always forcing his celebrated monopoly, had it suppressed. Yet there was nothing to be feared from these pathetic showmen: their jointed dolls were certainly no danger to real opera singers!

Little by little, real theatres were built where fairs had been held: actors seized upon the repertoire of the Italians who had just been expelled and presented genuine comedies. The Comediéns-Français sued them because of their monopoly. La Reynie had Alexandre Bertrand's theatre pulled down; in 1699 d'Argenson condemned Bertrand to pay 1,500 livres to the King's players. The lawsuits at the Châtelet and before Parliament were endless. The judges were extremely embarrassed and they tried new methods: dialogues were forbidden but monologues were allowed. The French actors objected and started a new lawsuit, which they won in 1708. Fairground showmen had to rely on puppet shows and rope dancers alone, and those who objected had their theatres pulled down, though they rebuilt them overnight. The whole business was taken to the Grand Conseil, then to the Conseil Privé and finally to the Conseil d'Etat. The fairground players finally lost their case in 1710. They had to act in dumb shows without speaking, merely miming parts which were printed in large type on cards which they took out of their pockets or which were lowered from the ceiling. When there were sung parts, the orchestra struck up and choristers, scattered among the spectators, sang. The public supported the fair actors against the official comedians, but this comic little war, which tickled public opinion, ended in the complete defeat of the fair shows, which were suppressed in 1719. From that time on, the only shows at the Paris fairs were rope dancers and marionettes.

CHAPTER EIGHT

THE BIRTH OF OPERA (1669–1673)

During the last quarter of the seventeenth century the French opera took first place in the theatrical life of Paris. The magic of music, singers and dancers, together with gorgeous costumes and sets, held the eyes and ears of the spectators. If to this one adds Louis XIV's taste for this kind of spectacle, in which his own glory was constantly eulogized in the mythological adventures of Apollo or Hercules, and the extraordinary favours he granted Lulli, even going so far as to ennoble that adventurer of most objectionable habits, making of him a King's Secretary, it is easy to understand the court's enthusiasm, which was promptly shared by the people of Paris. It should be added that the opera arrived at the right moment to replace the already declining tragedies in the public taste.

It is well known that the origins of the opera are ancient and varied, including the court ballet, the ballet-comedy, the Italian opera, the pastoral and the play with effects and music, singing and dancing. We have no need to summarize again the history of the French opera under Louis XIV, or to recall the achievements of Quinault and Lulli. But the conditions in which it was created, and which were important at the time, belong to the daily life of the French theatre in the seventeenth century and are part and parcel of the history of the companies. Molière's *Psyché* was already an opera; Lulli wrote the music and he even acted the part of the Mufti in *Le Bourgeois Gentilhomme*.

The year 1669, which still appears above the curtain at the Opéra, is only a starting point; in fact, opera was born as the result of a long and difficult maturation which lasted for four years, in an atmosphere poisoned by intricate lawsuits, crooked deals and furious quarrels about money.

The first idea of opera in French, over which specialists had argued long and which was even regarded as a contradiction in terms, undoubtedly originated with Pierre Perrin. He was born in Lyons about 1625; he was a poet who had translated the *Aeneid* into French verse and had arranged many poems for setting to music: some were sacred, others were profane and all were poor. Boileau harshly criticized the poems of this pitiful versifier, though Jean de Sablières, Michel Lambert, Robert Cambert, J. B. Boesset and Etienne Moulinié wrote music for them.

When he was twenty-seven or twenty-eight he had married Elisabeth Grisson, who was well over sixty and had been widowed twice. Of course, this marriage, which has been mocked by Talle-mant des Réaux, was a mere matter of money. The widow brought a pretty portion which enabled Perrin to buy an office of Gentle-man Usher for the Ambassadors to Gaston d'Orléans, the King's uncle. But the widow had a son, La Barroire, first councillor, then President of a Parliament, who refused to let his mother be fleeced by a young upstart. Four months after the marriage, which had taken place on January 22, 1653, the son made her lay a complaint against her husband and ask for an annulment, which was granted very quickly, thanks to the son's powerful friends. She then fell ill, gave all her properties to her son and died soon afterwards.

This brief and unbalanced marriage was the beginning of Perrin's troubles: for fifteen years his step-son, the President La Barroire, worried him to death, dragging him through endless lawsuits which ruined him and took him on several occasions to prison, a rather unsatisfactory place for the director of the Paris Opera.

Pierre Perrin had written a pastoral which had been set to music by his friend Cambert, a harpsichord player and the organist of the church of St Honoré. He was in prison at St Germain des Prés when it was privately performed by amateurs at Issy, in the house of one of the King's jewellers. This was 'the first French comedy set to music to be acted in France', its author proudly wrote. Mazarin had it performed with great success at Vincennes for the King and Queen.

Between two spells in prison, Perrin had written another opera, *Ariane et Bacchus*, and a tragedy, *La Mort d'Adonis*, set to music by Boesset, the King's Superintendent of Music, with drinking songs set to music by Cambert. After another imprisonment at the Conciergerie, again because of his enemy La Barroire, the librettist presented Colbert with a gorgeous manuscript of his *Paroles de Musique* and suggested the creation of an Academy of poetry and music. The idea caught the fancy of a Minister who had already founded other academies, younger sisters of the Académie Française.

On June 28, 1669, the date of the official creation of the Paris Opera House, Perrin, thanks to Colbert's protection, was granted a royal privilege for twelve years, giving him the exclusive right to 'establish in our good city of Paris, and elsewhere in our Kingdom, academies of as many members as he thinks fit, to perform and sing in public operas and shows in French verse and music similar to those in Italy'. One of the clauses of the deed was that noblemen could sing in an opera without losing caste.

Perrin, associated with his friend Cambert, recruited singers and began rehearsals for his opera *Ariane et Bacchus* at the Hôtel de Nevers. During these ultimate preparations those two very shady figures, Sourdéac and Champeron, whose dealings with the Comédie-Française we have already related, again made their appearance.

On December 12, 1669, Perrin and Cambert, expecting to get from their partners the financial help they needed, entered into partnership with Sourdéac and Champeron, who were to 'provide all the money necessary for the payments in advance until the day of the first performance'. The receipts were to be divided equally between the four associates.

But these two men soon realized that they had been tied up by this contract, and three months after it had been signed they induced Perrin and Cambert to cancel it and sign a mere deed of association. Deprived of a contractual guarantee, Perrin and Cambert were delivered into the hands of their associates who were both daring and unscrupulous.

Rehearsals of *Pomone*, which was to replace *Ariane*, began at Sèvres in Sourdéac's country house. On May 13, 1670, Perrin rented from the lawyer Patru's family the tennis court of Béquet, or *Bel Air*, in the rue de Vaugirard, close to the Luxembourg palace. But by a police decision that was far too convenient to have been uninspired, the lieutenant of police, La Reynie, banned its performance.

Sourdéac and Champeron then took charge and on October 8, 1670, rented the *Bouteille* tennis court in the rue des Fossés de Nesle, where the company of the Hôtel Guénégaud was to settle much later. It was richly decorated and organized as a theatre, and on March 3, 1671, the first public performance of *Pomone* was given there.

In spite of the jeers that greeted Perrin's very poor poem, the sung pastoral was a great success; the Paris public, always keen to see something new, flocked there in such numbers that there were disturbances at the doors, with free fights among the servants. The receipts were copious, but they were gathered in by Sourdéac and Champeron, who had been the only ones to sign the lease. Neither the singers, nor the librettist Perrin, nor the composer Cambert received a penny. They sued their dishonest associates and the Opéra was temporarily closed. On June 14, 1671, Perrin, having had enough of his associates' dishonesty, signed a new deed with Sablières, the superintendent of the Duc d'Orléans' music, granting him half his privilege. But on the very next day, La Barroire, who had never ceased to worry him and who was probably in league with Sourdéac and Champéron, had him arrested and sent to the Conciergerie.

Performances began again on August 8th, the imprisoned Perrin signed a new contract with Sablières, handing over to him all his rights, though there was a second contract in the form of a letter by which it was understood that they were still exploiting the theatre jointly. Most likely, the fictitious renunciation was made so as to enable Sablières to run the theatre by himself while Perrin was in prison.

Harassed by La Barroire, who continuously demanded the repayment of old debts, Perrin, with incredible thoughtlessness, signed another deed on August 17th, which made over to La Barroire, in repayment of debts, half his properties, including the income of the Opera House, which he had already surrendered to Sablières a week earlier. He was therefore set free. From dire necessity he had put himself into an impossible situation, which delivered him into the hands of his enemy, his step-son.

His liberty was short-lived. Contract in hand, Sablière informed Sourdéac and Champeron, demanding that they hand the rights over. Hearing of this, and furious at having been swindled, La Barroire had Perrin arrested again on August 29th. This time, he was to stay in prison for over a year.

While Sourdéac and Champeron were running the Bouteille tennis-court, Sablières had set *Les Amours de Diane et d'Endymion* to music and it had been performed in Versailles. The libretto had been written by H. Guichard, one of the noblemen attached to the Duc d'Orléans, who was later to be involved in numerous lawsuits with Lulli. On November 23, 1671, Sablières joined forces with Guichard, giving him a one-third share in the profits to exploit the rights relinquished to him by the imprisoned Perrin. Sourdéac and Champeron were also claiming them. The situation was hopelessly involved. Perrin, robbed and imprisoned, left behind him two opposing groups to take over his privilege, Sourdéac and Champeron on one hand, Sablières and Guichard on the other. There were two opera houses at the same time. While Sablières and Guichard performed *Le Triomphe de l'Amour* (a new version of *Les Amours de Diane et d'Endymion*) before the King in February 1672, Sourdéac and Champeron continued at the Bouteille tennis-court with Gabriel Gilbert's *Peines et Plaisirs de l'Amour*, set to music by Cambert.

Then Lulli stepped in. His music had just met with a tremendous success at the Palais-Royal with Molière, Corneille and Quinault's *Psyché*. Lulli, who had not believed at first in operas sung in French, was converted, in view of its striking success. He endeavoured to settle the whole matter by acquiring a monopoly of opera for himself.

He was a clever, resourceful, cunning man, not overburdened with scruples. With good reasons, he thought that both groups had equally doubtful rights to Perrin's succession. He did not intend to allow himself to be dragged into endless lawsuits by such business-men. After all, it was to Perrin that the original privilege had been granted, and it was with Perrin alone that he intended to deal direct, ignoring all others. Together with a notary, he went to see Perrin at the Conciergerie where, apparently, plenty of business was debated at that time. Bankrupt and heavily in debt, Perrin was defenceless. Lulli had no difficulty in persuading him, in exchange for a reasonable pension, to revoke his privilege, which was to lead automatically to the loss of rights of all the people he had previously dealt with. The transactions were agreed to at once and in proper form.

It has often been said that Lulli had shamelessly robbed Perrin. It is not completely true. Of course, they were not on the same footing. The poor man, imprisoned in the Conciergerie without hope or money, was not in a position to hold out against the Florentine, the King's favourite, Colbert's protégé and the darling both of the court and of Paris. But the transaction was loyal and was adhered to. Lulli paid what he had promised, which made it possible for Perrin to obtain his freedom and leave the prison. Besides, in a power of attorney Perrin expressed 'his great joy that his Prince has cast his eyes upon Lulli' to replace him. Through a curious irony of fate, this privilege, which he had never been able to use personally and which had never brought him in a penny, now that he had relinquished it, was providing him with the money that he had badly needed.

From the day when he was handed Perrin's legal renunciation, Lulli was the master of the situation. As a man who was well used to business and who wanted also to exploit the vogue for opera while it lasted, Lulli undertook to realize his project at top speed. He had friends everywhere: ministers, police lieutenants, and a president of Parliament were going to act like marionettes for the Florentine, who pulled the strings and collected the money. Though he had promised Molière, who had launched him in the Palais Royal, to associate him in this privilege, he shamelessly betrayed his friend and worked only for himself. He even tried to forbid Paris theatres to have more than two singers and two musicians, which meant ruin for Molière, as he would have been unable to present his ballet-comedies. Molière appealed to the King, who suppressed this exorbitant clause.

Consequently, within a few days, most likely on March 13, 1672, Lulli was granted a privilege formally cancelling the one granted to Perrin, who, according to the King, 'had not been able to carry out his intentions and raise the music to the level he had wanted'. Lulli was allowed to 'keep a royal academy of music' in Paris during his lifetime, 'and after him it would descend to one of his children, who would be provided and accepted as an heir to the office of superintendent of the music of the King's chamber, with the right to associate himself with whoever he likes'. For the first time, the Academy of Music was described as 'royal': Louis XIV thus intended to take it under his protection, like the other academies. Lulli, and then his heir, were its supreme directors.

All those who were defrauded by Lulli's new privilege, Sourdéac, Champeron, Guichard, Sablières and also Molière, opposed its registration, but Lulli did not let himself be involved in further lawsuits.

On March 30th Louis XIV ordered La Reynie to close the theatre in the rue des Fossés-de-Nesle, supressing Sourdeac's and Champeron's competition by a stroke of the pen. On April 14th the royal council made Lulli's privilege effective in spite of opposition. Colbert intervened personally with President de Lamoignon in Lulli's favour. The King's will was clear: his favourite should win his suit. On June 27th Parliament obeyed and decided that the privilege should be entered upon payment to Sourdéac and Champeron for their sets and machinery. On July 20th a new decree decided that Lulli was not responsible for this indemnity and left to his adversaries the ownership of the tennis court in the rue des Fossés-de-Nesles, its sets and machinery.

On August 12th—the quick succession of events is edifying—Lulli rented for eight months the *Béquet* tennis court in the rue de Vaugirard, formerly let to Perrin and from which the Opéra had been expelled before the works had been completed. On the same day a royal decree barred players from renting the hall in the rue des Fossés-des-Nesles. This was the death sentence for Sourdéac and Champeron, who had given up their indemnity to keep their sets. Now there was nothing more they could do, since they were formally forbidden to use the only free and properly equipped hall in Paris. The royal decree forbade the players to use more than six violins and twelve singers in their performances. Thus was Molière granted partial satisfaction.

On September 2nd Perrin was at last set free: he could have been witness, had he wished, of the triumph of his successor, who had worked with the celebrated decorator Vigarini. In November 1672 Lulli's music was triumphant throughout Paris, while the Palais-Royal was reviving *Psyché* with great splendour, the opera in the rue des Vaugirard was opening its doors with *Les Fêtes de l'Amour et de Bacchus*, a hasty concoction of already performed plays, including some ballet-comedies by Molière. But it was not until the spring of 1673 that Lulli, superintendent of the King's music and director of the Royal Academy of Music, produced his first real grand opera worthy of that name, *Cadmus et Hermione*, on a libretto by Quinault. The King's presence on April 27th gave emphasis to his interest in opera.

The King was not long in bestowing further striking proof of his patronage. Molière had died on February 17, 1673, in semi-disgrace. Four days later, on February 21st, just a few hours before:

> *Qu'un peu de terre obtenue par prière*
> *Pour jamais dans la tombe eut enfermé Molière*[1]

the King, annulling his former and more liberal dispositions, signed at Lulli's request a decree according to which actors could not employ more than two violins and six singers. Lulli's greed and haste were striking. He had struck while the iron was hot. For his sake Louis XIV betrayed Molière on the very day he was buried,

---

[1] 'When a little earth, obtained only by urgent request, had closed over Molière for ever.'

forgetting all the pleasure the great actor had given him for fifteen years and the glory he had brought to his court. But Lulli was the man of the day and Louis XIV, in his royal ingratitude towards Molière's memory, gave him gratuitously the Palais-Royal where Molière's company was then acting.

Having lost its leader, the company settled later in the *Bouteille* tennis court, and, as we have seen, suffered also at the hands of Sourdéac and Champeron.

Meanwhile, Lulli was at the height of his success. When one thinks of the financial difficulties with which poor Perrin had to struggle, one can only be staggered by the magnificent conditions the Florentine had been able to secure for his Academy of Music: a free hall, with sets and costumes paid by the King, since the operas were first to be shown at court and only afterwards in Paris. From the receipts he had only his singers and musicians to pay. Brushing aside all his rivals, sacrificing even friendship to his immoderate ambition, Lulli remained the one undisputed master of the musical world of Paris, after a four years' fight which had made many victims.

CHAPTER NINE
THEATRICAL PERFORMANCES

During the first half of the century the days on which there were performances seem to have been variable, but it is clear that they did not take place every day. During the classical era, the days on which the theatres were open were 'ordinary' days, Tuesday, Friday and Sunday, first nights usually taking place on Fridays. But there were exceptions. When a play proved successful, there were extra-ordinary performances, with seats at double the normal price. As for the Italians who shared the Palais-Royal with Molière, they usually acted on 'extraordinary days', Monday, Wednesday, Thursday and Saturday. But after 1680 the Comédie-Française, in return for its exclusive privilege in Paris, performed every day. Between comedies and operas there were about 800 performances a year.

A police regulation of 1609 fixed the beginning of a performance at 2 p.m., so that in any season it would be finished before night-fall, to avoid incidents. But in fact comedies were always late, for late-comers were always awaited patiently. Thus there were only matinées; there were no performances in the evening, except at court.

The performances were advertised in various ways to be des-cribed later; there were rehearsals, of course. *L'Impromptu de Versailles* gives us a very lively picture of one of the rehearsals in which Molière, the director of the company, pictures himself as the producer giving last-minute advice to his players and settling the conflicts that arose from the allocation of roles and the consequent jealousy and rivalry. This very delicate problem was sometimes solved by the contract of association drawn up by the company, by which the type of character—1st, 2nd or 3rd role—king, peasant, clown, were allocated. Some even went further and comprised an allocation, agreed upon by all the contracting parties, of all the roles in the repertoire. But if the director was a strong personality, he made the decisions himself, as did Molière, who wrote most of his characters for this or that player in his company.

With new plays the author had his say, and he usually succeeded in giving the main parts to the actors he liked: Corneille selected Mlle des Oeillets for Sophonisbe, and Racine selected Mlle du Parc and Mlle Champmeslé for Andromaque and Phèdre. After 1680, when the Comédie-Française had been given a strictly regulated organization, the First Gentlemen of the Bedchamber, under the Dauphine's authority, settled the problems raised by the distribution of parts.

So let us enter the Hôtel de Bourgogne or the Palais-Royal at about two o'clock, 'before the candles were lit'.

The performance had been advertised by posters set at crossroads. Of small size, about 16 by 20 inches, these posters were red for the Hôtel de Bourgogne, green for the theatre in the rue Guénégaud, and yellow for the Opéra. They merely gave the title of the play and the author's name; there was nothing about the caste. Their setting and printing were part of the functions of the company's 'orator'.

The curtain was still down. Was there, in fact, such a thing as a curtain in the seventeenth century? Scholars have argued the matter for long. It is a fact there was a curtain for court ballets, to judge by prints and written documents, at the very beginning of the century. At public performances the curtain did not exist early in the century, but it came into use shortly afterwards. A curtain in two parts, which are drawn to either side of the stage, is shown in the print of the first performance of *Mirame* at the Palais-Cardinal in 1641. When the Hôtel de Bourgogne was repaired in 1647, the estimate for the work definitely mentioned the nailing of a beam above the stage 'for rolling up the curtain'. At the same time, the Marais, too, had a curtain which completely closed the stage before the beginning of the performance. Each stage, therefore, had its curtain, but it was probably not moved during the intervals if the play had a single, unmovable set. It may have been different for plays with stage effects which required considerable changes of sets.

The halls were badly lit. What would most surprise a modern spectator was that, at least after the curtain had gone up, a number of spectators sat on the stage on cane chairs. They were mostly men of quality in rich garments who, according to Chappuzeau, 'provided the theatre with much ornament'. Some of these privileged spectators abused the privilege, like the man Molière depicts in *Les Fâcheux*, who drags his chair into the middle of the stage, in front of the actors, instead of sitting to one side. These choice seats were more expensive than the rest. A letter written by Montdory suggested that this custom dated from the first triumphant performances of *Le Cid*.

Neither La Mesnardière in his *Poétique* (1640) nor d'Aubignac in his *Pratique du théâtre* (1657) alluded to this custom, which seems not to have been general, but which spread to the Italian theatre later and then the opera, arousing justifiable protests. Tallemant des Réaux regarded it as 'something frightfully inconvenient'. But the Abbé de Pure thought that this led to intolerable confusion: 'How often, when the actor had to declare: '*Mais le voici!*" or "*Mais je le vois!*" the audience confused the actor with a well-dressed, well-built man who suddenly entered the stage, looking for his seat even after several scenes had already been acted?' This survived throughout the seventeenth century and was only suppressed in Voltaire's day.

The little beribboned, silk-clad Marquises who sat on the stage were in contrast with the rest of the audience, which at that time was very mixed. Of course, pretty bejewelled women used to shine, as they still do, in comfortable boxes, but in the pit, where the audience stood, there was a large number of idlers, valets, pages, musketeers, cavalrymen, artisans, students, prentices, many of whom had managed to slip in with the crowd but without paying. A royal edict of 1673 forbade these abuses, probably without great effect. To those idlers were added a number of blackguards, thieves, pick-pockets, girls of little virtue who were out to find adventure or some lucky pick-up. This vulgar public, frothy and more interested in farces than in noble tragedies, shouted, joked or abused other spectators and sometimes organized brawls which brought in the police. Sometimes the spectators started playing cards or throwing dice. As soon as the curtain went up, the pit organized an uproar, violently applauding the actors or cat-calling; those who were at the back could not see well and could scarcely hear the actors. Hubbub filled the hall, and from the top of the amphitheatre more spectators took part in this agitation and yelling. Little by little during the century this unruly public became rather more polite, but no one was able to enforce the silence of a modern audience. The theatre remained a public place where a motley noisy crowd would gather. Till the very end of the century there were scandals and brawls at the theatre.

In 1642 Charles Sorel wrote: 'The pit is very uncomfortable because of the crowd of blackguards to be found there who sometimes tried to insult respectable people and, after having quarrelled for nothing, drew their swords and stopped the play.' The same year, Colletet spoke of the 'scandalous assignations' which took place in the pit, 'offensive to female modesty and honour', and the quarrels, fights and even murders that were committed there. The Abbé d'Aubignac stated that, as 'the theatre is attended very little by respectable people, it remains quite discredited and a dishonest form of entertainment'. And yet Molière was full of confidence in the taste of that disreputable audience, because to him they represented solid popular commonsense much more than did the scholars and fashionable people in the boxes of the amphitheatre.

Finally, when the audience had shouted: 'Begin! Begin!' often enough, the curtain went up. Early in the century there was a comic prologue, recited by some clown like Broscambille to put the audience in the right mood, but this was soon dropped.

The performance began with the main play, either a tragedy or a comedy. When the curtain went up, the audience admired the set, and we must deal at some length with that important part of the display which changed a great deal during the century.

At the beginning of the century, according to a tradition inherited from the Middle Ages, theatres still used a manifold set. The stage was partitioned into four or five compartments, each depicting a definite place, a street, a palace, a room, a mountain, a forest or the sea, sometimes very far apart from each other in space and time. According to the Abbé d'Aubignac, one could sometimes see 'France in one corner, Turkey in another and Spain in the middle'. According to the text, actors moved from one compartment to the other, across the proscenium. There were also compartments hidden by the curtains which could be drawn aside when the action moved towards them. The *Mémoire* of the decorators of the Hôtel de Bourgogne has been preserved, written by Mahelot and his followers, with many drawings of those multiple or simultaneous sets, with notices and long lists of required stage properties.

But soon after 1630, dramatists discovered in Italian plays Aristotle's rule of the three unities. The unities of action and time were the first to be adhered to: Mairet was the first to formulate them in the preface of his *Silvanire,* published in 1631. Corneille's *Médée* (1635) and *Le Cid* were still acted with multiple sets, and the text required them. But after that date, the usual five or even seven compartments were reduced to two or three. As for the unity of time (twenty-four hours technically, but often very much less) it was better respected; it compelled the dramatists to concentrate the action. A single set grew more and more useful: it was the *palais à volonté* (any palace hall) used in tragedies situated either in Greece, Rome, or in the East. By 1645 manifold sets had fallen into disuse.

But from this new type of décor, so very convenient to the performers, no archaeological local colour was required. The setting itself was still fairly simple. In Rosidor's *La mort de Cyrus* (1662), for example, in the fourth act, Thomiris exclaimed: 'Guards, come here!' From the ceiling a curtain unrolled on which was painted a fighting army crossing a bridge!

It must be admitted that since the spectator was now deprived of the 'visible satisfactions' previously provided by changes of scene, he was treated to tragedies or pastorals full of extraordinary adventure and incident. But the classical theatre brought much more to cultured people, on account of its high psychological and dramatic value. Literary work offered new pleasures to refined minds who could easily be satisfied with the sobriety of a single scene.

That was all very well for tragedies and comedies written according to classical rules, but there was another kind of play which could please those intent on feasting their eyes on something spectacular: it was the *genre* in which the Marais specialized, still giving ample scope to scenery and machinery, and requiring a large and gorgeous collection of sets. The Italians were masters of that kind of show, and their best men were Jacques Torelli and his successor Charles Vigarini, who organized the setting of the royal ballets and of the magnificent *Plaisirs de l'ile enchantée*. It was from them that French decorators and effects specialists learned how to organize the gorgeous productions which were later used in operas.

But each company usually had its own stage-designer; Molière first used Mathieu, then Jean Crosnier. But for the particularly spectacular plays they had to rely on specialists, painters for the scenes and engineers for the mechanical contrivances which had been used for a long time by authors of pastorals and mythological plays. A number of contracts signed for that kind of production have been found: for instance, the contract for Corneille's *Toison d'or*, signed for the Marais company by the actor François Juvenon, called La Fleur, on behalf of the Marquis de Sourdéac, for whom the play was created at his Normandy castle of Neubourg. Nicolas Bellot, the royal painter, made the six sets, including a garden 'as magnificent as possible' and 'a hideous palace full of monsters'.

For *Dom Juan* Molière summoned two painters, Jean Simon and Pierre Prat. His contract provides very valuable information on the six sets the painters had to create for 900 livres, everything included. Each of them was made of a back curtain and three or five side-frames, the heights of which were eighteen feet at the front of the stage, decreasing towards the back. The sets were a garden for the first act, a bower with a cave for the second, a forest with a temple for the third, the inside of the temple for the fourth, a room for the fifth. A last set depicted a city. Painted bands across the stage represented clouds. Those useful but dry descriptions in a legal deed cannot recreate the richness of the sets nor of the machinery which delighted a public still passionately fond of numerous changes and supernatural episodes.

Other documents are more helpful from that point of view. The Cardinal de Richelieu, for the celebrated performance of Desmarets' *Mirame* at the Palais Cardinal in 1641, had given a sumptuousness unknown hitherto. The *Gazette* described it as follows:

'Neither France nor possibly foreign countries have ever seen such a magnificent theatre, with a prospect displaying so much delight to the spectator's eyes: enchanting gardens decorated with caves, statues, fountains, and large terraced lawns above the sea complete with what looked like the natural waves of vast size, and two large fleets (one of which was supposed to be two leagues away), passed before the eyes of the spectators. Then it was as if night fell, with the progressive dimming of the light, both in the garden and at sea and of the sky, which were then lit by the moon. Day next drove away the night, which slowly passed into dawn, and then the sun rose in the sky.'

After Richelieu's death, Mazarin, with the help of Italian scenedesigners, surpassed even these marvels for the production of *Finta Pazza* and *Orfeo*, on which he spent some 500,000 écus.

Shortly afterwards, when the Marais had made a speciality of spectaculars, creations of that kind became increasingly frequent. They began with Corneille's *Andromède*, Boyer's *Ulysse dans l'Ile de Circé* and *La Naissance d'Hercule*. Everything possible was brought in to delight the audience: gods flying through the air, tempestuous seas on which whole fleets were tossed, stars and lightning, mountains, rocks, gardens, caves, statues, splendid palaces, a hell that was horrifying, and fearful prisons.

The Marais had its own stage-designer, Denis Buffequin, who painted all the sets, the beauty of which was even further enhanced by the spell cast by the music, the songs and the dances. He was a member of the company and drew a regular salary over and above what he earned as a designer. Corneille's *La Toison d'or*, Boyer's *Les Amours de Jupiter et de Sémélé* and *La Fête de Vénus*, Donneau de Visé's *Les Amours de Vénus et d'Adonis* and *Le Mariage de Bacchus et d'Ariane* maintained the audience's taste for the sumptuous display of scenes and effects in the service of pagan marvels which for them were more appealing than austere classical tragedy and the strict control of the three unities. This unfettered kind of theatre allowed playwrights to give their imaginations free play.

In 1665, for *Les Amours de Jupiter et de Sémélé*, the machinery that had been used for *La Toison d'or* could be used, but with Jean Simon's help Buffequin painted new sets, the latter having provided the scenery for Molière's *Dom Juan*. Boyer's play had a set for each act. At the end, Semele and Jupiter were seen in their palace among the clouds, while Mercury and Fame flew away to the end of the hall. Louis de Mollier had organized the musical setting and the players had engaged instrumentalists and a dancing master.

A journalist emphasized the richness of the scenery:

> *Le machiniste avait, je crois, le diable au corps,*
> *Lorsqu'il fit de telles merveilles,*
> *On ne conçoit point les ressorts*
> *De ses machines sans pareilles.*[1]

Louis XIV who was not satisfied with what was produced at court, came to the Marais to see *Les Amours de Jupiter* and started the applause. It was often revived; yet, in spite of very good takings, the outgoings were such that the theatre had difficulty in facing the cost, and was even obliged to borrow 2,700 livres from attorney Rollet, the one whom Boileau had called a blackguard.

Five years later the industrious Donneau de Visé gave to the

---

[1] I am sure the engineer was possessed of the devil when he contrived such wonders. One cannot imagine how these unparalleled contraptions work.

Marais his *Les Amours de Vénus et d'Adonis*. Several flights of gods across the stage delighted the audience. Here is the description of the prologue by Visé himself:

'The whole theatre represents the sky, with nothing to be seen but masses of cloud. A halo soars up at the back and the clouds at the top are different from those lower down.

The Graces appear in a globe with Cupid, seated on a pile of clouds, from which he rises at once and crosses the entire hall, passing above the amphitheatre; from thence, being summoned by the Graces, he returns and halts above the stage to recite the prologue with them, then disappears up-stage. The sky closes and the scene changes to represent an Italian forest.'

Two years later, to make the most out of his success, Donneau de Visé brought out another play, *Le Mariage de Bacchus et d'Ariane*, with the same display of luxury, music and dancing. After one of those very spectacular plays, the *Gazette* wrote: 'The spectators wondered whether they themselves had not been wafted to other places.'

Let us now see how the actors moved among those rich sets. Early in the century the use of the mask and of flour was still common in the performance of comedy. We now know that Molière wore a mask when acting Mascarille in *Les Précieuses ridicules*, and that in the same play Jodelet had his face covered with flour as he usually did. But masks soon disappeared.

Players were very careful with their costumes and we have plenty of information on the subject. A few contemporary engravings, mostly those which represent clowns, and above all inventories drawn up after a player's death, are very informative about theatrical costumes. They were as rich and as varied as the scenery.

First of all, costumes were usually the player's private property; we know that a player's wardrobe was well stocked, though early in the century costumes belonged to the director, enabling him to dress all the actors he engaged. Tallemant des Réaux claimed that at this time actors got their clothes from rag shops and were 'disgracefully dressed'. This was probably true of some miserable strolling companies. In fact, Charles Sorel agrees. He wrote in *La Maison des Jeux*:

'I saw in Paris some people who had but a single costume in which to act all sorts of characters, and could only disguise themselves

128

9. Molière Breakfasting with Louis XIV at Versailles

with false beards or similar feeble features, according to the characters they were acting. Apollo and Hercules were dressed in hose and doublet. You can imagine what mortals looked like.'

On the Paris stage costumes were splendid. As early as 1606, Valleran le Conte was provided with robes and tunics of cloth of gold, crimson velvet, damask and taffeta. Among inventories which have come down to us, those of Molière, of several of his companions and of Le Noir of the Marais, we find rich costumes of velvet, taffeta, satin, bunches of multi-coloured feathers, skirts of cloth of gold or watered silk, and gold or silver embroideries (often false, in spite of Chappuzeau's declaration to the contrary). At a time when manufactured fabrics were very expensive, the players had to go to great expense to acquire them. On several occasions, Louis XIV gave generous grants to Molière for this purpose during court performances. This was great good luck for actors who afterwards wore those costumes on their own stages. Sometimes noblemen presented the actors with their own court costumes. One of the founders of the Marais, Charles Le Noir, owned twenty-one complete costumes, all of them of precious material, decorated with lace and ribbons and identical with those worn at Louis XIII's court. In the inventories these costumes were valued very low, a few hundred livres, but these figures were certainly far below the purchase price. To the man who drew up the inventories, the silk costumes with lace, ribbons, and gold and silver trimmings which had glittered in the candlelight, were no more after their owner's death than faded rags fit for the rag shop.

Chappuzeau, who was a good observer of everything connected with the stage, has made a note of those rich garments: 'That item of expense was to the player greater than one imagines. There are few new plays which do not oblige them to buy new costumes. . . . A single Roman costume may cost 500 écus. They prefer saving on other items in order to give greater satisfaction to the public and there are players whose outfits are worth more than 10,000 francs each.' Several actors, Molière among them, pawned part of their wardrobes for money when in difficulty.

The descriptions of those costumes in the inventories sometimes give us an idea of their owners' personal tastes. For instance, Molière liked yellow and mostly green; these colours are also found in the furnishings of his house. Was not Alceste in *Le Misanthrope* 'the man with green ribbons'? The inventory of his wardrobe is

I

especially valuable, for it specifies the role in which each costume was worn.

Yet the richness of the costumes made local colour impossible: shepherds in pastorals wore silk dresses and carried silver crooks. Tragic parts were acted in contemporary costumes. At most, Eastern potentates were provided with turbans, but heroes in the tragedies were dressed like courtiers at Versailles. Alexander wore a wig, a plume in his hat and a lace cravat. Cuirasses were replaced by silk, velvet or satin bodices embroidered in gold or silver. Mlle de Villiers, as Chimène, looked like Anne of Austria; Mlle de Champmeslé, as Phèdre, looked like Mme de Montespan; and Polyeucte walked on the stage in a Spanish velvet doublet, slashed hose and a feathered toque. In spite of d'Aubignac's protests against such anachronisms, one had to wait until Lekain or even Talma to find an attempt at some historical accuracy in dress.

Those tragedy costumes, which would seem to us ridiculous, helped the seventeenth-century spectators to gather a general impression quite different from what we feel today. For many a twentieth-century spectator, tragedy is a dead literary genre in which kings and princes of antiquity are seen dressed in costumes which, though stylized, retain a historical look. As ancient history is little known, those characters are equally unfamiliar to a modern audience; their language, abstract and full of archaism, is not easily understood when heard for the first time.

The seventeenth-century spectator did not see tragedies as we do now. The palace on the stage resembled Versailles or St Cloud, which at least he had heard of, if he did not frequent it; costumes were those of his contemporaries, exactly like those of the little marquises who crowded the stage, serving as a link between actors and spectators; Greek and Roman history was the basis of culture and was much more familiar than it is now; even the language, if not exactly what the public spoke, at least was familiar; finally, the tragedies contained allusions, more or less obvious, to contemporary events. Louis XIV from various points of view reminded the public in many respects of Alexander or Julius Caesar, and Nicomède made them think of the Prince de Condé. The Marais spectator of *Cinna* thought of the numerous plots against Cardinal de Richelieu's life, and the one who saw *Bérénice* at the Hôtel de Bourgogne naturally remembered Tacitus' *invitus invitam* and applied it to Louis XIV's sorrowful parting from Marie Mancini. All those associations which today are perceived no longer, but which the historian of literature tries to unravel, gave an even greater interest to the tragedies and a touch of reality which has now vanished. For all these reasons seventeenth-century spectators felt much more at home in Corneille's and Racine's plays than does the modern Frenchman, to whom such works remain literary museum pieces.

How did the actors of the Palais-Royal or the Hôtel de Bourgogne deliver their lines? On this subject we have very little evidence. The modern actor or literary historian would give a great deal for a recording of Montdory in *Le Cid*, Molière in *Le Misanthrope*, or Mlle de Champmeslé in *Phèdre*, even though any such evidence would probably produce more disillusion than admiration.

Yet it is possible to glean some information from written documents. It is certain that declamation in tragedy was stilted and that the lyrical effects of the text were rather heavily stressed by the actor. The result was a pompous form of diction, droned out in a singsong manner, interrupted by shouts and fearful howls. Corneille's lines lent themselves especially to this 'elevated' speaking. There is a tradition according to which Montdory, nicknamed the Roscius of his time, had a vocal accident which compelled him to retire as a result of his efforts in declaiming Herod's imprecations in Tristan's *Marimne*. It is also said that Montfleury died of a similar excess in Orestes' mad scene, and that Mlle de Champmeslé killed herself performing Longepierre's Médée. All this may not be altogether true, but the mere fact that it seemed likely to contemporaries is a proof that such unrestrained declamation really did exist.

It is also certain that Molière vigorously reacted against these excesses at the Hôtel de Bourgogne. In *Les Précieuses ridicules* he made fun of the royal players who are the only ones able to 'drone out the verses' and created an uproar. He attacked again, more pointedly and aggressively in *L'Impromptu de Versailles*.

As Molière himself has given us such an opportunity, let us look closely at his criticism of his rivals: it will help us to understand what he objected to and consequently what he approved of and himself practised.

First of all, there was fat Montfleury, who had been cruelly and wittily abused by Cyrano de Bergerac in a well-known diatribe. Instead of a 'well-built young man' to perform the parts of kings, Molière ironically wrote, 'one needs a king as large and as fat as four men together, a king, zounds! with plenty of guts, and of a vast circumference, properly filling his throne. Is there any point in a slim king?'

So here was the first silly convention. Why should not a king be good-looking? And why should not a king speak naturally? But Montfleury, 'an excellent actor of the Hôtel de Bourgogne', according to a footnote, declaimed bombastically, through Molière's mouth, a few lines of *Nicomède*: Why should a king assume this 'voice of a man possessed by the devil' when talking to the captain of his guards? Because you had to draw the attention of the audience: 'If you recite as *you* usually do, I bet you wouldn't get an "ah!" '. Obviously, Molière was against bombastic diction and lack of naturalness.

He addressed the same reproach to other members of the royal company and made mock of them: for instance, Mlle de Beauchâteau, whom he caricatured in her part of the Infanta in *Le Cid*: 'Look how natural it is and impassioned! Look at the smile she maintains, even in the greatest affliction!' Beauchâteau in the stanzas of *Le Cid*, Hauteroche in *La Mort de Pompée*, de Villiers in *Oedipe*, all lacked naturalness and acted in the conventional way, not bothering to attune their acting and speech to the text and the feelings it expressed.

Molière's gift of mimicry gave to this scene a comic force which must have delighted his audience. It is not without interest to note that all the texts cited were drawn from the tragedies of Corneille, whose pompous style was most likely to induce actors to grandiloquence and bombast.

Casting the parts of the comedy that is about to be rehearsed, Molière as producer gave his instructions to his companions: 'Try to get right into the character of your part and to feel as if you are the person you act.' Molière wanted acting to be true and natural. The poet had to assume 'a pendantic aspect which he keeps even when mixing with fashionable people, a sententious voice and an exactitude of pronunciation which stresses every single syllable'; the honest courtier must 'have a quiet air, a natural tone of voice and gesticulate as little as possible'. Each actor has to bear constantly in mind the character of his part, so as to 'render his features well'. Molière explained and described to each actor the character he was to impersonate: 'I will tell you all about your characters, so that you can imprint them deeply upon your minds.'

There was no question of impressing the audience with conventional tricks: acting and speaking close to the text had always the aim of naturalness and truth. Such was Molière's teaching to his companions, and what he practised with them at the Palais-Royal.

That was probably why all his contemporaries, either hostile or friendly, praised his comic acting but agreed that he was an 'execrable tragedian', because the public, used to the Hôtel de Bourgogne species of declamation, found that Molière's style was flat and artless, avoiding all the bombast he had denounced among his rivals. We may think that the latter, when plotting against Molière, did not forget to stress the miserable diction of a clown who, according to them, could only amuse a low-class audience by the grimaces he made when performing in farce.

We have good evidence, recently discovered, concerning this fundamental opposition on the concept of dramatic method which added to the commercial rivalry between the two companies. It is a note by Jean-Baptiste Racine about his father, explaining all the trouble over *Alexandre*. 'He did not like the too-fluent diction adopted by Molière's company. He wanted verses to be given a certain tone which, together with the measure and rhyme, distinguish them from prose; but he could not stand the exaggerated and screeching voices used which some wished to substitute for natural beauty, and which could be written, so to speak, like music.' Thus Racine stood half-way between the two schools when training Mlle du Parc as Andromaque and Mlle de Champmeslé as Phèdre.

Another rather unexpected piece of evidence comes from Vincent de Paul. In a letter to a priest of his order, the date of which is unfortunately unknown, but definitely written at the end of his life, and possibly thinking of Molière and his company, he wrote:

'Some time ago, I told you that our Lord blesses speeches spoken in an ordinary and familiar tone, because he himself taught and preached in that fashion and because this manner is natural, it is also easier than the more stilted one, and the people enjoy it less though they benefit more from it. Will you credit that actors have discovered this and have changed their way of speaking, so that they no longer speak their verses in a high-pitched tone? They do so in a low voice, as if speaking familiarly to those who are listening to them. It was a man who had been in that profession who told me so a few days ago. Now, if a desire to give greater pleasure to the world has brought such a change in the minds of actors, what humiliation for the preachers of Jesus Christ if the affection and the zest to save souls had not the same power on them!'

Molière, in the name of truth and simplicity, led an onslaught against the stilted elocution of the time. We know too well that he failed and that the Comédie-Française after his death and for a long time returned to the Hôtel de Bourgogne tradition.

Besides, spectators, whatever their ideas or prejudices concerning dramatic art, were perfectly able to impose their ideas. We have mentioned that the spectators who stood in the pit were an unruly and often rebellious public. They had been told that booing was 'un droit qu'à la porte on achète en entrant'[2] and they did not fail to use it generously against the actors or the authors. Moreover, they sometimes stopped a show or compelled the company to change the play. Donneau de Visé, who was a playwright and joint editor with Thomas Corneille of the *Mercure galant*, complained of booing: 'a bad habit which began a short time ago at the comedy with such violence that the actors are often interrupted and even sometimes compelled to abandon a new play at the third act and to revive an old one if the hooligans ask for it'. To soothe his colleagues' pride and possibly his own, Donneau de Visé added: 'In condemning the booing, I do not mean to justify all the plays that were booed, but one must not thereby conclude that all the plays that have been booed were bad.'

Of course, those who liked the play reacted against the boos, and this sometimes lead to plenty of noise and possibly to brawls. The police tried to step in but booers protested. A charming rondeau was written on the subject:

> *Le sifflet défendu, quelle horrible injustice!*
> *Quoi donc, impénement un poète novice,*
> *Un musicien fade, un danseur éclopé*
> *Attrapperont l'argent de tout Paris dupé,*
> *Et je ne pourrai pas contenter mon caprice?*
> *Ah! si je siffle à tort, je veux qu'on me punisse*
> *Mais siffler à propos ne fut jamais un vice;*
> *Non, non je sufflerai, on ne m'a pas coupé*
> *Le sifflet!*

[2] 'a right you buy at the door on entering'.

134

Un garde à mes cotés, planté comme un jocrisse,
M'empêche-t-il de voir ces danses d'écrevisses,
D'ouir ces sots couplets et ces airs de jubé?
Dussè-je être, ma fois, sur le fait attrapé,
Je le ferai jouer à la barbe du Suisse,
        Le sifflet![3]

But as disorders increased players complained and the police were more severe. On January 15, 1696, the Minister Pontchartrain wrote to the police-lieutenant La Reynie: 'The Comédiens-Français having given me the report I send you, I mentioned it to the King, who agrees to have appropriate measures taken to prevent henceforth the disorders brought about by booers at the Comédie, and his Majesty has ordered me to ask for your advice and what you think should be done.'

La Reynie's propositions were accepted by the Minister who answered: 'As for the disorders at the comedies, nothing could be better than what you have planned; after you have issued a new decree and it has been made public, if some persons of whom one can make an example are found guilty, I will send you orders to have them shut up for correction in the General Hospital.' A few booers were arrested and imprisoned in the Petit Châtelet and were given several weeks to meditate; meanwhile, the audience replaced the booing with yawns and sneezes.

Disorders in the theatre usually went much further. Either in the pit, or when leaving, arguments turned into quarrels and sometimes into free fights, and people were injured or sometimes killed. In 1641, Louis XIII had forbidden valets to carry swords, daggers or pistols when going to plays. Louis XIV renewed that order several times, proof that it was not obeyed. La Reynie wrote to Colbert: 'They carry [disorder] to such an extent that hardly anybody in town dares go.' But the main trouble-makers were not the people of Paris; members of the King's household, and his musketeers especially, created serious disturbances by refusing to

---

[3] To forbid booing, what dreadful injustice! What! can an inexperienced poet, a dull musician, a lame dancer pocket the money of an audience that has been fooled, and I cannot express my feelings? If I boo at the wrong place I am willing to be punished, but a well-timed boo has never been a vice. No! I shall boo; I haven't been deprived of my voice— Does a guard, standing next to me and looking like a fool, hide from my sight these crab-like dancers, or prevent me from hearing those silly ditties and idiotic chants? Even at the risk of being caught red-handed, I am going right under the nose of the Swiss guard, to use my right to boo.

pay for their seats. The King had to issue a special decree which was read at the crossroads, to compel those unruly warriors to pay for their seats, just like any *bourgeois*. One day the Marquis de Livrey came to the Comédie-Française with a great dane, 'which began its tricks on the stage. . . . People in the pit, to encourage it, gave voice to all the hunting calls they could think of.'

Thus the theatrical performances of the seventeenth century were much more lively than those of today. But all the incidents we have described did not prevent the classic theatre from triumphing on the Paris stage or from ensuring good receipts at the door.

Companies made their own publicity. For each of them, a player acted as *orateur*, or spokesman, though the custom fell into disuse at the end of the century. The spokesman had the task of composing and supervising the printing of the posters. That meant writing a long advertisement, telling the reader about 'the large audience of the previous day, the merit of the play which was to be acted and the urgent necessity of booking boxes in advance, as the play was new and fashionable people were flocking to see it'. The spokesman was such an important person that the function was often carried out by the director himself: Montdory, Floridor and La Roque at the Marais, Floridor and afterwards Hauteroche at the Hôtel de Bourgogne, Molière and afterwards La Grange at the Palais Royal.

It is probable that the spokesman provided the gazetteers with information about plays that were being rehearsed and their castes, thereby increasing the publicity given by the authors when they read their plays to fashionable circles. After the performance, the spokesman, still dressed for his part, delivered a little speech to the audience. Chappuzeau gives interesting information concerning this lost usage:

'The speech he makes at the end of the play is meant to propitiate the audience. He thanks them for their pleasant attention. He announces the next play and invites them to come and see it by the few words of praise he gives it. These are the three main parts of which his speech is made. Usually it is brief and improvised. At other times it has been studied and learnt by heart when the King, Monsieur or some prince of the blood is in the audience, as happens in the case of the spectacular plays, since the machinery cannot be moved elsewhere. He does the same when announcing a new play which needs to be praised, and also when bidding farewell to the audience on the Friday before the First Passion Sunday, when the theatre reopens after Easter to revive the public's taste for comedy. In his ordinary announcements, the spokesman promises plays by various authors, to be acted in a distant future, to keep the people primed, and enhance the merit of the company. . . . When the spokesman comes to make his announcements, the whole audience listens in great silence and his brief, well-spoken words are often listened to with as much pleasure as the comedy. He produces each day some new witticism which tickles the audience's attention and marks the fertility of his mind, and either in his speech or in his posters he is modest in the praise lavished on the author and his play, as is customary, and on the company which is to act it. When praise is too great, the impression is that the speaker is speaking to deceive, and the audience feels less persuaded by what he is trying to instil into their minds. But, as customs are changing, all these habits are falling into disuse. Both in the farewell announcement and in the poster, long discourses have been dropped, and they make do with simply naming the play to be performed.'

Molière was outstandingly good at this function: it was he who, in October 1658, when his company arrived, made a speech to the King in the Louvre before presenting *Le Docteur Amoureux*.

So, by their care in embellishing their theatres, by the ingenuity of their scenes, the beauty of their costumes and publicity as broad as the period permitted, Paris companies did all they could to give lustre to their performances, while serving, at the same time, their own and their authors' interests.

CHAPTER TEN

HOW THE COMPANIES LIVED

We have followed the actors through their various theatres and on the stage; now we must take a look at their professional life, how their companies were organized, their relations between themselves and with the authors, and at the administrative and financial organization of their theatres.

First of all, we must mention the fact that in the seventeenth century all the theatres of Paris, as is still the case with the Comédie-Française, were run as associations in which actors had full, half or quarter shares. Sometimes a half or even a full share was given to an actress in consideration of her husband (as was the case with Armande Béjart) and less often to the husband in consideration of his wife (as was the case with Champmeslé). As often as possible, when a good actor married he tried to find a wife able to deserve a share like himself. Those matters were settled by legal deeds. The financial organization was of the simplest: after each performance, the treasurer-actor extracted the expenses from the receipts and at once distributed what was left in proportion to the shares held by each actor. This is revealed by La Grange's register, which for each performance states how much was received and how much was given to each. Every month the company met and checked the accounts, and all the actors and actresses were present.

But though they were private associations and therefore free in their activities and their administration, at least until the last quarter of the century, when the Comédie-Française came under strict supervision, all the Paris companies were subsidized by the King, which compelled them to attend court whenever the King summoned them. Their performances at Versailles brought them fame and money, as the Office of Entertainment repaid their expenses for the journey, their stay in town and for their costumes. 'When they moved to St Germain,' wrote Chappuzeau, 'to Chambord, to Versailles or elsewhere, besides their subsidy, which is always paid, their coaches, wagons and horses, which are provided by the King's Stables, they have a joint bonus of 1,000 écus a month, each member has two écus a day for his expenses, their servants in proportion, and they are housed by the King's intendants.' They sometimes remained at court for several weeks on end.

They were also often requested to perform in private houses by princes, ministers or foreign ambassadors and they could not decline these invitations. There, too, they received presents in cash, but far less generous than at court. Sometimes, too, they gave free public performances to celebrate some happy event, the signature of a peace treaty or the birth of a Dauphin or of a prince of the blood. On the other hand, court mourning compelled them to close for a long time, to which was added the compulsory closure for Lent.

Among the various financial problems they had to face, a vital one was the price of seats. In the sixteenth century the Italian players charged four sous for a seat. A police regulation of November 12, 1609, forbade charging more than five sous in the pit and ten in the boxes and gallery. At that rate, which was still usual in 1620, adequate receipts could only come from a completely packed auditorium! It is true that it had already become a habit to double prices on the first night of new plays, which was called 'acting double'. On the other hand, one must take into account the number of those who entered without paying: authors, members of the King's household including musketeers (until the Royal interdiction of 1673), and those who had no right at all but entered all the same. As Chappuzeau writes, 'there were many people and very little money', on account of all those spectators who slipped in by stealth and sometimes by sheer strength. Actors had also to take into account the doorman's crooked fingers, for he made as much as he could out of the tickets he sold and, according to Scudéry, 'an honest man in that profession is something like the philosophers' stone, perpetual motion or the square of the circle, that is, something possible but never found'.

Yet the poor players sometimes found a generous protector like the Comte de Belin or the Duc de Guise, who gave them costumes and money. They also made more money out of performances at the Louvre or at some great lord's house. But it was only in 1641 that the Hôtel de Bourgogne, thanks to Richlieu, received a royal subsidy of 12,000 livres, while the Marais had to make do with 6,000. In the summer, tours in the provinces added a little to their meagre income, and during all that time they still had to pay rent to the Confrères de la Passion.

But the players of the early periods were already conscious that they were acting a noble part, delivering a message to a rather limited audience. They were therefore very haughty towards the mountebanks of the Pont Neuf who were taking part of their audience away from them.

In the classic period the situation was very much better; the audience was much larger than at the time of the early farces, and it is likely that players, if they did not all of them own coaches, as La Bruyère wrote, made a substantial profit out of their profession. The property inventory drawn up after the death of Molière or Baron revealed a very prosperous situation. We lack documents about the Hôtel de Bourgogne or the Marais, but La Grange, who was as meticulous in his own private accounts as in those of Molière's company, stated that in fourteen years between 1658 and 1673, he had received 51,670 livres, which is about 250,000 new francs. The receipts were constantly increasing, with a specially prosperous year in 1669, when *Tartuffe* was produced. They diminished after Molière's death, but increased again regularly until the end of the century. At that time Dancourt renounced his author's share. The Comédie-Française, like the Hôtel de Bourgogne, received a royal subsidy of 12,000 livres, the payment of which was always in arrears. Molière was granted a double share as an author; with his salary of upholsterer[1] to the King, his royalties on his printed plays, and his share of the royal subsidy, it has been reckoned that during the same period he received some 160,000 livres, the equivalent of 800,000 modern (new) francs. Grimarest stated that he had an income of 30,000 livres, which seems excessive.

It is true that from the middle of the century the seat prices had risen: it was fifteen sous in the pit, one livre in the third row boxes, one livre ten sous in the upper boxes, three livres in the amphitheatre, and five livres ten sous in the first boxes and on the stage.

The same prices were charged by the Italian players. But the pit was still accessible to the common people as Boileau says:

> *Un clerc pour fifteen sous, sans craindre le holà,*
> *Peut aller au parterre y siffler* Attila.[2]

As for the Marais, it also charged more for the plays with stage effects, as expenses were heavy.

As from 1699, the year when the poor tax was instituted, prices

---

[1] Which he had inherited from his father.
[2] For fifteen sous a lawyer's clerk can go to the pit to boo *Attila*.

went up by a sixth. If the bourgeois paid for their seats when entering the theatre, lords had no such scruples and often forgot; imitating the King, they were not in a hurry to repay their debts. According to the account books of the Comédie-Française, they sometimes waited for three or four years before payment was made. For instance, the Prince de Turenne argued over a matter of a few livres in a debt of thirty-three livres. The Marquis de Rochefort asked for credit for a balance at debit of fifty-five sous. On the whole, receipts at the door of 2,000 livres were reckoned as very good for an evening; more often it was about 1,000. We must also take account of the fact that until 1680 Paris theatres opened only three times a week, and closed on days of mourning and during Lent. On July 17, 1676, 'there was no performance on account of Mme de Brinvilliers'. That day's spectacle was in the Place de Grève, where Mme de Brinvilliers was executed; not for anything would Mme de Sévigné have failed to be there!

Theatres had very heavy expenses to settle before the takings were divided: the rent (except for the Comédie-Française, which owned its theatre), sets, costumes, musicians, salaried people such as door-keepers, copyists, prompters, fiddlers, receivers, comptrollers, candle-snuffers, usherettes, porters, printers and billstickers. In 1673, Chappuzeau reckoned these expenses at the Hôtel de Bourgogne at 15,000 livres. To these were added taxes, legal expenses, alms to various religious bodies and finally pensions to retired actors. It was the Hôtel de Bourgogne which in 1664 started this 'retirement of old players', to whom the company paid 1,000 livres for a full share, and 500 for a half-share, which could not be distrained. Molière's company followed that example soon afterwards: it was Louis Béjart who retired from the theatre in 1670 and was the first to receive the pension in order 'to live honourably', as the deed described it. But finding those pensions too heavy, the companies formed the habit of putting the pension to the charge of the player who had been engaged to replace the retired one. If a player died while still active, the company made a gift of 1,100 livres to his heirs. Sometimes, but very seldom, the company gave a pension that was supplementary to his share to an actor of very high repute, to bind him to the company: this is what happened with the Champmeslés when the Hôtel Guénégaud had succeeded in grabbing them from the Hôtel de Bourgogne. Talent and fame were at a premium.

A last source of expenses had to be faced by the actors: royalties

141

to the authors who provided the plays. This needs careful examination as, by checking various documents, we shall be able to appreciate how much comedians had to pay, and how much seventeenth-century playwrights could make by their writing.

Early in the century, while their only repertoire consisted of outdated Renaissance plays, Parisian companies tried to hold on to certain dramatic poets. Such was the case with the forerunners of classic tragedies, Alexandre Hardy and Rotrou.

It seems that Hardy was the first author to make some money out of his creations, but he met with many difficulties in this connection. In 1598 he associated with Valleran le Conte, who made deserving but vain efforts to force these plays upon the public. Hardy, an actor and an author, at first acquired the honorary right of first signature on the contracts drawn by the company whose paid poet he was, and the pompous title of 'poet ordinary to the King', a title which was neither of more value nor more authentic than the 'King's comedian' assumed by strolling players. Yet his large production brought him some repute.[3]

In 1620 he had become the salaried poet of Bellerose when he succeeded Valleran le Conte and was in Marseilles with his company. Bellerose was an exacting and hard director, and he literally exploited the luckless Hardy. He bought his plays at a price still unknown, against a deed of cession which gave him the monopoly of performances and prevented the author from publishing them. When Bellerose joined the Hôtel de Bourgogne company in 1622, he took Hardy with him. Hardy's reputation had increased, but Bellerose still refused to allow him to publish his plays, so that they might not be performed by rival companies. Held in tight bondage by his director, Hardy went on writing plays which he sold to Bellerose under the same draconian terms because he needed the money.

Hardy protested, argued and finally was allowed to publish at least some of his plays. Thus, in 1625 he handed twelve of them over to a Paris printer for the very respectable sum of 1,800 livres, a proof of his popularity. He obtained 100 livres for his *Jaloux*.

---

[3] I recently made a note of a curious contract (Cat. St Hélion, no. 171, 4th trim, 1964) between the author of a play entitled *La Généreuse Allemande* and a touring company led by Pierre Daré, who undertook to perform it, upon the payment to the author of half the profits. But was this half the net profits with expenses deducted, or the gross takings? Even in the former event, it was much more profitable to the author than what was granted by the Paris theatres mentioned later.

In the end, strengthened by his success on the stage, having become aware of the value of his merchandise, Hardy broke with Bellerose and offered his services to another company, managed by Villiers. This time he was given part of the takings, but death soon ended his career.

Rotrou succeeded him at the Hôtel de Bourgogne. At the outset, Bellerose tried to press on him the same terms that he had made with Hardy, but Rotrou soon freed himself and, as both he and Bellerose had need of his plays, they came to an agreement: Rotrou was to hand all his plays over to the Hôtel de Bourgogne for 600 livres each, with a copyright of eighteen months. After that time he was free to have them printed. So Rotrou remained with the Hôtel de Bourgogne until his death in 1650.

Meanwhile, Corneille was most successful at the Marais. As a Norman he was very careful of his money, checking his royalties minutely and the income he could draw from his plays. He did not hesitate to dedicate *Cinna* to a financier, M. de Montauron, from whom he got a fair bag of écus in return for some undignified flattery. It is not known how much he was paid for his plays. But we do know that he was furious when, after they had been printed, the Hôtel de Bourgogne revived them without paying him a thing.

He then conceived a brilliant idea: to have these revivals banned. So in 1643, the year when *Cina, Polyeucte* and *La Mort de Pompée* were published, he made a draft of letters patent to be submitted to the King for signature. But as this text was aimed at the King's company essentially, the privilege was refused and Corneille secured nothing but a deterioration of the already unpleasant dealings of the two main Paris theatres.

During the classical period, the relations of authors and actors, which had been quite bad, improved. Chappuzeau, very well informed in his capacity as a playwright, provides first-hand information about the conditions offered to authors in the second half of the seventeenth century:

'The most usual and just condition, on either side, consists in giving the author two shares in each performance of his play for a certain time. For instance, if in a *chambrée* (which is what players call that which comes to them for one performance or a day's receipts) they receive, as I have said, 1,660 livres, and the company holds fourteen shares, on that night the author will have 200 livres for his two shares, the other 60 odd livres being collected in advance for ordinary expenses, such as candles or wages. If the play is a great success and goes on at double price for some twenty performances, both author and actors are rich; if the play is unlucky and fails, either because it cannot stand by itself or lacks admirers, thus giving the critics a free hand to maul it, no one is stubborn and it is performed no more, and both sides try to draw comfort as best they can, as in this world one has always to do concerning all unpleasant happenings. But that happens very seldom [?] as the players know very well what to expect from a play. Sometimes, the players buy the play outright, even for as much as 200 pistoles or more, taking it from the author and gambling on its success. But the risks are not great when the author has a high reputation and all his former works have been successful, and it is only with men of that kind that such fine conditions are made. When the play has been very successful, above what the players had expected, because they are generous they make a few gifts to the author, who is thereby led to remain on friendly terms with the company.

'But for a first play by an unknown author they give no money or very little, regarding him only as an apprentice who has to be content with the honour of having his play produced. When a play has been accepted on the footing of a cash payment or two shares, most often the author and the actors do not separate without a feast together, during which the agreement is signed.'

It was thus, in fact, that things happened, though there were special cases which varied from the general rule. For instance, Racine, when a young and still unknown dramatist, received two shares in the Palais-Royal receipts for *Thébaîde*, his first play. This favour, granted by Molière, who was making his début in Paris, gives an even worse aspect to the trick played on him when, some time later, Racine took his *Alexandre* to the Hôtel de Bourgogne without warning. It is easy to understand how grieved and furious Molière was; he never forgave Racine for this treacherous behaviour.

Before he received his author's share, Molière was granted 1,000 livres for *Les Précieuses ridicules*, 1,500 for *Le Cocu imaginaire*, and 1,100 for *Les Fâcheux*. Payments for his books were equally large. He sold *Psyché* for 1,500 livres and *Tartuffe* for 2,000. The Abbé Boyer, a young playwright, only received 550 livres for his *Tonnaxare*, 'in a gold-embroidered purse'. But Corneille received 2,000 livres from the Palais-Royal company for his *Attila* and also for *Tite et Bérénice*. For *Circé* Thomas Corneille, a very fashion-

L'ESCOLE DES FEMMES

11. Scene from *L'École des Femmes* (Molière)

12. La Fontaine, Boileau, Molière and Racine dining

able playwright who, according to Dangeau, 'died as poor as Job', received in addition to his royalties a present from the company of 60 louis d'or.

His verse version of Molière's *Dom Juan* brought him 100 livres, and a similar sum was paid to Armande Béjart. *La Devineresse* by Thomas Corneille and Donneau de Visé had an enormous success and brought almost 6,000 livres to its authors. The loss of the Hôtel de Bourgogne registers deprives us of information concerning this theatre, but we know that Pradon reecived 2,000 livres for *Phèdre et Hippolyte*, Boyer 1,600 for *Judith*, Boursault 2,050 for *Esope à la ville* and 2,500 for *Esope à la cour*.

But the best-paid of all dramatists was Quinault, who was under contract to Lulli for his opera libretti: he had to provide one a year, for the sum of 4,000 livres. By his monopoly Lulli acquired exclusive rights over Quinault's operas, who thus lost all ownership of his own works. Quinault had gone ahead at a great pace, for when he began the Marais had given him only 150 livres for a libretto in 1653.

As from 1683 the Comédie-Française set a new and simple rule: authors would receive a ninth of the takings for a play of five acts, and an eighteenth for shorter plays of from one to three acts. But such conditions only applied to the first performances of new plays: revivals produced for the author no royalties whatever.

Not before the end of the eighteenth century did this anomaly come to an end, and it was the Italian Comedy which set the example, which the Comédie-Française could only follow.

We now know that, like Molière, the great Paris actors were fairly well off. Charles Le Noir, one of the founders of the Marais, bought a house in Paris in the rue de Périgord for 9,800 livres and when he died he left his widow enough to bring up their five children in a very respectable way. Montdory retired to Thiers and lived there in his own house, very comfortably off, with a pension from the Cardinal de Richelieu and also from a few noblemen who sought to attract the minister's attention. La Roque, the manager of the Marais, bought several houses. Mlle Baron and Mlle des Oeillets had many jewels. Jodelet and his brother L'Espy owned properties in Anjou; Bellerose had a country house near Conflans-Ste-Honorine; Mlle Beaupré lent large sums of money to the Marais when the theatre was in difficulties, and even when Molière's company was touring the provinces, Madeleine Béjart

K

made big investments. Floridor, besides his professional income, was granted by the King, in 1661, the right to provide ropes for boats from the Quai des Bonhommes de Chaillot to the Porte de la Conférence, and, two years later, together with Quinault, the privilege of transport between Sarlat and Cahors. Often summoned by the King, actors attended court, where they were in great demand among courtiers and drew substantial profits of various kinds. The glamour of the theatre under Louis XIV put them very much into the foreground; the nobility pampered them, even if only to please the King.

In the seventeenth century, more than at any other time, actors were also playwrights. Molière stands out as the most illustrious of them all. Of about 100 plays he produced during his fourteen years in Paris, thirty-one were written by him and they were the most successful of all; many others were acted ten or twenty times at most, and often less. Molière kept his theatre alive by his comedies, with which he was always successful, and it is obvious that, tragedies (apart from those by Corneille or Racine) being so poor, he could never have survived the rivalry of the Marais or the Hôtel de Bourgogne, the tragedy company of which was better than his own.

During his lifetime Molière the author kept the company of Molière the actor alive. The best proof of this, apart from his companions' fidelity, is the fact that his death is a landmark in the history of the theatre: after it there was such a gap that theatres had to be reorganized.

But if Molière is the one player whose dramatic writings have survived, he had many imitators in his lifetime. Without mentioning provincial companies which included a number of actor–authors like Rosidor, Dorimond or Nanteuil, of whom we shall write later, there were many others on the Paris stage: Chevalier at the Marais, at the Hôtel de Bourgogne and later at the Comédie-Francaise; Montfleury *fils*, Poisson, Hauteroche, de Villiers, Champmeslé, Brecourt, Rosimont, Baron, Raisin, Dancourt, La Tuilerie, and Le Grand, all of whom provided their theatres with comedies. Yet it is likely that more than once those actor–authors merely lent their names or were the modest collaborators of authors who did not care to offer their own names as a prey to public slander, just for some quite insignificant piece of work.

So actors, authors and actor–authors worked closely together. Each of them was tied to a theatre which he helped and for which he fought. For the three Paris theatres were in constant bitter rivalry, which sometimes led to open warfare. *Les Précieuses ridi-cules* and *l'Ecole des Femmes* set Molière's company and that of the Hôtel de Bourgogne at loggerheads, and their quarrels often went beyond the limits of dignity and courtesy.

One of the most frequent forms of this commercial rivalry was for a company to produce a play on the same subject as its rival. This stimulated public curiosity and in the end helped both plays. This practice went far back: in 1633 Gougenot published *la Comédie des Comédiens,* which put the Marais actors on the stage. Scudéry replied the next year with another comedy with a similar title in which the actors of the Hôtel de Bourgogne appeared. Throughout the century there was a number of double plays pitted one against the other. In 1635 the Marais produced Mairet's *Cléopâtre* in opposition to a play on the same subject by Benserade which was performed at the Hôtel de Bourgogne, and a little later Quinault plagiarized Boisrobert's *Coups de l'amour et de la for-tune* in a tragi-comedy of the same title written in haste for the royal company. Donneau de Visé wrote: 'It is not enough for me to attract people to my play; I must have others to praise it on the other stages and to abuse the new plays produced in opposition to mine.' The public was induced to take sides and to become involved in the scheme. This malicious pastime always appealed. When Molière produced *Les Précieuses ridicules,* Somaize, prompted by the players of the rue Mauconseil, brought out *Les Véritables précieuses*; a third-rate scribbler wrote *La Cocue imaginaire* to rival Molière's *Cocu imaginaire. L'Ecole des Femmes* and *Tartuffe* gave rise to famous quarrels and satirical comedies; Montfleury *fils* produced his *Impromptu de l'Hôtel de Condé* in rivalry with *L'Impromptu de Versailles.* From the day when the Spanish theme of Don Juan was imported into France by the Italians, everybody seized upon it—de Villiers, Dorimond, Molière and Rosimont after him. Two *Mères Coquettes* were produced in the same year, one by Donneau de Visé and the other by Quinault; each accused the other of having stolen his subject and the public had a good laugh at both. When Molière produced Racine's *Alexandre,* the Hôtel de Bourgogne, before grabbing the author, revived Boyer's *Alexandre* at top speed. In 1668 Molière opposed Subligny's *Le Folle querelle* to Racine's *Andromaque.* Two years later the Corneille–Racine duel took place with the two plays called *Bérénice,* inspired, according to Fontenelle, by Princess Henrietta Anne, the Duchesse d'Orléans. Molière had not forgiven Racine,

147

and when the latter's *Iphigénie* was performed with great success at the Hôtel de Bourgogne, he put on another *Iphigénie* by Le Clerc and Coras, which was a total failure in five nights, and was finally killed by Racine's epigrams:

> *Entre le Clerc et son ami Coras*
> *Tous deux auteurs rimant de compagnie,*
> *N'a pas longtemps sourdirent grands débats*
> *Sur le propos de son* Iphigénie.
> *Coras lui dit: 'La pièce est de mon crû';*
> *Le Clerc répond: 'Elle est mienne et non vôtre'.*
> *Mais aussi tot que l'ouvrage a paru,*
> *Plus n'ont voulu l'avoir fait l'un ni l'autre.*[4]

As usual, Chappuzeau was too optimistic. He wrote about those rival plays: 'They sometimes try to hurt each other by sly stratagems, but it never comes to much.' It is true that he was writing in 1673; four years later the *Phèdre* affair was to give him the lie.

This story has to be related in some detail, for it provides an excellent example of the bitterness of some theatrical rivalries. On January 1, 1677, Racine's *Phèdre* was produced at the Hôtel de Bourgogne with Mlle Champmeslé in the name part. But the Corneille party, very much opposed to Racine and led by the Duchesse de Bouillon and her brother the Duc de Nevers, conjured up a rival to Racine in the person of Pradon, who hastily turned out a *Phèdre et Hippolyte*, which was produced at the Hôtel Guénégaud two days after the first performance of Racine's play.

The Duchesse de Bouillon, who was the life and soul of the plot, had reserved in advance all the boxes of both theatres for six performances to create a furore round Pradon's play and a desert around Racine's. On January 1st, Mme Deshoulière, who was party to the Corneille plot, wrote the following satirical sonnet about Racine's play, which was widely distributed in the salons and in literary circles:

> *Dans un fauteuil doré, Phèdre, tremblante et blème,*
> *Dit des vers où d'abord personne n'entend rien.*
> *La Nourrice lui fait un sermon fort chrétien*
> *Contre l'affreux dessein d'attenter à soi-même.*

---

[4] Between Le Clerc and his friend Coras, both of them poets who made their verses together, there was a heated discussion a short time ago about their *Iphigénie*. Coras said 'The play is mine,' Le Clerc answered: 'It is mine, not yours.' But as soon as it was published, neither would have anything more to do with it.

Hippolyte la hait presque autant qu'elle l'aime,
Rien ne change son air ni son chaste maintien,
La nourrice l'accuse; elle s'en punit bien.
Thésée a pour son fils une rigueur extrême.

Une grosse aricie au cuir noir, aux crins blonds,
N'est là que pour montrer deux énormes tétons
Que malgré sa froideur, Hippolyte idolâtre.

Il meurt enfin, traîné par les coursiers ingrats,
Et Phèdre après avoir pris de la mort-aux-rats,
Vient en se confessant mourir sur le Théâtre.[5]

Racine, the victim of the Duchesse de Bouillon's plot and the satires of Mme Deshoulière, took them very hard and got some friends to answer in the same style, with the same rhymes. They believed, or pretended to believe, that the first sonnet had been written by the Duc de Bouillon, and it was him they attacked:

Dans un palais doré, Damon jaloux et blème,
Fait des vers où jamais ne sonne n'entend rien.
Il n'est ni courtisan, ni guerrier, ni chrétien
Et souvent pour rimer se dérobe a lui-même-

La Muse par malheur le hait sutant qu'il l'aime
Il a d'un franc poète et l'air et le maintien;
Il veut juger de tout et n'en juge pas bien
Il a pour le phoebus une tendresse extrême.

Une soeur vagabonde aux crins plus noirs que blonds
Va par tout l'univers étaler deux tétons
Dont, malgré son pays, Damon est idolâtre.

---

[5] In a gilded armchair, Phèdre, wan and trembling all over, babbled verses of which nobody at first understood a thing. Her nurse read her a most Christian sermon against her terrible intention of committing suicide. Hippolyte hated her almost as much as she loved him. Nothing could alter his chaste look and behaviour; the nurse accused him and paid for it dearly. Theseus was very harsh with his son. A stout Aricie, swarthy and yellow-haired, was only there to display her enormous breasts, which delighted Hippolyte in spite of his coldness. He died at last, dragged along the ground by his ungrateful steeds, and Phèdre, having dutifully swallowed rat-poison, came, confessed and died on the stage.

149

> *Il se tue à rimer pour des lecteurs ingrats,*
> *L'Eneîde est pour lui pire que la mort-aux-rats,*
> *Et selon lui, Pradon est le roi du théâtre.*[6]

The counter-attack was witty, though rather stilted. The third stanza was aimed at Hortense Mancini, Duchesse de Mazarin, the crazy adventuress for whom, it was rumoured, her brother, the Duc de Nevers, revealed feelings that were rather too fond.

The Duc de Nevers took this sonnet very badly and ascribed it to Racine and Boileau, though they both denied authorship. But, if they did not write it, they were certainly diverted. The Duke spoke of using a cudgel to defend his honour and rhymed this third and last sonnet:

> *Racine et Despréaux, l'oeil triste et le teint blème,*
> *Viennent demander grâce et ne confessent rien.*
> *Il faut leur pardonner parce qu'on est chrétien,*
> *Mais on sait ce qu'on doit au public, à soi-même.*
>
> *Damon qui, pour l'honneur d'une soeur qu'il aime,*
> *Doit de ces insolents abattre le maintien,*
> *Devien drait le mépris de tous les gens de bien*
> *S'il ne punissait pas leur insolence extrème.*
>
> *Ce fut une furie aux crins plus noirs que blonds*
> *Qui leur coula, du pus de ses affreux tétons,*
> *Ce sonnet qu'en secret la cabale idolâtre.*
>
> *On vous verra punir, satiriques ingrats,*
> *Non pas en trahison d'un bol de mort-aux-rats,*
> *Mais de coups de bâton donnés sur le théâtre.*[7]

---

[6] In a gilded armchair, wan and jealous Damon writes verses no one understands. He is neither a courtier, nor a warrior, nor a Christian and often, when attempting to rhyme, has to run away from himself. By sheer bad luck, his muse hates him as much as he loves her; he has the free air and the demeanour of a true poet; he has ideas about everything, and they are all wrong; he is passionately fond of gibberish. His wanton sister, whose hair is far from fair, displays throughout the world her two enormous breasts, which delight Damon, in spite of his Italian origin. He kills himself for the sake of ungrateful readers. The Aeneid for hm is worse than rat-poison and, according to him, Pradon is the king of playwrights.

[7] Racine and Despréaux, with sad eyes and pale faces, came to implore pardon and confessed nothing. Being a Christian, I must forgive them, though

The quarrel worsened and took a dangerous turn, which required the attendance of the Grand Condé. There was no love lost between him and the Duc de Nevers, the nephew of Mazarin who had clapped him in prison years before.

So Monseiur le Prince stated that 'he would take revenge, as if he had been the victim himself, for any insult offered to two clever men whom he loved and was taking under his protection'. At the sound of this great voice the Duc de Nevers desisted. Racine and Boileau had had a narrow escape.

The affair of the sonnets amused all Paris and served as splendid publicity for both plays, both of which were very successful. The only difference is that Pradon's tragedy left the bills for ever after three months, while Racine's is still the object of admiration for scholars and theatre-lovers everywhere.

The theatrical life of Paris in the seventeenth century lacked neither liveliness, quarrels and cabals nor skirmishes. All those episodes were a godsend to actors, for they meant excellent receipts.

I know what I owe to the public and myself. Damon, to revenge the honour of the sister he loves, must crush the arrogance of those impertinent scoundrels; he would become an object of contempt to all respectable people, would he not punish their unprecedented insolence. A fury, with dark, and not fair hair, gave them, from the pus of her hideous breasts, this sonnet, secretly admired by their confederates. O you ungrateful satire-mongers, you will be punished not treacherously, with a draught of rat-poison, but with cudgels wielded on the stage.

PART THREE

THE THEATRES IN THE PROVINCES

CHAPTER ONE

LIFE IN THE PROVINCIAL THEATRES

In Paris, thanks to the emergence of a dramatic literature of great worth, thanks also to the talents of the players and to the taste of a cultured and even refined public, the life of the theatre was becoming more and more active throughout the century. But what was going on in the provinces, which were a long way from the Court at Versailles, where a play was made or broken, and whence spendour spread its light to the contemporary stage?

Of course, the provinces had touring companies, the most famous of which was Molière's. But those companies which frequented the chief cities, where they could find large audiences, were not interested in boroughs or villages at the back of beyond.

Meanwhile the need for the theatre and its pleasures is so deeply embedded in the human heart that, wherever man lives, even under the most primitive circumstances, the theatre emerges. Amateurs, though very poorly gifted, take the place of professionals when necessary.

In the sixteenth century, at a time when the Court itself lived in the country, great and small noblemen prided themselves in protecting playwrights, and strolling companies already existed. The Grand Siècle, from that point of view, was a victim of centralization. Every playwright wanted to be acted and printed in Paris.

In those places where the strolling companies did not pass, the first amateurs were the pupils of the various colleges, mostly those run by the Jesuits, and they acted in the schoolrooms themselves. A few noblemen also invited companies to their castles: the Marquise de Rambouillet had Mairet's *Sophonisbe* performed in her château at Rambouillet. Sometimes amateurs came together to act a new play. That is why Fortin de la Hoguette, a patron of the brothers Dupuy, having read Corneille's *Le Cid*, wrote in March 1637: 'We have received from Paris a comedy called *Le Cid*, which is so beautiful that in my view it surpasses all that the ancients or the moderns have written in this genre. We are going to act it here to amuse ourselves, and I am going to be one of the performers, Don Diègue. Is it not strange that, at fifty-two, I should be studying how to become a mountebank?' But such a case was very rare.

To amuse the public there were also games included in traditional local festivities, performed by groups of gay dare-devils like the *Conards* of Rouen, the *Mère Folle* of Dijon, or the *Suppots de la Coquille* of Lyons, but parliaments were hostile and quickly suppressed them. Plays performed by religious communities to celebrate Christmas, Corpus Christi, or a local saint's day enjoyed a longer spell of life. These were always religious plays, edifying and funny at the same time, in the medieval tradition of mystery plays. Producers were still making use of the manifold sets which had not been used in Paris for more than fifty years. There were also puppet shows, performing animals, mountebanks or quacks, who provided a sort of free entertainment and delighted passers-by with 'monkey-tricks, buffoonery and juggling'.

Yet none of this would have been enough to create and maintain a genuine theatrical life in the provinces. We must return to the touring companies which, intermittently if not permanently, gave some continuity in dramatic art to the provinces.

Contemporaries scarcely bothered with them, and we have to rely on Chappuzeau's testimony alone, despite his naïve optimism.

'As far as I have been able to discover, they amount to some twelve or fifteen companies, the total number not being restricted. They follow more or less the same rules as in Paris, so far as their itinerant life permits.

It is in these companies that people pass their acting apprenticeship, and it is from them that we draw those actors and actresses who are thought good enough to fill the gaps in the Paris theatres. They sometimes come to Paris at Lent, a period during which few people go to the theatre in the provinces, as much to take good lessons under the masters of their art as to draw up and sign new deeds of employment. Some are pretty poor, either in number or talent; others are reasonably good. They are a success in the main cities and only leave them when they have made plenty of money.'

Recent researches have detected the constantly increasing number of touring companies. Throughout the seventeenth century, some 200 of them are known, totalling about a thousand identified and classified players, not counting dancers, singers and mounte-banks.

How were those companies organized? Our information comes from their contracts, drawn up by notaries. Just like the Paris companies, they were all organized as societies. We have something like 100 contracts, kept in the archives of Paris notaries, and they are almost identical.

Of course, the company had a chief who had gathered his companions together, and his authority was freely accepted and not just endured, as players were very independent. Says Chappuzeau:

'They don't accept any superior. The very word hurts them. They all want to be equal and to call each other comrade. The leader has the same income as the rest, though he usually owns the sets, but not the costumes, which belong to each actor. Beginners have sometimes a half or a quarter share. Along with the members of the society, the company has a jack of all trades, paid after each performance, a musician and a decorator.'

Early in the century, the actors were taking 'au pair' young beginners whom they trained. Bellerose and Montdory got their training in Valleran le Conte's company. But contracts of apprenticeship disappeared after 1620: beginners were progressively replaced by the actors' children, who followed the *bande* and began acting children's parts at a very early age.

The deeds very often stated that the selection of plays and of the cities where they should be performed would be made by vote, but women were sometimes excluded from the meetings where accounts and profits were checked. Usually, the kind of part taken by each player—king, peasant, lover, and so forth—was stated in the contract.

Contracts were almost always signed in Paris; but occasionally in the provinces, too, when extended or renewed. In fact, Lent meant compulsory idleness, so actors gathered in Paris, where there was a real labour market and recruiting office. The company leaders there recruited their companions for the next season and they went to the notary; this explains why almost all contracts were dated in February, March or April. The company thus constituted about twelve people, men and women brought together by ties of friendship and especially by kinship: one finds whole families and even dynasties of players.

Most often, the contract was drawn up for a year, from one Lent to the next; they seldom covered two or three years. Sometimes trouble started at once between fellow-members, and one could see companies calling on the notary to annul what they had accepted the day before. Quite often a company went bankrupt and its members were scattered before the year was over. It is not unusual to find players who belonged to several companies in the same year. Chappuzeau did not fail to mention the fact:

'Their companies changed very often and at least at each Lent. They are so unstable that as soon as one company has come together they immediately talk of disintegrating and, either through that state of things, or through lack of means to rent good theatres and convenient places, or the lack of experience of members who have not the necessary gifts, it is easy to see the difference between the Paris companies and those who moved through the provinces.'

Nanteuil's career, which we shall describe later on, is a good example of the destiny of members of these unsettled touring companies. Some players led five or six companies, one after the other.

In their struggle against such great odds, actors always mention a clause which is a sort of insurance against their own infidelity. The penalty was great: between 500 to 1,000 livres. For Molière's *Illustre théâtre*, which ended in bankruptcy, it reached the astronomical figure of 3,000 livres, not one penny of which was owned by any actor of the group. That forfeit clause was a mere matter of style, for when the company failed or when an actor wanted to break away, it was practically impossible to take action or squeeze the money out of people who were virtually destitute.

These strolling companies performed wherever they could find a stage, a tennis court by preference. There were three courts in Rennes and nine in Poitiers; if none was available, then the company performed during the summer in barns or in the open air. No provincial town had a real theatre: they began to appear only at the end of the century, in Rouen in 1688, in Lille in 1702, in Strasbourg in 1701, in Metz in 1703. They were usually built to house operas, a new genre the popularity of which had grown very quickly after Lulli's success in Paris.

The repertoires of the itinerant companies are obscure; sometimes the list of the plays has been retained in the town archives. Strolling players obviously performed contemporary plays mostly, as soon as they had been printed: Molière, Racine, the Corneille brothers, Boursault, Montfleury, Dorimond, and (less often) authors of the last generation but one, Rotrou, Tristan l'Hermite and Scudéry.

It would be interesting to discover each company's itinerary across France: yet apart from a few privileged companies, protected by noblemen whom they followed in their travels, we have scanty information. The companies mostly visited the principal cities, where the provincial governors or parliaments resided and where they could rely on good audiences. Research into local archives has led to some rather surprising facts: although Molière went into the south-west, the south and the Lyons neighbourhood, the northern half of France, Belgium and Holland were much more frequented than the south. Where it is possible to discover the dates when companies arrived in various cities during the seventeenth century, the following figures are found: 72 companies in Dijon, 57 in Lyons, 53 in Nantes, 51 in Rouen, 48 in Lille. South of the Loire the figures dwindle to 22 in Marseilles, 21 in Bordeaux, and 11 in Toulouse. We must not forget that south of the Loire were mountain districts, the Massif Central, the Alps, the Pyrenees, poor regions with backward populations and bad roads, difficult for heavy wagons with scenery and costumes. Another cause seems to be the fact that in these regions southern vernaculars were spoken and the French repertoire was less understandable, but the figures quoted may have to be revised, for they rely upon performances about which written documents are available: many others are still unknown, and city archives have not all been investigated.

CHAPTER TWO

FREE COMPANIES

About three-quarters of all the touring companies were free; that is to say, they had no recognized protector and could achieve success and fortune only by their own endeavours.

As early as the end of the sixteenth century, itinerant companies were already travelling the French and foreign roads despite the wars of religion which overwhelmed the kingdom in blood and fire. Some of the companies appeared in Nancy in 1572, in Bordeaux in 1592, in Frankfurt in 1593 and 1602, in Basle in 1604. But they were more numerous under Louis XIII's reign, and even more so under Louis XIV. According to Scarron, in 1641 the Duc de Longueville gave to one of them, as an unexpected gift:

> *. . . deux mille livres*
> *En argent, vêtements et vivres*
> *Dont les pauvres comédiens,*
> *Gueux comme des bohémiens,*
> *Devinrent gras comme des moines*
> *Et glorieux comme des chanoines.*[1]

On receiving such generous gifts a company assumed the patron's name. Otherwise they assumed the proud title of 'Players to the King', which meant precisely nothing and implied neither the King's recognition nor his subsidy.

At that time the theatre was for the public a meeting-place as well as a show, and they came 'as much to find friends as to hear actors, and as many love affairs took place there as on the stage', says Scarron.

Under the management of players with the flowery stage names of Bellerose, Rosidor, Richemont, Longchamp, Beauchamp, du Boccage, Jolimont, La Couture, du Rocher and Champmeslé, itinerant companies multiplied. Scarron gives a lively description

---

1 2000 livres in money, clothes and food, so that the poor players became as fat as monks and as proud as canons.

of the arrival of one such company in the city of Le Mans, where people were as fond of plays as of poultry:

'The sun had run more than half its daily course, and its chariot, having reached the top of the world, was rolling down more quickly than was desirable. . . . To be more precise, it was between five and six when a cart entered the market-place of Le Mans. The cart was dragged by four lean oxen, led by a mare, whose foal was running round the cart like the mad creature it was. The cart was loaded with chests, trunks and large bundles of painted canvas piled up like a pyramid, on the top of which sat a girl whose dress mingled town and country fashions. A tall young man, very good-looking but very badly apparelled, was walking alongside the cart. He had a large plaster on his face, which hid an eye and half a cheek, and he carried a big gun over his shoulder, with which he had slaughtered several magpies, jays and crows, which he carried like a bandolier, at the lower part of which were tied by their legs a hen and a goose very much as if they had been shot in a private war. Instead of a hat he wore a night-cap, and round it were twined garters of various colours. . . . His doublet was a cheap grey cloak, fashioned with a strap, which served also to hold a sword so long that it could not have been used without a prop. His breeches were tied like those worn by actors when representing a hero of antiquity, and instead of shoes, he had laced boots of an antique kind covered with mud up to the ankles. An old man, whose dress was less strange but still much worn, walked beside him. He was carrying on his shoulders a bass-viol and, as he stooped slightly when walking, he looked from afar like a large turtle walking on its hind legs. Some critic may object to this comparison on account of the big difference in size between a man and a turtle, but I have heard speak of giant turtles in the Indies; besides, this was my own impression! Let us go back to our procession. It passed the gaming house, *La Biche*, at the door of which had gathered most of the leading citizens. The strangeness of the apparel and the noise made by the rabble which had gathered round the cart induced all these respectable burghers to stare at the strangers. A lieutenant of the provost, named La Rappinière, approached them and asked what sort of people they were. The young man I have already mentioned answered and, without removing his turban, because with one hand he held his gun and with the other he held the hilt of his sword, to prevent it from getting between his legs, told him

L

that they were French by birth, actors by profession, and that his own name was Le Destin, that his old companion was called La Rancune and that the lady perched like a hen on top of their luggage was La Caverne. This bizarre name made some of the group laugh, whereupon the young actor added that the name La Caverne could not sound stranger to clever men than La Montagne, La Vallée, La Rose or L'Epine. The conversation ceased when fisticuffs and swear-words were heard from in front of the cart. The gaming house valet had attacked the coachman, because his oxen and mare were helping themselves too freely to a heap of hay in front of the door. They stopped the noise and the lady of the house, who was fonder of plays than of sermons or vespers, with a generosity unheard of in the mistress of a gaming-house, allowed the beasts to eat their fill.'

But as soon as the enthusiasm of arrival had calmed down, difficulties would begin for the leader, even before the performance.

Sometimes a company, arriving in a city, found that another company was already there, which made thing very tricky. That is what happened to Molière at Nantes in 1649, where there was a puppet show, and also in Pézénas in 1653, where Cormier's company was installed, over which he triumphed thanks to the effect of Mlle Du Parc's beautiful eyes on the poet Sarasin, who was the Prince de Conti's secretary. According to Chappuzeau that sort of thing was quite frequent.

'Emulation goes with them through all the provinces of the kingdom, and it is very unlucky when two companies happen to come together at the same place, with the intention of staying there for some time. I saw it quite often and very recently in Lyons, when the Dauphins [that is, the Dauphin's company], who know how to keep everybody's esteem, did not relinquish the place until very late to another company that had been kicking its heels there for over three weeks. In such circumstances each company has its own cabal, especially when they persist in acting, as in Paris, on the same day and at the same hour. It is a question of who has the most supporters, and cities are often divided on such subjects. . . .'

Even when a company met no rivals, they had to find the cheapest possible lodgings in an inn, where they paid their way, if possible, by acting a scene from a farce. Next they had to obtain permission to perform, which was not always easy. The leader called on the mayor with the list of plays to be performed and promised to avoid scandal. Town authorities were very touchy about their prerogatives. In the town registers of Grenoble, in February 1658, when a company turned up (Molière's most likely) there appeared a strange note about 'the incivility of players who have displayed posters before being allowed to do so; it has been suggested and then decided that the posters will be removed and the performance of any comedy forbidden until they have received the permission that should be granted by the consuls and the council'.

Of course, no performances were allowed during Lent, and sometimes they were forbidden also during Advent and the week of Corpus Christi; on Sundays they were allowed only after mass. Moreover, in times of famine, want or plague, which were so frequent in the seventeenth century, civil authorities refused permission to actors in order to avoid offence to public misery. In 1632 the *jurats* of Bordeaux refused Charles Dufresne permission to act for fear of fire. In 1648 Molière's application was turned down in Nantes, because M. de la Meilleraye, the Governor, was ill. At Poitiers, in the same year, actors were sent away 'because the time we live in compels us rather to pray to God and attend the Jubilee rather than public spectacles.' The same refusal was given at Dijon in 1676, the times being such that 'we need prayers more than entertainments'. The Rouen Parliament dismissed a company 'because such performances lead to vain and useless expenditure'. The Poitiers town council, in November 1649, rejected Molière's application because of 'the destitution of the people and the high price of wheat'. In Nantes, in 1639, they were turned down for even vaguer reasons, described as 'various'.

Sometimes, local authorities came into conflict with parliaments, provincial governors or intendants representing the central power. In 1629, at Poitiers, the lieutenant-general sought to expel the players who had received permission from the municipality, 'which was greatly detrimental to the authority of the Mayor who, apart from all other considerations, has the right to accept or reject the players'. The Mayor stuck to his prerogatives and was successful. In 1667 the Dijon magistrates refused Mademoiselle's company the right to perform; the players appealed to parliament and won. In 1677 there was a further refusal because, the president of the parliament explained to the Prince de Condé, 'everybody was suffering on account of taxes which put families in despair . . .

163

and the people would not tolerate such entertainments when they were in such sorrow'. There were attempts also to drive away companies, not temporarily but for ever, because it was said that they debauched young people, that school children were less assiduous to their studies, 'and that this amusement should be placed with those that are forbidden and that, as it could not be indulged without money, it induced young sons and servants to rob their brothers and masters'. A long quarrel followed between the Mayor and the intendant on one side and parliament on the other; there was some talk of 'sending the mayor to court'. In the end the matter was settled in the player's favour by the Prince de Condé, who was Governor of Dijon and a great lover of the theatre.

Yet, most often, local authorities were at one in persecuting players. In 1670, in Château-Thierry, the players found united against them the local Lieutenant-General, the General-Attorney of the Parliament of Paris and the Bishop of Soissons. They had no choice but to clear out.

When permission was eventually given, there were further questions to be settled with the local authorities: the repertory had to be submitted and the price of seats had to be decided. Again, the authorities had to make the decisions, trying not to overcharge spectators and often demanding a free bench for the town councillors: Here are some figures—rather modest examples—found among the records: in Frankfurt, in 1593, the price of a seat was 4 pfennigs; in Nantes, in 1648, 10 sous for the old plays, 15 for the new ones, those recently acted in Paris, and prices were raised to 15 and 20 sous in 1660. Prices were lower in Dijon: in 1648, 6 sous, one going to the man who provided the chairs. The next year a company asked 20 and 30 sous, but had to agree to 10 and 15; in 1660, 15 and 20. In 1662–3 prices went down to 10 and 15; and (exceptionally) 20 for some plays with stage effects. The 'effects' machinery of the itinerant players must have been quite rudimentary. In 1668 the Dauphin's company, having charged 15 and 20 sous instead of 10 and 15, was fined. In 1669 the Duke of Savoy's company received for the first time 20 sous, 'whatever play they perform'. A few years later prices went up to 30 sous for new plays, 'extraordinary plays and spectacular plays'.

The tennis court or the inn courtyard had to be well filled if the company was to cover its expenses. But the municipalities not only taxed the price of seats but imposed charges on the players for the sick and the poor, doubtless to atone for the moral scandal which a dramatic performance still signified for certain persons. The poor tax was only enforced in Paris in 1699, raising prices by one sixth, but it already existed in the provinces at the beginning of the century, and the poor actors had to bear not only their own poverty but part of the general poverty too.

At Nantes the town council taxed players 40 livres for the hospital. At Poitiers it was 20 livres a week, payable in advance without prejudice to the receipts from one of their best-attended performances. As the players did not cover their expenses, the tax was reduced from 20 to 10 livres, but the owner of the tennis court was made responsible and had to pay the difference. In Bordeaux, in 1635, permission to act was granted on condition that they paid '120 livres, one half to the hospital and a half for the city walls'. The *jurats* made itinerant players pay for public works!

As early as 1609, in Bordeaux, two companies were sentenced to pay 3 écus for each of their 10 performances, that is 30 sous, on penalty of having their luggage confiscated and being sent to prison. In 1632 Dufresne paid 60 livres; in 1647 the Nantes municipality demanded a day's receipts for the poor. In 1660 Richemont paid 2 pistoles and Philandre in 1664 paid 30 livres. In Dijon, in 1632, the poor tax was 4 livres a performance, or a lump sum of 100 livres; in 1648, the whole receipts of a performance were demanded. In 1654, as a company had not given a special performance for the poor, they were compelled to pay 50 livres, again on penalty of having their baggage confiscated. In 1661 actors replied 'by rebellion, insolence and swear words' when asked to pay 100 livres, and they were properly sent to prison. In 1668 the Dauphin's company had to pay 60 livres as poor-tax.

It is easy to realize the extent of the worry and expense which town councils inflicted on strolling companies. Besides, when these troubles were over they still had to secure at least the neutrality of the Church, for there were priests who exploited every single rule in the ritual against the players. In other cities they had to face the hostility of lay associations, branches or imitations of the Compagnie du St Sacrement of Paris, who also used all their ingenuity against the theatre in general and actors in particular. In Grenoble, Chorier, in his *Vie de Boissat*, mentioned that 'ferocious animal' who cursed Molière and counted him as 'an excommunicate among scoundrels and blasphemers'. In Chambéry in 1673, the Bishop of Grenoble, Le Camus, preached against the players: needless to say, all this was very detrimental to the company. In 1599 a bishop publicly complained of the permission given by a town council and threatened that if they dared perform their theatre would be destroyed and that he would 'pray to God for strength to do this'. In 1607, in Bourges, the Jesuits tried to prevent La Porte from acting by threatening to 'excommunicate those who went to see him'.

If we consider the endless applications the town and church authorities forced the actors to make merely for permission to perform, which had to be renewed in every city, that week after week they had to dismantle their theatre, reload their baggage and take to the road again, not knowing what might happen the next day, it must be admitted that their life was not pleasant. It was a free and varied life, of course, but was interspersed with worry and failure. They needed courage and a strong sense of humour to endure the lack of comfort on such journeys. Yet most of them were carried along by a sense of vocation. Throughout the centuries the theatre has been an exacting master to its devotees. All through their journeys they were comforted by the distant but ever-present hope of finding a place in one of the great companies of Paris and performing before the King. That is how Moliére and his companions, after thirteen years of wandering in the provinces, finally succeeded in settling in Paris, rivalling the Hôtel de Bourgogne and the Marais, whose actors had also trained in the provinces.

The arrival of a company in any new city was an outstanding event. Of course, their performances were not all on the same level. Mme de Sévigné mentioned a company which in Vitré 'made her shed six tears'. On the other hand Fléchier is very hard on another company which he saw in Auvergne:

'They spoke their parts as well as they could, but they changed the order of the lines and of the scenes, sometimes imploring the help of one who prompted whole lines and tried to assist their memories. I confess I was sorry for Corneille, and I would have preferred that M. d'Aubignac had written dissertations against his tragedies than to have seen them performed in this way by such people.'

All provincial actors were not like Roscius, and they could only learn their trade by practice. Let us be kind to their memories,

166

remembering all their efforts and all the worries they encountered in the daily exercise of their profession.

To get an idea of the vicissitudes of such a life, we might follow the biography of one of them. He was a colleague of Molière, forgotten now but fairly well known in the seventeenth century as an actor and a playwright. His professional name was Nanteuil, but his real name was Denis Clerselier and he may have been one of the fourteen children of the philosopher Claud Clerselier, who published Descartes. He came from near Meaux and probably borrowed his stage name from the town of Nanteuil-le-Haudouin.

He began acting in 1667, when he was seventeen, in the Espérance company. Charles Guérin, called L'Espérance, was an experienced actor, with forty years of experience behind him; together with Philandre, he had for a long time been a member of the Prince of Orange's company. He was the father of Guérin d'Estriché, who ten years later was to marry Molière's widow. For a year L'Espérance grouped around him, besides Nanteuil, Longueil and his wife, Liancourt, Mlle du Tressay (who married Liancourt), Mlle Rosidor, Mme de Champclos and Mlle Robin. L'Espérance knew by long experience of itinerant companies that it was very difficult to live by the profession without help of a generous patron. So he took his company to Lyons, where he secured the patronage of the Governor, Marshal de Villeroy. With these resources the company went to act in Marseilles in September 1667.

By the next year Nanteuil had already moved to another company, the Queen's players. For a few years Maria-Theresa subsidized a French company, but she personally preferred her Spanish actors. Her French company, which she never summoned to Paris, was constantly on the roads. It consisted of actors from the Espérance company (l'Espérance himself, Nanteuil, Liancourt) and from Mademoiselle's company (La Source, Boncourt and Jolimont). At first, it seems, they went abroad. They were in Brussels and on August 9, 1668 rented the theatre of the Montagne Ste Elizabeth until the following Whitsun. They wandered across the Spanish Netherlands and performed in Lille in 1669. They were probably satisfied with the financial results, since they renewed their lease and their association contract for a year.

Nanteuil played an important part in the company, in which he was given the first and second lovers' roles, while La Source acted the fathers. His prestige derived from the fact that he provided his companions with light comedies which they added to

167

their repertoire. He probably tried on the Brussels public the plays he acted and printed in The Hague. For the company abandoned the lease which was valid until Whitsun 1670 and was acting in The Hague in November 1669. Nanteuil had three comedies performed and printed in Brussels. *L'Amour Sentinelle* was 'his Muse's first child'; it was dedicated to the Prince of Orange and implored his patronage. It is a rather dull comedy concerning a silly marquis in the Molière tradition and an amorous tutor borrowed straight from Arnolphe. Then came *Le Comte de Roquefeuille, ou le Docteur extravagant,* dedicated to M. de Nassau, the same prince's grand equerry, a short comedy in one act in octosyllabic verses, rather clumsily rhymed and fairly coarse; two of its characters are named Gorgibus and Pancrace, as in Molière's plays. *Les Brouilleries nocturnes* is a comedy in three acts in which figures a peasant named Gareau, as in *Le Pédant Joué* and the *Docteur Amoureux,* and also a valet named Moron, who addresses a monologue to his lantern which is obviously lifted from *Amphytrion.* It is a comedy of intrigue, with misunderstandings and disguises.

In The Hague Nanteuil met Rosidor, who had acted in the English King's company, at the Marais theatre and also in the Duke of Hanover's company. Now King Frederick III of Denmark also wanted to have a company of his own, and charged Rosidor with forming it. The conditions were tempting: travelling expenses paid 400 écus to each actor. Nanteuil joined Rosidor's company and they left for Copenhagen, where they arrived in December. Alas! the company's brilliant hopes of the Danish episode soon evaporated. An unexpected event occurred in February 1670, when the King of Denmark died and the company was dismissed. Rosidor, who was not afraid of long journeys, took his company to Germany and Italy, but Nanteuil had no wish to run further risks in such distant countries and left his companions after the first stages in Germany.

It seems that he was then on quite bad terms with Rosidor, and a few years later he did not hesitate to speak of his former director harshly. In fact, when leaving the Hague, Rosidor had taken with him his mistress, Marianne Vole, a hairdresser's wife. At the request of the deceived husband, Nanteuil testified to a notary that Marianne Vole had followed Rosidor to Venice.

Yet Nanteuil did not return to France and he went to try his luck with the company of the Dukes of Brunswick, Celle and Luneburg. Chappuzeau wrote:

'The Bishop of Osnabruck and the Dukes of Celle and Hanover have for several years maintained an excellent company of French players, with fine costumes, who act their parts admirably, and when the three groups of violins play together, they make a string orchestra of twenty-four members, most of them French and masters of the profession.'

It seems that Nanteuil was the leader of the Brunswick and Luneburg company, to which he had brought Boncourt and his wife. The other players were Lecocq and Lavoy and their wives, Mme de La Mettrie, Bruneval and Mlle Bénard. The players remained in Hanover for three years, probably handsomely paid by the Duke. As in The Hague, Nanteuil performed his own comedies, which were dedicated to the Duchess of Brunswick, Luneburg and Hanover, in the delightful little theatre of the castle of Celle, which had been built by Italians in 1645 and is now the oldest in Europe.

His new comedies were different from those he had performed for the Prince of Orange. The difference is obvious in a single reading. The verses are easier, the style firmer and dignified, the tone nobler. After comedy of intrigue, Nanteuil was now writing 'heroic comedies' of a romantic style, quite akin to tragi-comedy. The characters of *La Fille Vice-Roi*, *L'Amante invisible*, *L'Héritier imaginaire* are the princes and princesses of Valencia, Naples or Genoa who speak with great dignity and whose adventures sometimes achieve a certain dramatic grandeur.

After three years in Hanover, the Duke's company seems to have been reorganized under the management of the comedian Clavel, who took them through Holland and Germany. But no actor of the former company remained with him. Pierre Boneuil in 1675 rejoined the company led by Jolimont; Lecocq and his wife that of the Prince de Condé. As for Nanteuil, we find him again in Brussels in 1675 and probably in Nijmegen the next year. In that city the diplomats negotiating the peace treaty asked for passports for a company summoned from France. Was this the Queen of France's company, to which Nanteuil may have returned? It is doubtful, for this company was in Brussels at the beginning of 1676, so could not have been 'summoned from France' to Nijmegen.

However, if Nanteuil did pass through Nijmegen in 1676, he did not stay long. On March 23, 1677, he was in Paris, joining the Duc d'Enghien's company. This was led by Richemont and its members were Nanteuil and his wife, Clavel, who had left the Duke of Hanover's company, with his wife, Jean Fonpré and his wife, Germain le Riche, du Fort and Clotilde Le Riche. The presence of Nanteuil's wife, Marthe Lhomme, should be noticed. Henceforth, she will follow her husband, at least until 1685. It is not known where the Duc d'Enghien's company acted in 1677. Nanteuil was with them only for a year: when they signed a new contract of association on March 23, 1678, he was not a member. A few days earlier, in fact on the 17th, he had joined the Queen of France's company for the second time. During the ten years he had been away from it, the company had acted in Dijon, Château-Thierry, Auxerre, Amiens, Charleville, Brussels and Maastricht. The members were La Source (until 1671), Antoine Le Febvre and his wife, du Boccage and his wife, Beautemps, Alcidor, Dominique Longchamp and his wife, and DuFresne and his wife. No members of the 1668 cast were with the company in 1678. Had there been a break at that time? Or did the company act in two different theatres at the same time? Nothing is certain, but it is known that, on November 26, 1678, du Boccage in his own name had a theatre built in the riding school at The Hague, which he rented until mid-Lent 1679; also that two days earlier, Nanteuil, as director of the company, had had another stage built in the tennis court of Brussels. It is possible that the company travelled backwards and forwards between the two cities during the 1678–79 season.

We have already recorded that in Brussels the company met the Duke of Hanover's company under Clavel. As usual under such circumstances, they put on rival performances and this helped neither. The Hanover company, besides Clavel, comprised Desmarets, du Boccage, Isabelle and Jacques Valliot, Romainville, Richemont, Germain Le Riche, Châteauneuf (who became manager in 1680), Jean Fonpré, and Lecocq and his wife. The Brussels newspaper, *Les Relations véritables*, announced on November 12, 1680: 'H.E. the Prince of Parma on Tuesday last paid the Duke of Hanover's players the compliment of attending their performance of *La Toison d'or*, which pleased him very much.' As the Prince was probably generous, the company then assumed the title of Prince of Parma's company in a deed signed on January 17, 1681. At that date, Nanteuil had left the Queen's company to join Clavel.

After the Brussels season, Nanteuil went back on the road with the Prince of Parma's company. On January 25, 1681, he signed a deed with a 'master carter' for the transport of his company and baggage to Ath, Lille and Valenciennes. He engaged an embroiderer, no doubt to mend and decorate stage costumes, and also a dancing master. Then the company returned to Hanover and Cologne.

Nanteuil did not follow it so far. On March 24, 1681, he was back in Paris and again in the Duc d'Enghien's company. This company was still led by Richemont and its members were, besides Nanteuil and his wife, Bergé and his wife, Champvallon, La Marche, Marianne Richard and Madeleine Poirier. But thenceforward all trace of the company is lost.

Next Lent, Nanteuil formed another company (La Cassagne, Guérin d'Estriché, Valois and his wife); he took the lead and they went to Holland. It seems that by now he was thinking of reviving the lost title of the Duc d'Enghien's company for his own use. Consequently, he went to Chantilly to ask for old Prince de Condé's patronage and permission to perform in Dijon, which hitherto had been reserved for the M. le Prince's Company. On March 8th Condé wrote to his secretary: 'Nanteuil hasn't come yet. If he does, I shall speak to him properly.' On the 15th the secretary answered: 'Nanteuil is delighted with the kindness he received from Your Highness, and Monseigneur le Duc [d'Enghien, his son] promised his approval regarding Dijon; as soon as the deed is signed, I send a copy to Your Highness.' Provided with M. le Prince's agreement, Nanteuil gave his company the vague and pompous title of 'Players of the Royal Company'. He arrived at Dijon on April 30, 1683. He returned there in 1684, but brawls in the pit led to the closing of the theatre. It seems that the company he had created, thanks to the Condés' patronage, had lasted for three years, an unusually long time.

But at the end of his life Condé was converted, and this drew him away from the theatre and the actors he had loved and helped so generously. Nanteuil had to look for opportunities elsewhere. We find him in Angoulême on February 3, 1685, where he organized another company with his wife, his sister Madeleine, Jean Bergé, his wife and daughter Hippolyte, Champvallon and his wife, Jean Fleurs, Longchamp and his wife, Mlle de Champclos (a former member of the L'Espérance company of 1667), Jacques Troche, the sisters du Bocage and Rosidor. The company built a stage 'with a trap door' for *Le Festin de Pierre*. In December they were in Rennes. They performed Donneau de Visé's *Amours de Vénus et d'Adonis*, created at the Marais in 1670 and recently revived at the Hôtel Guénégaud, *Le Bourgeois Gentilhomme*, *Andromède* and Dorimond's *Le Festin de Pierre*.

That new company did not survive the usual year. On March 15, 1686, Nanteuil joined the Dauphin's company with his wife and his sister. This company had been very active since 1662, performing mostly in Dijon and Rouen, in close association with the Prince de Condé's company, and their successive managers had been Haute-feuille and Michel Siret. It is not known how long Nanteuil stayed with them, but he had certainly left them by the beginning of 1688.

For on March 10th of that year, Nanteuil and Dominique Pitel rented the Bordeaux theatre for five years at 300 livres a year. The local magistrates, who did not mean to pay for their seats, gave their agreement on condition that 'according to custom, they would act their first comedy free for their Worships the *Jurats* and any person they might care to invite, and each time they perform they will provide the Jurats, the Syndic attorney and the town clerk with two seats each, either in the boxes or in the pit to their choice'.

Nanteuil's new company went to the end of the five years' lease in Bordeaux. The first year, business was fairly good, as the receipts went up to 46,000 livres against expenses of 43,600. But they began to dwindle from the day when an opera house opened in Bordeaux which, being something new, drew the audiences. At the end of their lease, the Jurats granted Nanteuil and his company a release of a year's rent, that is 300 livres.

Their lease expired in March 1693. In 1693-4 we find Nanteuil in Strasbourg and Metz, though we do not know to which company be belonged. On May 3, 1696, he was putting together a new company with his second wife, Marie Baroy, Charles and Jacques de Beauchamp, François de la Barre and his wife, Mlle Lefebvre and her daughter, Renaud and Mlle de Lanone. The company acted in Angoulême on February 6, 1697. Did it survive until 1698? It is not likely, as Nanteuil is mentioned in Tours in 1698 with the Rosélis and the Chaumonts, who did not belong to the former company.

In 1699, Nanteuil went back to his former companions of the Duc de Celle's company. With the Lecoqs, Boncourt, Lavoy and Mlle de Beauchamp, he undertook the long journey to Warsaw.

Three years later he was back in France, and undiscouraged he collected a new company. At Grenoble, on January 10, 1702, he

172

joined forces with Jacques St-Fray, about whom nothing else is known, and built a theatre in a tennis court of *La Dame Blanche*. While it was building, he left for Paris to select a company.

Did this company ever come into being? The answer is unknown. For thirty-five years had this courageous man travelled the roads of France and Europe behind the chariot of Thespis. After 1702 we finally lose track of him, without knowing how many more attempts he had yet to make in the service of the theatre.

What we know of his career gives a very clear idea of the vicissi-tudes, adventures, successes and failures which formed the daily life of an actor in the seventeenth century. Let us draw up a summary of Nanteuil's career:

1667:   L'Espérance Company (Lyon and Marseilles)

1668:   The Queen of France's Company (Brussels and The Hague)

1669–70:   King of Denmark's Company (Copenhagen)

1672–74:   Duke of Hanover's Company (Hanover)

1675–76:   Unknown Company (Brussels and Nijmegen)

1677:   Duc d'Enghien's Company

1678:   Queen of France's Company (Brussels and The Hague)

1680:   Duke of Hanover's Company, later known as the Duke of Parma's Company (Brussels and Lille)

1681:   Duc d'Enghien's Company

1682–84:   First Nanteuil Company (Dijon)

1685:   Second Nanteuil Company (Angoulême and Rennes)

1686:   Dauphin's Company

1688–93:   Third Nanteuil Company (Bordeaux)

1693–94:   Unknown Company (Metz and Strasbourg)

1696–97:   Fourth Nanteuil Company (Angoulême)

1698:   Unknown Company (Tours)

1699:   Duke of Hanover and Celle's Company (Warsaw)

1702:   Fifth Nanteuil Company (Grenoble)

Eighteen companies, eighteen changes, eighteen attempts in thirty-five years to find fame and fortune! And this is the minimum figure, because we are not certain that the documents available cover the whole of the comedian's career, and that we know all its episodes. But the figure is impressive without being exceptional, and it reveals an unflinching and indefatigable will, as well as a true vocation for the theatre.

Like Nanteuil, and throughout the century, strolling players, more than a thousand of them, wandered through France and Europe. Many of them remained unknown; a few of them, like Floridor and Champmeslé, reached Paris and fame. But all of them, with the same devotion, carried to the most distant cities of France the rich message of the contemporary theatre which today stands as the classic drama of France.

CHAPTER THREE

PATRONS

Parallel to free companies, whose instability and precarious fate we have just recorded, there were other companies, far less numerous, which toured the French provinces and also foreign lands. Their life was much more pleasant, for they had been able to find patrons, a prince of the blood, a member of the royal family, or the governor of a province, who took them into his service and paid them. Pensions and subsidies from the princely treasury were very timely in supplementing the ever-uncertain receipts from public performances.

But they had not always the benefit of their patrons; the company might act in his Paris house during the winter and in his country château during the summer, and the patron had first call. Meanwhile, the company took to the roads like the rest.

This peculiar situation had several important consequences. First of all the actors, being better paid, were keen to join those favoured companies whose manager could be more exacting in his choice and recruit actors of quality. It is clear that members of the poorer free companies tried to join those companies that were better than the rest. On the other hand, the mere presence of a patron gave the company a cohesion and a durability quite unknown to others. Some of these protected companies remained the same under several managers during several years or even for decades.

As an example, here is a list of the main companies, with the length of time they survived and the regions where they performed:

Queen Marie-Theresa's Company (1661–78; North of France, Belgium, Holland)
The Dauphin's Company (1662–96; Dijon and Rouen)
The Dauphine's Company (1680–90; Nantes, Dijon, Aix and Marseille)
Monsieur's Company (Gaston d'Orléans) (1644–58; Lyons)
Prince Henry II of Condé's Company (1614–43; Orléans, Dijon)

Louis II of Condé's Company (1660–98; Rouen, Dijon, Chantilly; tours in England and Germany)

The Duc d'Enghien's Company (1674–78; Dijon)

The Grande Mademoiselle's Company (1651–78; Dijon, Lyons, Turin, Belgium, Holland)

The Prince de Conti's Company (Molière's company) (1653–56; west and south of France)

Marshal de Villeroy's Company (1663–68, 1692–97; Lyons and Nantes)

The Duc d'Epernon's Company (Molière's) (1632–50; west and south of France)

Monsieur's Company (Philippe d'Orléans) (1662–82; Vienne, Avignon, Nantes, Thionville)

Madame's Company (Princess Henrietta-Anne Stuart's) (1667–68; Alençon)

At a time when all cultured persons in Europe spoke French, it was not surprising to see a number of foreign kings and princes with a company of French actors in their pay. Here are the most important:

The King of England's Company (1662–63; 1687–1701; Belgium and Holland)

The Queen of Sweden's Company (1655–58; Brussels)

The King of Sweden's Company (1699; Sweden)

The King of Denmark's Company (1682–1732; France and Denmark)

The King of Prussia's Company (1706–11; Brussels, Cologne, Berlin)

The Prince of Orange's Companies (1618–31; 1638–64; 1673–1703; Belgium, Holland, Grenoble, Narbonne, Angers, Lille)

The Prince de Liège's Company (1696–97; Belgium, Holland, Lorraine)

The Duke of Hanover's Company (1676–79; 1681–96; Hanover, Holland, Belgium)

The Duke of Lorraine's Company (1667; 1688–1720; Lorraine, Alsace, Dresden, Bordeaux, Holland)

The Duke of Savoy's Company (1658–98; Lyons, Dijon, Mâcon, Chambéry, Turin)

The Duke of Luneburg-Celle's Company (1668–99; Hanover, Warsaw)

Troisième Journée.
Le Malade imaginaire, Comédie représentée
dans le Jardin de Versailles devant la Grotte.

Dies tertius.
D. Robinson, seu Æger imaginarius, Comœdia acta
in hortis Versaliarum ad forva Cryptæ.

13. *Le Malade Imaginaire*. Played before Louis XIV and his Court, 1676

14. Scene from *Le Malade Imaginaire* (Molière)

German princelings, such as the electors of Bavaria, Saxony and Cologne, also had their companies. On the whole, these companies kept a constant dramatic stream running through France and elsewhere throughout the seventeenth century.

Dressed in gorgeous costumes, for their patrons prided themselves on the splendour of their companies, very well paid and familiar with all the European courts, these actors had nothing in common with the poor creatures described by Scarron in his *Roman Comique*. They were part of their patron's household and enjoyed a high public reputation.

Molière was one of those company leaders; he belonged first to the Duc d'Eperon and afterwards to the Prince de Conti, whom he followed in Guyenne and Gascony; during the thirteen years of its wandering life, this company kept together and after 1658 continued its career in Paris. During that long spell, the players acquired a lasting reputation, and we know that, at that time, its affairs prospered, Molière certainly was well known in the provinces before he came to Paris.

Le Boulanger de Chalussay, in his *Elomire Hypocondre*, a pamphlet in the form of a comedy, did not fail to record that Molière had his failures in the provinces:

> *Nous prîmes la campagne, où la petite ville*
> *Admirant le talent de mon petit troupeau,*
> *Protesta mille fois que rien n'était plus beau,*
> *Surtout quand sur la scène on voyait mon visage;*
> *Les signes d'allégresse allaient jusqu'à la rage;*
> *Car ces provinciaux, par leurs cris redoublés,*
> *Et leurs contorsions, paraissaient tout troublés.*
> *Dieu sait si, me voyant ainsi le vent en poupe,*
> *Je devais être gai! Mais le soin de la soupe*
> *Dont il fallait remplir vos ventres et le mien*
> *Ce soin, vous le savez, hélas! l'empêchait bien;*
> *Car ne prenant alors que cinq sous par le personne,*
> *Nous recevions si peu qu'encore je m'étonne*
> *Que mon petit gousset avec mes petits soins,*
> *Ayent pu si longtemps suffir à nos besoins.*[1]

[1] We took to the country, and the little towns admired the talent of my little troop, swearing that nothing could be finer, especially when I showed my face on the stage. Their signs of pleasure rose to frenzy; these provincial people, with their shouting and contortions, looked beside themselves. God knows I looked pleased, seeing that things were so favourable. But I had also to provide

M

There is a more truthful account, written by an eye-witness who lived three months with Molière's company. This was Dassoucy, master of the burlesque, poet, musician, composer of the score for Corneille's *Adromède,* and a renowned pilferer. In his *Adventures Burlesques,* he writes about the delightful hours he spent with Molière and the Béjarts:

'I was then richer and happier than I had ever been, for these generous people helped me not only as a friend; they wished to treat me as a relative. As they had been summoned to the Etats, they took me with them to Pézenas and I cannot tell how very charming everybody was to me. There is a saying that the most devoted brother is bored after a month of feeding his own brother; but they were more generous than any brother and did not tire of having me at their table the whole winter; and I can say:

> *Qu'en cette douce compagnie*
> *Que je repaissais d'harmonie,*
> *Au milieu de sept ou huit plats,*
> *Exempt de soins et d'embarras,*
> *Je passais doucement la vie.*
> *Jamais plus gueux ne fut plus gras;*
> *Et quoiqu'on chante et quoiqu'on die,*
> *De ces beaux messieurs des Etats,*
> *Qui tous les jours ont dix ducats,*
> *La musique et la comédie*
> *A cette table bien garnie,*
> *Parmi les plus friands muscats,*
> *C'est moi qui soufflais la rôtie*
> *Et qui buvais plus d'hypocras.*[2]

In fact though I was their guest, I could well say that I was at home. I never saw more kindness, frankness or courtesy than among these people, who were the worthy servants of dramatic art.'

---

them and myself with supper, and so much worry prevented me from feeling too happy; we charged five sous a seat, and we got so little money that I still marvel how my tiny purse and all my efforts could provide us with all we needed for so long.

[2] Among this delightful company which I provided with sweet harmony and a choice of seven or eight dishes, free from care and worry, I passed a tranquil life. Never was a beggar fatter; and whatever may be said or sung of the worthy members of the Etats who cash ten ducats every day to enjoy music and comedy at this well-provided table, drinking the choicest muscatelle, I was the one who drank the toast in the largest tumbler of *hypocras.*

What he conjures up of this delightful life does not lead us to be sorry for the company. One does not feed a parasite for months when one lacks a bare minimum. Good humour does not blossom on poverty.

We think it is superfluous to repeat the story of Molière's provincial career, so often told already and to which we can add nothing new. We think it is more interesting to follow the journeys of two other touring companies whose history is far less familiar: those which had the patronage of the Grand Condé and the Grande Mademoiselle. Among them will be found a good many players of some renown.

Patronage had a long tradition among the Condés. Helping men of letters and artists, and especially actors, was part and parcel of the prestige of the younger Bourbon branch. The Grand Condé's father, Henri II de Bourbon, in spite of his legendary avarice, already kept a theatrical company at his own cost. Its director was Vautrel, who had gathered around himself, to serve M. le Prince, a number of actors who were well known in Paris: Longueval, Gasteau, La Fontaine, Nicier, du Maine. They had all been former companions of Valleran le Conte who, having failed to force the new repertoire of Alexander Hardy on the Paris public, had gone to find a precarious fortune in the Low Countries.

Vautrel had collected together what was left of Valleran's company, to which he added the inimitable trio of clowns Gros Guillaume, Gaultier-Garguille and Turlupin. The Prince de Condé's company opened up on the old stage of the rue Mauconseil, where farce had replaced the old mystery plays formerly given by the Confrères de la Passion. They performed there from June 1614 to January 1616, then again in April 1618.

M. le Prince fell from favour and was imprisoned in the Bastille: after he had been set free but was still feared and under suspicion, living in semi-exile in the country, the company which still bore his name, but probably was no longer in receipt of subsidies, took to the roads of France, like many other touring companies. It was in Orléans in 1623, in Bourges (where the young Duc d'Enghien was studying at the Jesuits' college) in 1639, in Dijon in 1632 and again in 1643. Its presence in the latter city is easy to account for as M. le Prince was Governor of Burgundy. But, kept in Guyenne with the army, he did not live in his governorship. The Duc d'Enghien, who was eighteen, had been designated by the King to

179

replace his father. The young man was pleasure-loving and when he received the King in Burgundy in September 1639 he wanted to treat him to a comedy; from that time on it was M. le Duc rather than M. le Prince who looked after the players. When the father died in 1646 that was the end of the company.

However keenly he loved the theatre M. le Duc had no time to devote to it: neither as the youthful conqueror at Rocroy, Lens and Nordlingen, nor as the leader of the Fronde, intent on fighting Mazarin, nor when in prison at Vincennes, nor as a rebellious prince who for eight years kept the royal troops at bay. But on his submission and his return to France after the Peace of the Pyrenees he revived the family tradition at once and got a theatrical company together which, through many changes and tribulations, survived him and after his death was taken in charge by his son, Henri-Jules de Bourbon. Its first leader was an actor known as Philandre.

He had probably taken his pseudonym from the title of Rotrou's comedy, *Le Philandre*, printed in 1637. His real name was Jean Monchaingre, but he also turned up under the name of Jean Mattée, and, while acting in farces in Lyon, as Paphetin. Actors at that time often had several names, their real one, another for comedy and a third one for farce. Philandre, like all his colleagues, had begun his career in itinerant companies. Born about 1616, he was little more than twenty when, in 1637 or 1639, he became manager of a company at that time in Saumur. There he met another itinerant actor, Floridor, who was to have a most brilliant career in Paris. Usually the arrival of two companies in the same town at the same time meant catastophe, with jealousy and struggles from which no one benefited. The more reasonable people preferred to come to an understanding and, instead of quarrelling about an uncertain audience, offer them a joint performance. That is what Philandre and Floridor did at Saumur. Their companies 'found it more advantageous to come to an agreement, and were praised for it by all respectable people, who were pleased by their good intelligence'.

During their provincial wanderings the hazards of the journey one day took Philandre, his wife Angélique Meunier and their companions to Le Mans, a city renowned for its tasty capons and hazel-hens. This was about 1635; companies on the road from Paris to Rennes passed fairly regularly through Le Mans. Scarron wrote:

'That kind of people—like many others—move along a set course, like the sun in the Zodiac. In that country they go from Tours to Angers, from Angers to La Flèche, from La Flèche to Le Mans, from Le Mans to Alençon, from Alençon to Argentan or Laval, according to the road they take to Paris or Britanny.'

Le Mans was probably reached with particular pleasure, for the companies knew they would find the help of a patron very enthusiastic about the theatre: François d'Averton, Comte de Belin, always generous towards actors and even more so towards actresses.

A historian of Le Mans has written that Philandre and his wife had been Scarron's models for Léandre and Angélique in the *Roman comique*. In fact, this suggestion merely rests on the resemblance between the names of Philandre and Léandre, and the fact that Philandre's wife was called Angélique. These are rather meagre elements to build on. Besides Léandre, as a young student who runs away from the college of La Flèche to follow Angélique, the beautiful actress, has a very secondary role in Scarron's novel, in which he only appears as valet to Destin, the leader of the company who plays a game of tennis at Biche's inn.

Whether Philandre and his company did or did not pass through Le Mans to Scarron's benefit, they certainly continued touring in the provinces: their tracks have not so far been found but, like all his colleagues, Philandre certainly dreamt of Paris. His dream came true at last in 1647, thanks to Floridor's friendship; Floridor had not forgotten his companion of Saumur days. He had been a member of the Marais company since 1638 and had brought much applause to Corneille's tragedies; he was now about to go over to the Hôtel de Bourgogne and assume its management at Bellerose's request. His departure left an empty office at the Marais and deprived it of Corneille's plays, which he was now to produce in the rue Mauconseil.

As his own replacement he summoned his former companion Philandre, whom he thought worthy to succeed him. Floridor owned a sixth of the wooden theatre built in the Marais after the 1644 fire. On April 10, 1647, he sold this share to Philandre for 550 livres, which enabled him to settle unpaid rents and a debt to his bill-printer.

Philandre must have been fairly successful at the Marais, since he was honoured with an engraved portrait by Duret, which is

181

preserved in Fossard's print collection. In his theatre costume, with curly hair framing his face, moustache and peaked beard, according to the fashion of the time, he looks like an elegant nobleman, with feathered hat and lace collar, his sword at his side and his cloak draped over his arm.

Yet for unknown reasons the newcomer did not stay long at the Marais; he was still there on May 14, 1648, but as early as 1650 we find him in the Netherlands, a member of the Prince of Orange's company. The Prince died on October 26, 1650. With the disappearance of their patron, the French company which had flourished since the beginning of the century, both at the Hague and in Paris, where it had often performed during the summer at the Hôtel de Bourgogne, found itself in serious difficulties. Chappuzeau wrote:

'Since the death of the late Prince of Orange, who kept a company of French players, they were not greatly pleased with that part of the Low Countries where he had ruled, and they found themselves better off in Brussels, near to court.'

On November 24, 1650 they received a safe-conduct for Brussels where, a few days before, Beaulieu, Guérin and Philandre had rented the Gracht tennis court for thirteen florins per day. The Governor-General since 1647 was the Archduke Leopold-Wilhelm, a keen lover of the theatre, who showed himself perfectly willing to succeed the late Prince of Orange and take the company under his patronage. Indeed, he gave them large grants for their performances in the theatre of the Emperors' Gallery.

In the summer of 1651, keeping the title of 'Prince of Orange's Company', they acted in Ghent. In December they were back in Brussels, where they renewed their lease—twelve florins a day instead of thirteen—and had a new stage built by François Drion, master carpenter. The next year they rented the theatre of the Montagne St Elizabeth for three years, but they soon quarrelled with the owner and sued him. For a time they went back to the Gracht tennis court, and in November 1652 they signed a contract with a carpenter to build, wherever they willed, a theatre twenty-five feet wide by thirty-two feet deep, with boxes, amphitheatre and pit, for 825 florins. The contract was signed by Philandre and Villabé, the former manager of Gaston d'Orléans' company.

The next summer they came back to The Hague. Meanwhile they

had won their lawsuit in Brussels; the proprietor of the theatre
of the Montagne St Elizabeth had to accept their conditions and
he agreed to a new lease, as from St John's feast, 1653. In September,
at His Imperial Highness' request, they gave performances in
Valenciennes to entertain the Princesse de Condé, who had come
to see her husband. At that time the conqueror of Rocroi had
rebelled against his king and had his general headquarters in
Brussels where, between two campaigns against the royal troops,
he led a gay life in great splendour. Quite certainly he had
Philandre and the French company to act for him.

But the company was soon to find a new patron. At that time
Christina, the wayward and extravagant Queen of Sweden, had
abdicated on June 6, 1654, had reached Antwerp on August 12th
and Brussels in December. The importance of her French entourage in Stockholm is well known: artists, writers, scholars and
philosophers of the highest esteem, such as Chevreau, Naudé,
Saumaize, Descartes, Huet, Sébastien Bourdon and Bourdelot, had
gone there. Life at the Stockholm court was lively and libertine,
but this had not prevented Christina from secret adherence to the
Church of Rome.

In Brussels Christina did not meet the Prince de Condé much:
ridiculous questions of protocol had kept them apart, but they were
both very keen on the theatre, which they visited often. Christina
wrote to one of her correspondents: 'I am on excellent terms with
everybody in Brussels except with the Prince de Condé, whom
I only see at the comedy or out riding.'

Philandre and his companions, in the absence of a Prince of
Orange old enough to pension them, were now without a patron,
but they enjoyed Queen Christina's generosity and kindness. Consequently, and very naturally, the Prince of Orange's company became in 1655 the Queen of Sweden's company. There are other
instances in the history of the seventeenth-century theatre of companies changing their name as they changed their patrons: a little
later Mademoiselle's company, for the same reason, became the
Duke of Savoy's company.

The title of 'Players to the Queen of Sweden' appeared for
the first time in a deed of April 24, 1655, in which a neighbour of
their theatre, the brewer Van der Borcht, allowed them to make
a window at their own expense, opening over his garden. Relying
on the Queen's protection, they renewed their lease of the Montagne St Elizabeth theatre on April 30, 1655.

Monsieur le Prince never ceases to take an interest in the theatre, even during his Brussels exile; he especially appreciated Philandre and gave a striking proof of this by standing godfather to his son Louis at Ste Gudule, on May 14, 1656.

Despite the Franco-Spanish war, the French company was warmly greeted everywhere in the Spanish Netherlands: for instance, they acted Corneille's *Mort de Pompée* at Bruges in December 1656.

But soon Christina of Sweden left Brussels to travel to Rome via Paris, and the company was deprived of her patronage and support. That was not the only difficulty they met with. The Archduke Leopold-Wilhelm had been replaced in 1656 by Don John of Austria, who did not care for the theatre. This was the end of the brilliant and fruitful performances at the Archduke's palace. But that was not all. The unlucky Philandre was running into domestic trouble. In Brussels he had had a daughter, Jeanne, by his servant, Marthe Boisseau.

The mother had gone to Paris for the birth of her baby; she refused to keep the child and bring her up, and she lodged a complaint against the player who had seduced her. Philandre decided to reach an agreement about this unpleasant affair. He agreed to take the child into his own care and, by a transaction, got the mother, who lived on St Sauveur parish, to withdraw her complaint against a lump sum of 30 livres. So that Philandre had now with him a baby girl 'to bring up, instruct and rear in the Roman Catholic and Apostolic faith' at the very moment when he and his company were in difficulties. The child was to follow her father's destiny; we shall see her later as Mlle Beauval, a greatly admired actress.

Meanwhile, the company had no hope of paying its way in Brussels and they left for Holland. They were in The Hague on October 1, 1657: on that day, Philandre, Guérin and Beaulieu, under the very modest title of 'French players', signed a contract with Hendrik van Erp for the building of a theatre for 400 livres. Everything was to be ready by October 11th, as the company was anxious to get going.

Yet Philandre was still in The Hague in February 1658. For months secret diplomatic negotiations had been going on between France and Spain and they finally led to the Peace of the Pyrenees and to Condé's homecoming. Had he sent Philandre in advance to recruit a company under his name? We do not know, but what is certain is that the Prince of Orange's and the Queen of Sweden's former companies were dissolved.

Hautefeuille took up the Dauphin's company, with which he was in Nantes in 1658 and 1662. Guérin continued his itinerant life; he was in Marseilles in 1663, then became the leader of another company in 1667, was 'Player to the Queen of France' in 1668–70, and to the Duke of Savoy in 1673. As for Beaulieu, his tracks are lost, but he soon died, at any rate before 1664.

Philandre was back in France. With his wife and 'adopted daughter' Jeanne, named Jeanneton, he was in La Rochelle, 'living in the house of Pierre Coccoison, seller of bread at the sign of the Cock'. He also formed another company, signing in the members in a legal deed, to last from Ash Wednesday 1660 to the same day in 1661. Among the actors he engaged were La Couture and his wife. La Couture was none other than Georges Pinel, Molière's former writing master, who fifteen years earlier had started his dramatic career in his former pupil's Illustre Théâtre. When it collapsed in 1645 he remained on the stage. In 1649 he was a member of the Company of the Duc d'Orléans. In 1651, with his wife Anne Pernay, he created his own company and went with it to Rochefort the next year. In 1656–57, again as manager, he was in the neighbourhood of Nantes; he was an experienced player.

The other actors whom Philandre assembled were mere beginners: Michel de Rieu (whom he was to take along with him into Monsieur le Prince's company), Marguerite Marcoureau (who was probably the sister of Beaulieu, his old Netherlands companion), Beaumont, Besnard, Marie Coutelier, Pierre Mercier, who do not seem to have been long on the stage.

We know nothing about this company's fate, but it was short-lived anyhow. It is even possible that the company never actually put on a performance. At that time, and also between Bordeaux and La Rochelle, another company was performing, that of Raymond Poisson, who was later to create the part of Crispin. It is probably that company which is mentioned by young Marianne Mancini, Mazarin's youngest niece, the future Duchesse de Bouillon, in her childish verses to her uncle, dated La Rochelle September 7, 1659:

> J'ai été à la comédie,
> Où je me suis fort divertie,

Mais je ne pourrai plus y aller,
Parce que l'argent a manqué.[3]

At the very moment when Philandre was building up his new company in La Rochelle, Louis XIV, on his way to St-Jean-de-Luz wrote this curious letter to the mayor and Jurats of Bordeaux:

'*On the King's behalf.*
Very dearly beloved.
The company of actors of our cousin the Prince of Orange, who wish to return to our city of Bordeaux to perform their own plays and to entertain with their plays those who may like them; we have ordered this letter to be written to warn you, and order you to allow them to get a convenient place to erect the stage and boxes, according to custom, meanwhile paying a rent for the place they use. For such is our will.
In Toulouse, November 15, 1659.
(*Signed*) *Louis*
   Phélypeaux.'

Which was this company said to be under the patronage of the Prince of Orange? We know that since 1655 there had been no company of that name, as it had taken the name of the Queen of Sweden and then abandoned the new name in 1656. In 1657 in The Hague we have seen that Philandre and his companions simply called themselves the 'French players'. May we assume that, when the company disintegrated, some of its members came together and maintained the title? Or was it rather Philandre himself, the former director, who, with or without right, resumed the use of that title for the new company he had started at La Rochelle?

Meanwhile, political events hurried on. The Peace of the Pyrenees had been signed on November 9, 1659, bringing Artois and Roussillon to France. On November 29th Condé left Brussels; on January 27, 1660, he reached Aix-en-Provence, where the court was staying, and was coldly received by Louis XIV and Anne of Austria. He was back in favour, but he refrained from attending the King's wedding, and went straight back to his Paris residence. Yet he wanted his presence to be felt in some degree at the wedding festivities in St-Jean-de-Luz, so he summoned Philandre, whom he had often applauded in Brussels, and entrusted him with

---

[3] I went to the playhouse and amused myself very much, but I can't go any more as there is no money left.

186

recruiting a new company under his name. We do not know when and how it was constituted. It seems certain that, of all the actors he had got together in La Rochelle a few months earlier, Philandre kept but one, Michel de Rieu. He had probably collected some of the experienced actors who were to be found later in the Prince de Condé's company: Henri Pitel, called Longchamp, who had belonged in 1651 to the Grande Mademoiselle's company, then to that of Raymond Poisson, whom he followed from Toulon to Bordeaux, and had then joined Villabé in 1656. Longchamp, who had married a daughter of the famous clown of the Hôtel de Bourgogne, Turlupin, was an excellent actor who in 1672 became director of M. le Prince's company.

Another good recruit was Antoine Le Febvre, probably the son of Mathieu Le Febvre, called Laporte, a former actor from the Hôtel de Bourgogne, who had gone to the Marais in 1654 and afterwards to Villabé in 1656, acting the roles of kings.

François Serdin and his wife Catherine Bourgeois had belonged to various companies before entering the Marais in 1654. Then, like Longchamp, they joined Villabé's company. There was also a young couple, Jean Biet called Beauchamp, and his wife, Claudine Mellet, who were also probable members of the 1660 company.

Monsieur le Prince's new company, under Philandre's management, gave performances to the court in St-Jean-de-Luz in May 1660. On the 25th of that month Longchamp had a son baptized in that town; the godfather was Monsieur, the godmother the Grande Mademoiselle, who had not forgotten that Longchamp had been a member of her company.

After its début at St-Jean-de-Luz for the royal wedding, Philandre's company had a long and brilliant career. Condé was always faithful to his actors, himself distributing the parts, stepping in to settle differences between actors. That summer the company performed in Dijon, where Condé was governor, in the autumn at the chateau of Chantilly and in the winter at the Hôtel de Condé in Paris. They made journeys to England and Germany, and toured the provinces, at one moment joining forces in Rouen with the Dauphin's company. When Condé died in 1686, his son Henri-Jules de Bourbon, Duc d'Enghien, who had had his private company from 1674 to 1678, gave his patronage to his father's company and maintained it until 1698.

For several years Philandre continued to preside over its fate. He was in Dijon in May 1662, and in Nantes and Rennes the next year. On July 3rd Longchamp had his daughter, Charlotte-Marguerite, baptized in the latter city. Her godfather was Beauval who was soon to marry Jeanneton, Philandre's natural daughter, and she signed the deed with her father, which is proof that she followed him on his journeys. Mme de Rieu was the baby's godmother. At the end of 1663 the company passed through Langres on its way to Paris to perform at the Hôtel de Condé; there they staged *l'Impromptu de l'Hôtel de Condé*, Montfleury-*fils'* reply to Molière's *L'Impromptu de Versailles*, which did not prevent Condé, in the folowing year, from supporting Molière's banned *Tartuffe*.

From 1665 to 1667 the company of M. le Prince was in England, producing the French classical repertoire. When back in Rennes on July 3, 1667, Beauval had his son François baptized: the mother was Philandre's natural daughter Jeanne. Surprisingly, the godmother was Philandre's own wife. The baby died on October 30, 1670. By that date Philandre and his wife had abandoned the stage under quite mysterious circumstances.

A deed in the registers of the Hôtel du Roi (March 16, 1667) tells us that there was an action pending beween Philandre and his wife on the one hand and M. le Prince's company on the other. What obscure quarrel, what kind of professional jealousy or sentimental intrigue could be the cause? We know nothing, but the conflict must have been serious as the Philandres told the magistrate that they had 'asked M. le Prince for permission to retire from the company, not wanting any longer to act, either in that company, or in any other, as they are advanced in years'.

The age reason for this untimely retirement is clearly nothing but a pretext; Philandre was scarcely fifty and, except if he were ill, this was no age to retire. We cannot but feel that there was something grave in the background, a professional or sentimental conflict putting them in opposition to the company they had created and led for seven years. This unaccountable retirement marks a break in their career which had been successful for thirty years.

Where would they settle for the rest of their lives? It was M. le Prince, who was always very generous, who provided them with a pleasant place for retirement. It seems that for several years Philandre had, thanks to his protector, owned an estate in Anjou Quincé near Brissac. It was in Brissac that his son Louis was buried on March 7, 1664. The boy, who was eight, had been

Condé's godson. In the burial certificate the father is called *écuyer, sieur de la Brosse.*

Yet it seems that the couple also lived in Paris in their house on the rue du Petit-Lion in the parish of St Sauveur. Meanwhile, M. le Prince's company was still travelling across France. Philandre's natural daughter, Jeanneton, had grown up. She had married Henri Pitel, 'Beauval', Longchamp's brother, the man who had started his career as a candle snuffer in a former company. Since then the Beauvals had gone far, passing through the Duke of Savoy's company and making a short stop in the Théâtre de Marais for a few years. In 1670 they were in Dijon. There they received a summons from the King, ordering them to go back to Paris to enter Molière's company at the Palais-Royal, together with Baron.

It is most likely that it was through his daughter and son-in-law that Philandre became acquainted with Michel Baron, Molière's pupil. On arriving in Paris the young man probably owned nothing but very poor theatre costumes. To enter 'the King's company of the Palais-Royal', Baron had to renew his wardrobe, and he applied to Philandre. On August 31, 1670, probably not without some melancholy, the retired actor sold Baron for 300 livres all the costumes he had worn in the Prince of Orange's and M. le Prince's companies. But poor Baron, who was just seventeen, had no money and could not produce the 300 livres. He borrowed them from the attorney Rollet, the very man whom Boileau had off-handedly called a blackguard, and Molière guaranteed the money.

It was probably through Condé's recommendation that Philandre was given a peaceful job, that of porter at the Chateau de Brissac, where we find him installed in 1675. From time to time he travelled to Paris to see the Beauvals; on January 16, 1688, for instance, he attended the wedding in St Sauveur of one of their numerous children, Louise, who married Jacques Bertrand, master wigmaker. Faithful to his patron, who was also in retirement at Chantilly, he proudly wrote, under his signature, 'officer to the Prince de Condé'.

Philandre and his wife continued their peaceful old age in the Chateau de Brissac. Philandre died on April 25, 1691, at Trèves, near La Flèche, when he was seventy-five; the barony of Trèves had come to Condé through his wife. Until his last breath, the name of the Grand Condé—the Prince had died five years earlier—was

Philandre's protection in his private life, as it had been earlier in his theatrical days.

Like Condé, the Grande Mademoiselle had inherited a taste for the theatre which she retained throughout her life. Her father, the delightful, unreliable Gaston d'Orléans, was already very keen. In his entourage were playwrights like Tristan and patrons of art like the Duc de Guise or the Comte de Modène, who was Madeleine Béjart's lover before Molière. In 1644, Louis XIII's brother took under his patronage the Illustre Théâtre which had been founded by Madeleine Béjart and young Poquelin, but nevertheless soon ended in complete failure. As early as 1626 the Duc d'Orléans made grants to the clown Gros-Guillaume for performances at Chantilly. In 1637, Monsieur summoned actors to his château at Blois. Anne-Marie-Louise d'Orléans, his daughter, was just ten years old, yet she attended their performances, for she later wrote in her memoirs: 'Finally, in Tours and Blois, I had a delightful time; it was in the autumn [1637]; Monsieur brought his players there and we had plays almost every day'. The Duc d'Orléans also invited Italian companies there, and those of the Hôtel de Bourgogne and the Marais.

Moreover, Gaston, like all contemporary princes, had his own company. It was first mentioned in 1645. That year, in Toulouse on May 9th, one of his actors had his little daughter baptized. Between performances in Blois or Tours, the company toured the kingdom. It is mentioned in Lyons in January 1646, in Troyes in 1647, in Lyons again in 1648 and 1650, in Poitiers and Saumur in 1651 to 1652, in Nantes in May 1652, in Orléans in October 1652, possibly in Rouen in 1653, and in Avignon in July 1654. Its members were, at that time, Boisvert and his wife, Gilberte Loiseau, Hugues de Lan and La Couture.

In October 1652, when the Fronde was quite finished, Mademoiselle, who had had a gun fired at the King's army from the tower of the Bastille, was exiled to St Fargeau. She had plays acted there to pass the time.

'I found players there; it was a very good company which had been all winter with the court at Poitiers and had followed it to Saumur. It had been widely praised by the court. I had this company act at my house one evening and His Royal Highness [Gaston d'Orléans] was there. The one subject of talk at that time was Cardinal Mazarin's return to court.'

A little later, she added:

'When I arrived, my only idea was to have a theatre organized as quickly as possible. In St Fargeau there is a large hall which was very convenient for this purpose: I listened to the play with more pleasure than I had ever felt; the theatre was well decorated and well lit. . . . The next year, I summoned players to St Fargeau and they stayed for two months. . . . The year after, I had players as usual. . . . I stayed the whole month (October 1654) at Blois; there were players there who were not watched by Monsieur or Madame. There were only myself and my sisters who went to their performances.'

After 1649 the manager of the company, which called itself 'H.R.H. the duc d'Orléans' company', was a certain Abraham Mitallat from Metz. This man wanted his stage name to conjure up an impression of soft and fresh running water, and he took the name of La Source. Nothing is known of his youth, during which he probably trained in some strolling company. His name does not appear anywhere until the date of his marriage in Sens, on February 27, 1634, to Jeanne de Roserat. She was probably of a good family, since her father was described as *écuyer, sieur de Belle-fontaine*. The witnesses were probably members of the company. One of them was Antoine Marcoureau, perhaps the brother of Pierre Marcoureau, called Beaulieu, the father of the actor-playwright Brécourt.

La Source must have been quite young, as he had had no time to save. The month before, on January 16th, he had borrowed 100 livres from Martin Caillou, sieur des Carnaux, to start his married life. For the ten following years nothing is known of the La Sources and their travels, but they appeared in Lyons in 1644, probably already members of the Orléans company. On February 1st of that year one of the actors, Toussaint Le Riche, called Hautefeuille, had a son, Jean-Jacques, baptized at Ste-Croix. The godfather was an Italian mountebank, Giacomo de Gorla, the father of a lovely daughter who was to become Mlle du Parc and join Molière's company. The godmother was Mlle de La Source. It is likely that these two were then acting with Hautefeuille. In 1648 La Source and his wife were still in Lyons, and this time definitely in the Duc d'Orléans' company.

We have already mentioned the journeys of that company along the Loire, from Nantes and Saumur to Orleans, and its visits to

St Fargeau between 1651 and 1654. At Dijon, in 1655, they were mentioned under the new title of 'Players to His Royal Highness the Duc d'Orléans and Mademoiselle'. The next year the company found new members and signed a new contract of association on March 24, 1656. Villabé, an old hand from the Marais, became manager and collected Raymond Poisson, called Belleroche, Antoine Le Febvre, Serdin and Longchamp and their wives. La Source and his wife were no longer members. Of the old company only Boisvert and his wife remained. The new company acted in Luxembourg and the Netherlands in 1656 and 1657, and in Rouen in 1658. By that time Mademoiselle had been pardoned and was back at court.

In November 1658 the French court went to Lyons to meet that of Savoy: there was some idea of marrying Louis XIV to the Princess of Savoy. It came to nothing: it was probably only one of Mazarin's manœuvres to compel the court of Spain to take action and offer the Infanta Maria-Theresa as a pledge for the peace treaty which was under discussion. Nevertheless, the meeting of the two courts in Lyons was an opportunity for entertainments among which the theatre was prominent. Mademoiselle, who was in Lyons with the King, summoned her company from Marseilles—for it was now hers alone, as Gaston was no longer interested. 'I forgot to say,' she wrote in her memoirs, 'that there were two companies in Lyons, one of which was very good. They were billed as *Les Comédiens de Mademoiselle*, and that was right.'

La Source and his wife, who had vanished some ten years earlier, do not seem to have been back by the time of the official beginning of Mademoiselle's company. Nothing is known about them at that time. In 1658 the company was led by Philippe Millot, who had belonged to Molière's Illustre Théâtre and who had joined Mademoiselle's company in 1651; with him came, among others, Anne Millot, (Philippe's sister), Nicolas Biet (called Beauchamp, the specialist of female impersonations) Joseph du Landas (called Dupin, who came from Rochefort's company), François de Lan and Nicolas Drouin. Dorimond had belonged to Monsieur's company since March 26, 1650, and had taken part in all their tours. His prestige among his companions probably came from the fact that he was also a playwright and added to their repertory a number of one-act comedies which the public liked to see following a tragedy.

It was in Lyons in November 1658 that Dorimond thought of

15. Molière and his Troupe, by G. Melingue

looking for a new comic plot in an Italian comedy borrowed from the Spanish, *Don Juan* by Tirso de Molina. His *Festin de Pierre ou l'Athée foudroyé* was successfully acted before both courts. It was the first French comedy on the Don Juan theme, which was soon rewritten by many other authors.

Proud of his success, Dorimond had his play printed in January 1659 by the Lyons publisher Antoine Offray. His wife, Marie Dumont, who acted in the company, has been harshly criticized by theatre historians, who have denied her any talent and only allowed her 'a very successful bust'.

It seems that it was then more or less that La Source rejoined Mademoiselle's company. He is to be found on April 1, 1659 in the church of Ste Croix de Lyons, standing as godfather to Claude Pélissier's daughter, and on the 14th in the same relation to a posthumous son of Hugues de Lan, former player in the company of the Duc d'Orléans.

Meanwhile Louis XIV and his train were back in Paris. Probably well received and well paid by the Duke of Savoy, Mademoiselle's players loitered in his lands. On August 31, 1659 they were in Chambéry, where the first nobleman of the city, the Marquis de St Maurice, was godfather to Nicolas Biet, Beau-champ's son. For a while, Mademoiselle's players went over to the Duke of Savoy. On September 8, 1659, the manager, Philippe Millot, married in Chambéry Marguerite de Lan, Hugues de Lan's very recent widow.

From Chambéry the company was summoned by the Duke to Turin. Before leaving Chambéry, on September 14th, they decided, in order to avoid trouble, that all they received from the Duke would be divided into eleven shares; Dorimond would get three of them (one as a player, one as an author and one for his wife); the eight other actors would have one each. The company remained in Turin until May. Having exhausted its success, and its repertoire, and filled its purse with the Duke's largesse, the company sought new fields to conquer. La Source suggested Holland, which was toured by numerous French companies, and he may have acted there during the ten unknown years of his career.

Baggage and scenery were loaded on a cart, and the company proceeded north, from city to city and from inn to inn. And as they had to live, at each stage they performed in a tennis court or on a village green. They performed in Dijon on May 28th, in Ghent from June 26th to August 7th, 1660. They took a whole year to

N

make the journey from Turin to The Hague, where they acted on October 20th, in the Buitenhof tennis court, rented for four weeks at the rate of 7.10 florins a day.

But Mademoiselle was bored without her theatrical company and she called them back to Paris, where they arrived by the end of the year, settling in a tennis court in the Faubourg St Germain. After such long journeying through the provinces and foreign lands, would they settle at last in Paris, thanks to Mademoiselle's patronage? This was the hope; but they had not reckoned upon the jealousy of the three royal companies, the Hôtel de Bourgogne, the Marais and the one that was soon to settle at the Palais-Royal with Molière. La Source soon realized that there was no room for newcomers, and that the King would not allow anybody to rival the theatres he subsidized.

For Mademoiselle's players there was no alternative but to return to the roads. By the middle of February 1661 they were in Brussels for Carnival and they acted in the theatre in the rue de la Montagne Ste Elizabeth. The Brussels gazette, Les *Relations Véritables*, wrote about them:

'Among the Carnival entertainments to which we were summoned by this pleasant and peaceful season, the most attractive have been the comedies performed with the greatest charm by the French actors of Mademoiselle d'Orléans' company, who perform each day the most excellent plays, full of diversity, art and skill, above all the great machinery of Corneille's *Andromède* which they acted this week to the full satisfaction and admiration of all the persons of quality of the court and an infinity of others.'

And a few days later:

'Carnival is over, with the usual entertainment, mostly comedies, as Mademoiselle's players surpassed themselves in the *Descente d'Orphée aux Enfers*, which is outstandingly beautiful on account of its surprising machinery and changes of scene, which delight the court and the other spectators.'

Mademoiselle's players returned to Ghent on August 7, 1661, and were in Brussels on April 1, 1662. La Source signed a contract with a master boatman to take them to The Hague with their luggage and costumes for 150 florins. When they arrived on April 14th they had a theatre built in the Gracht tennis court with eighteen benches for 356 florins and they rented it on January 7th

194

for 11 florins 20 sols a day. It was a three-tier stage sufficient to act *La Toison d'or* and similar plays.

This play had lately been performed to full houses in Paris. At about this time La Source engaged a musician, Marie Aucart, who for six florins a day played the harp and sang. She was probably a citizen of The Hague for, by the contract, the players promised to take her home 'in a coach, after the show'. To replace Mlle de Beauchamp, La Source engaged Mlle Rosidor, born Charlotte Meslier, Mlle Bellerose's daughter by her first husband. But the new actress did not like the company and in May went over to the King of England's company, then acting in Brussels.

Mademoiselle's players would not have done too badly but for the fact that in May 1662 the Dutch court, induced by the pastors' council, suddenly banned the theatre. The company returned to Brussels where, through the good offices of the master surgeon Bigot, they rented the theatre in the rue de la Montagne Ste Elizabeth until Easter 1663, for 920 patacons. Rather worried about its future, the company acted in Brussels in 1663. In December, at its own expense, it sent Bellefleur to organize a tour in England, but this came to nothing and Bellefleur was back in Brussels in January 1664. He had belonged to Rosidor's company, which he had left to enter Mademoiselle's, attracted by Françoise de Lan's beauty; he married her at Ste Gudule on January 3, 1665.

The company was pleased with the way they had been received in Brussels. On March 4, 1664, they renewed for a year their lease of the theatre of the Montagne Ste Elizabeth for 240 patacons. The lease mentioned two new members, Jean Godart, called Champnouveau, who did not stay long in the company as he joined the Marais the next year, and Vincent du Bourg-Jolimont, who also left to enter the company formed on March 26, 1665 by Nicolas Biet-Beauchamp. Mademoiselle's company went back to The Hague.

In The Hague they had a stage erected in the Buitenhof tennis court for 210 florins; meanwhile, they travelled up and down the Spanish Netherlands. In June they performed in Antwerp; in August in Ghent. They were back in Brussels in December and Philippe Millot had a daughter baptized there: her godfather was Henri de Ligne, Marquis de Roeulx, and her godmother Claire-Marie de Nassau, Princesse de Ligne. They spent the winter of 1664–65 in Brussels, apparently not earning much since La Source was compelled to borrow forty-six florins from an Antwerp merchant. The Prince d'Orange's largesse was already spent, and Mademoiselle was losing interest in her players. Yet La Source persevered and, after a journey to Metz in February 1666, gave a power of attorney to a Brussels *bourgeois* to renew the Montagne Ste Elizabeth lease until Easter 1667. But they did not stay all that time, for they turned up in Dijon as early as January 1667. New trouble was in store for them. The town authorities twice refused them permission to act.

On arrival at Dijon the company was exhausted and discouraged. La Source was expecting the worst and he had left, looking for better things elsewhere. Mademoiselle, probably aware of that desertion, took action. She reorganized the company under her name and gave its management to a young actor, François Mousson; none of the former company joined him. All the actors were new, Romanville and his wife, Boncourt and his wife, Charles Biet (Beauchamp), Coirat (Belleroche), du Raincy and Mlle de la Fratte.

La Source entered a new company, the Duc de Lorraine's, and took with him several friends from Mademoiselle's company, Philippe Millot and his wife, Louis Dorimond, the actor-poet's brother, and Mlle de Bellefleur. Touchingly naïve, the contract stated that they promised to live on friendly terms 'without quarrels or abuse, on pain of a fine of one pistole'. The company acted in Lorraine for a year; then it disintegrated.

Once more La Source had to find a new company to take him in: in the familiar Netherlands he came across the Queen of France's company. As it never acted in Paris, since the Queen was not interested in them, it was always on tour in the provinces or abroad. It acted in northern and western France, in the Spanish Netherlands, Holland, Denmark and Germany.

In 1668 La Source took command and brought in several former members of Mademoiselle's company, Boncourt and Jolimont, Mlle Boisvert, du Raincy and his wife. He remained in Brussels with his new companions and rented the Montagne Ste Elizabeth theatre in August 1668 until the following Whitsun. His wife was probably dead, for her name is not to be found in any deed of the Queen of France's company. In October he acted in The Hague.

From Lille, where the company was performing on June 13, 1669, they renewed their Brussels lease for the 1669–70 season. La Source was sharing the first parts with a young beginner who acted the lovers' parts and made the announcements: he was the player-poet Nanteuil, whom we have already met. The Queen's players performed not only in Brussels: by the end of 1669 they were in The Hague, where St Evremond, in exile in Holland, saw the new play *Tartuffe*, by which he was enchanted:

'Here we have players good enough for comedies, but detestable for tragedies, with the exception of one woman who is good in anything. They have performed *Tartuffe*, which pleased me immensely on account of its characters; and as I still keep a very vivid memory of things French, that portrait of a feigned bigot is so well done that it made on me exactly the impression it was meant to do. Here, where they find it enough to maintain some regular religious practice and where no one is deceived by a show of sham devotion, they wonder what a false bigot is, and they hardly believe that there is a country where such a character might serve any purpose. There are scarcely any more *cocus* here than *tartuffes*. . . .'

The Queen's company, with Rosidor, who had just left the Marais, was summoned to Copenhagen by the King of Denmark. In haste they made for the Danish capital, hoping for royal grants. They arrived in December, but the King died less than three months later, leaving the players at their wits' end. They left Denmark and toured several German—and possibly Italian—cities. By the end of 1670 they were in Dijon, in January 1671 in Château-Thierry, but the company disintegrated. It was reorganized on March 3, 1671, by Charles Floridor, the great Floridor's son, who had managed the Hôtel de Bourgogne. Charles Floridor and his wife Marguerite Guérin had joined the Queen's players two years earlier. La Source left him the parts of kings and fathers. But Floridor remained only a year as manager and Nanteuil took his place. La Source, Nanteuil, du Raincy, his wife and Desmarets were the only members of the old company to be admitted into the new one.

Once more, La Source, aged and tired but still full of courage, tried his luck. With difficulty he gathered together a few players —Charles Floridor and his wife, Pierre Châteauneuf, Préflery, Charles Guérin. On March 21, 1672, for better or for worse, they created an association, but the deed had scarcely been signed when they started quarrelling again and became aware they could never agree. The next day they returned to the notary to annul the deed signed the day before.

The following year it was Charles Floridor who took the same initiative. On March 23, 1673, Floridor, La Source, Pierre Château-neuf, Romainville and Beaubourg and their wives went back to the same notary to sign on for a year, but it is not known if the arrangement was more successful than its predecessor.

This is the last time that La Source is named. For forty years with one company or another he had wandered through France and Europe in search of success. He had had his great days when leading Mademoiselle's company, and he had been applauded by sovereigns and princesses. Old age came and then he was no more than an obscure strolling player, trying his luck with short-lived companies, without patrons or admirers. *Sic transit gloria mundi.* No one knows when or where he died.

CHAPTER FOUR

THE FAMILY LIFE OF ACTORS

In days gone by as well as today, actors formed a society within a society, because of the public aspect of their calling, the curiosity they aroused, and the publicity given to their smallest gestures. This was even more marked in the seventeenth century because of the frankly hostile attitude of the Church towards them in principle, despite certain compromises in practice. It is obvious that the harsh moral stricture passed upon them, by which players became 'infamous' and were placed on a level with usurers and prostitutes, incited the majority of Christian society to keep them at arm's length.

What is more, the majority of players belonged to strolling companies, which forced them into a sort of permanent promiscuity and a communal professional life. Such conditions were favourable to marriages between players as well as to extra-marital relationships.

In fact most players went through a church marriage; their children were baptized and most often had players for godparents. With a few exceptions, they were granted religious burial. The civil records in all the regions give evidence of this. Marriages multiplied in this little world that was turned in upon itself. Contracts of association prove that companies were organized on a basis of affinities and friendships; one often finds that groups of actors had moved in unison from one company to another. Family ties also determined the composition of companies.

So in the seventeenth century dynasties of actors came into being which endured until the Revolution. Children born on tour accompanied their parents and learnt their profession from an early age. In Scarron's *Roman comique*, Mlle de la Caverne says: 'I was born a player, the daughter of a player whose parents have always said to have been in the same profession.'

The best-known acting family were the Béjarts, who for thirty years, from his beginning till his death, were faithful to Molière. Five Béjarts, brothers and sisters, were members of his company.

The mother of the tribe, Marie Hervé, toured the provinces, and stayed with them in Paris.

Many other examples are less well known, among them the Barons. The father, a member of the Marais company, married Marie Auzoult, the daughter of a pair of players, and she followed her husband to the Marais. Their son, Michel Baron, Molière's much-loved pupil, acted for more than fifty years; he married Charlotte Le Noir, daughter of La Thorillière, who also was one of Molière's companions; their son acted with him at the Comédie-Française.

At the Hôtel de Bourgogne, Bellerose married Nicole Gassot, a player and the widow of a player; the daughter born of her first marriage married Rosidor. Montfleury, also born of strolling players, married Jeanne de la Chappe, daughter of a pair of players and the widow of Pierre Rousseau, who was also on the stage. Of their six children, three took to acting: Antoine married Floridor's daughter, Françoise Mathieu d'Ennebaut and Louise Joseph Dupin. Françoise's daughter married Mlle du Parc's son.

As for the Poissons, they were a real dynasty. The ancestor, Raymond, who created the part of Crispin, married an actress, Victoire Guérin, of the same family as Guérin d'Estriche. One of their daughters married La Tuilerie and another married Dauvilliers; when a widower, Poisson again married an actress, Catherine le Roy. Her son by a first marriage, Paul, who was at the Comédie-Française, married du Croisy's step-daughter. They had three sons who entered the Comèdie-Française.

There was exactly the same situation in the itinerant companies, so far as we know their composition. Henri Pitel-Longchamp was Beauval's brother and Mlle Beaubourg's uncle; he married Turlupin's daughter; of his nine children, at least three were strolling players. Nicolas Biet-Beauchamp married Villiers' niece; four of their sons were in travelling companies.

In the matter of manners, it is certain that the theatrical world shared the growing refinement created by the increasing public interest in the theatre, the birth of a remarkable dramatic litera-ture and the huge increase of audiences. The King's patronage gave them glamour both at court and in Paris. It is obvious that Bruscambille, who spoke fairly coarse prologues at the Hôtel de Bourgogne, was closer to the Pont Neuf mountebanks than to Molière and Floridor, the latter being descended from a noble family and specializing in the tragedies of Corneille and Racine.

At the beginning of the century many unfavourable remarks about the players could be heard. In his *Page disgracié*, Tristan l'Hermite always speaks of them as debauched. Yet even at that early period, there are opposite points of view. In 1592 Valleran le Conte was in Bordeaux with his company. A local writer mentioned the fact and also recorded that one actress, a lawyer's daughter,

'against all the usual rules of that profession, was honest, both in her life and talk. This woman, when visited by young men, liked honest and serious conversation, was interested in history, and freely and frankly rebuked those who spoke to her too licentiously on Mardi Gras, telling them that off the stage she was not a *comédiante* any longer. She gave such a good impression of herself that she was always welcome in the best Bordeaux houses among her own sex.'

This precious testimonial reveals the fact that as early as the end of the sixteenth century there were women in the travelling companies, which was not so in Paris, where they only participated early in the seventeenth century. Female parts were acted by boys.

A little later, in 1618, Mlle de Rohan wrote to the Duchesse de la Trémoille: 'We have seen in Nantes a very good company which claims to be under your brother's patronage. They are very respectable and do not speak coarsely, either in our presence or at any time, according to what I have been told.'

When we come to the classical period, Chappuzeau, for whom all is for the best in the best of worlds, takes a very favourable view of the morals of his actor friends:

'If there happen to be in the company persons who do not live with all the propriety one might like, this defect does not reflect on the whole company, for it is common to all nations and all families. Such people are only tolerated because of their great talent, a thing which in other surroundings also compels people to bear what they cannot prevent without incurring great loss. So it can be said that when an actor or an actress enters a company, they are examined not only to ascertain their theatrical talent, but also for an easy demeanour, an excellent memory, plenty of wit and intelligence, a peaceful temper to live with their comrades, a love for the common good beyond private interest; also it is hoped that good morals accompany such good qualities, and that no man or woman of scandalous behaviour shall enter the company. This

o

happens very seldom, for all the rumours that are heard everywhere, which are often false. It is a fact that actors' families are
usually well regulated and that life among them is honest; that is
what reasonable people know, so they are courteous towards actors
and help them when necessary.'

A little later, Germain Brice also wrote that 'the theatre is far
less dissolute than of late. Good manners and modesty are much
better observed than ever. . . . There is not much difference between
an actor and any other man.'

M. de Tralage, La Reynie's nephew, is more careful in his manuscript notes. Among players he finds people of two sorts: those
'who live well, regularly and even in a Christian fashion', like
Molière, La Grange, Poisson, Beauval, Floridor, Raisin, and the
'debauched' ones, like Baron, 'a great gambler and common pur-
suer of pretty women'; Molière's wife 'often kept by people of
quality and separated from her husband', Brécourt, La Tuillerie,
Rosimond and the Champmeslés, 'who parted because of their
debauchery. The wife was with child by her lover while Champmeslé himself, at the same time, had fathered a child upon his
servant. Their love adventures would fill a book.'

There were several well-known actors who lived a fairly riotous
life. Montfleury's daughter, Mlle Dupin of the Théâtre Guénégaud, who had a sensational lawsuit with Molière's widow and was
temporarily expelled, was compromised in the Poison Affair, and
so was Mlle du Parc. La Voisin swore that she had managed to
miscarry, that she wished her husband's death so that she might
marry a notary's son, and that her servant supplied her with 'love
potions'. One cannot believe what the sorceress said, but it is
certain that Mlle Dupin, like many women of the nobility and the
bourgeoisie, came to her kitchen.

Brécourt's story was darker. The son of Beaulieu, who had
married Etiennette des Urlis, he belonged to various theatres
(Marais, Palais-Royal, Hôtel de Bourgogne, Comédie-Française) as
an actor and a playwright. But he often left Paris to tour the
provinces and Holland with the Prince of Orange's company. He
had a violent temper, was a remarkable swordsman and had an
excessive love of wine, gaming and women. Among seventeenth-
century actors he stands out as an extraordinary scoundrel. His
contemporaries knew him as such. Brossette relates that Brécourt
once called on Boileau to read him one of his comedies, and coolly

told him that the author's character is always reflected in his works, and that one had to be a perfectly respectable man to look as such when writing. Then Brécourt reminded the satirist of his celebrated lines:

> *En vain l'esprit est plein d'une noble vigueur;*
> *Le vers se sent toujours des bassesses du coeur;*[1]

Boileau replied with irony: 'I agree that your example serves to confirm the rule.'

Brécourt was in The Hague in 1681. He was in disgrace. Thrice running had Louis XIV pardoned him for rather hurried blows of his sword, but in a further brawl he killed a coachman. He had therefore to go abroad, but after two years he felt his penance had lasted long enough. He sought an opportunity to draw the King's favourable regard.

At that time a man called Sardan, who had stolen the tax money in Le Puy and was compromised in many dirty episodes, had avoided punishment by escaping abroad and spying successively for Spain and Holland. Under various names, such as Mirande, Marquis, Dauphin, this unsavoury person had made treaties with Spain and with William of Orange to favour the actions of rebels.

M. d'Aveux, the French Ambassador in Holland, heard that Sardan was there and vainly asked his extradition from the Burgomaster of Amsterdam. The rogue had managed to get himself recorded as a burgher of Amsterdam under the assumed name of Comte de St-Paul. Louis XIV, to whom d'Avaux had explained the problem, decided to have Sardan kidnapped, entrusting the task to a man called Le Beau. Brécourt, who had just put on a comedy in The Hague for the Comtesse de Soissons (another exile), thought that by taking part in the kidnapping he might secure a pardon.

He made contact with Le Beau and the latter asked Louvois to send an officer and a few dragoons. Lieutenant La Garrigue was sent out from the Ypres garrison with ten men; they arrived at Brill on November 25, 1681. On the 27th, at nine in the morning, Le Beau, Brécourt and the soldiers were at Amsterdam. The next day Brécourt provided the soldiers with bayonets, hand grenades and pistols. The wily actor had called on Sardan and had managed to secure an invitation to dinner on the 29th so as to do his dirty trick more easily. But one of the soldiers, who was greatly worried, deserted and went to the Prince of Orange to confess, adding that the plot was directed against him. Meanwhile the others had

[1] Vainly is the spirit full of noble vigour; verses always taste of the heart's baseness.

surrounded Sardan's house and failed to grab him. After the failure, Le Beau ordered the soldiers to run away, which they did, throwing their weapons into the sea.

William of Orange thought he was in danger. He had the men closely followed and they were all arrested in Rotterdam, while Brécourt sought safety in Brussels, leaving the task of settling his debts to others. The lieutenant and his men were manacled and taken back to The Hague. Louis XIV told d'Avaux to claim the soldiers, but the Prince found there a good reason to discredit France. On December 13th the lieutenant was sentenced to death and the soldiers to permanent exile. After new explanations supplied by d'Avaux, La Garrigue was pardoned at the last minute, when he was already blindfolded, on the scaffold.

The plot was a failure, yet Brécourt's daring carried him through. He crossed the frontier, arrived in St Germain unannounced and 'threw himself at the King's feet, to thank him for his third pardon for the service he had only wished to give the King in Amsterdam'. Louis XIV pardoned him for the last time and Brécourt re-entered the Comédie-Française on half-pay, where he shared with Rosimont and Raisin the parts that Molière had once played. But he did not settle down. The next year he was arrested for debt and his companions had to club together to free him.

We have no wish to place these rather shady episodes on the same level as the actors' love affairs. But we cannot let them pass while writing about the manners of the time. Everyone knew of the liaisons between Racine and Mlle du Parc and Mlle de Champmeslé, and all the 'devilries' that developed from them, as they were described by Mme de Sévigné.

Paris theatres had no monopoly of society scandals. Mademoiselle's travelling company came to Paris in 1661 and gave performances in the Faubourg St Germain. They were managed by Dorimond for a short while. One day his wife, Marie Dumont, ran away with the porter of the company, Pierre Auzillon, taking her seven-year-old daughter and all her wardrobe with her. This family drama disorganized the whole company, which left for Brussels while Dorimond gave instructions to his father and his brother to find the fugitive and, if he could not get them censored by the church, to complain to the criminal lieutenant at the Châtelet. The girl was found and restored to her father, but the two culprits were safely hidden and not to be found. Indeed, they never were. Only after the death of Dorimond (who, strange to say, had written an *Ecole des Cocus* that same year) Marie Dumond and her lover were married in church, and they went back to the Hotel Guénégaud, she as an actress, he as the porter.

In Mlle Beauval, Philandre's natural daughter, we have a very different case; she led a most bourgeois life and, according to a tradition, had twenty-eight children! Tradition has obviously been too generous, but the registers still account for eleven Beauval children.

By the end of the century the court's intrusion into the administration of the Comédie-Française multiplied the number of patrons of actors and especially of actresses, leading to scandals, some of which were notorious, like the Dauphin's liaison with Mlle Raisin, who had a daughter by him. There were songs written about it:

> *Muse, célébrons la gloire*
> *De notre illustre Dauphin;*
> *Eternisons la mémoire*
> *Des amis de la Raisin.*

> *Elle porte dans son sein*
> *Un comédien d'importance*
> *On dit, mais je n'en sais rien,*
> *Que c'est un enfant de France*[2]

The King gave a 10,000 livres pension to the mother, but had it cancelled when Monseigneur died.

We ought to mention the flirtations of Armande Béjart which made Molière suffer so much, but whose infidelity has never been proved. Others were certainly much more fickle:

> *On dit que chez la Dancourt*
> *On y joue au jeu de l'amour,*
> *Ce n'est qu'une médisance;*
> *Son carrosse et sa dépense*
> *Sont les fruits de sa beauté,*

[2] O Muse, let us celebrate the glory of our illustrious Dauphin; let us immortalize the memory of Mme Raisin's friends. She has conceived a most important player. Some say he is a child of France but I know nothing about that.

> *Mais son automne s'avance,*
> *C'est la pure vérité.*[3]

Of course, dancers and singers, under the unflattering name 'opera girls', took the main part in this gallant chronicle. Usually they were unmarried, but were kept by rich protectors who often promised to marry them but hardly ever kept their promises. At least they collected large rewards. M. de Tralage wrote: 'There is usually one of them with a belly ache and a bodice that has to be enlarged. There is no year when that does not happen. Thus, the Academy of Music is also an Academy of Love.'

> *Ce beau lieu fournit de belles*
> *A tous les gens d'à présent;*
> *Des Matins pour de l'argent,*
> *La Moreau pour des dentelles,*
> *La Grande Diart pour son pain*
> *La Rochois le fait pour rien.*[4]

We must not, however, be too harsh regarding these pleasant girls, actresses or singers, or too severe about their love affairs. Let us rather remember that they served Corneille, Racine, Molière and Lulli effectively. That is enough to entitle them to an enviable place in the history of the theatre.

[3] They say that in Mme Dancourt's house they play a love game: this is but slander. Her coach and all she spends are produced by her beauty, but autumn is near: this is the truth.

[4] This wonderful place provides beauties for everyone today; Matins for gold, La Moreau for lace, the fine Diart for bread, and La Rochois does it for nothing.

INDEX

Accesi, Italian company, 106
Actae Ecclesiae Mediolanensis (Cardinal Frederico Borromeo), 15
Actors in the seventeenth century as fashionable personalities, 31
condemnation of by the church, 16
debauchery among, 202
family life of, 199–206
marriages of, 199–200
pension scheme for, 97–8
public opinion of, 27–41
'rehabilitation' of in public opinion, 17
taxes paid by, 165
voice production by, 131–4
Alexandre (Boyer), 147
Alexandre (Racine), 65, 66, 69, 144, 147
Alfieri, Jean-Paul, Italian company of, 49
Amours de Calotin (Chevalier), 36
Amours de Vénus et d'Adonis (Donneau de Visé), 172
Amphytrion, 88
Andreini, Gianbattista, 107
company of in Paris, 108
Andromaque (Racine), 66, 69, 70, 147
Andromède (Corneille), 80, 126, 172
Andromède et Persée, 79
Anne Christine-Victoire of Bavaria, influence on the Comédie-Française of, 98–9
Antiochus (Thomas Corneille), 66
Apologie due Théâtre (Scudéry), 29
Ariadne et Bacchus (Perrin), 114, 115
Arlecchino, 18, 108
Arminius (Capistron), 99
Artaxeres (Magon), 84
Attila (Corneille), 144
Aucart, Marie (musician), 195

Aurelio, 110
Auzillon, Pierre, 204
Auzoult, Marie, 200

Bajazet, 70
Ballet des Saisons, 69
Balzac, 29
Baptiste the Florentine, *see* Lulli
Baron, André, 60, 63, 77, 99, 146
transferred to the Royal company, 77
Baron, family of actors, 200
Baron, Mlle, financial position of, 145
Baron, Michel, 189, 200
Baron Pere, André, 76
Beaubourg, 198
Beauchamp, Jean, 187
Beauchamp, Nicolas, *see* Biet-Beauchamp, Nicolos
Beauchâteau, 53
as understudy to Floridor, 63
transferred to the Royal Company, 77
Beauchâteau, Mlle, 63
Beaulieu, 74, 182, 184, 191, 202
Beaupré, 73, 76
Beaupré, Mlle, 64
financial position of, 145
retirement of, 81
Beauval, 82, 202
Beauval, Mlle, daughter of Philandre, 184, 205
Béjart, Armande, 145, 205
married to Molière, 90
Béjart, famous family of actors, 199
Béjart, Madeleine, 23, 81, 84–5, 90, 190
death of, 91
financial position of, 145–6
Bellefleur, 195
Bellefleur, Mlle de, 196
Bellemore, 76
Belleroche, *see* Poisson, Raymond

Bellerose, 48, 54, 57, 58, 59, 66, 77, 142, 200
  achievements in the Royal Company, 60–1
  directing the Royal Company, 60
  financial position of, 145
  one of the great seventeenth-century actors, 67
  trained by le Conte, 157
  trying to disrupt the Théâtre du Marais, 75
Bellevilee, see Turlupin
Benserade, 62
Bergeries (Racan), 54
Bertrand, Alexandre, theatre of pulled down, 112
Biancolelli, Domenico, see Arlecchiono
Biet Beauchamp, Charles, 196
Biet-Beauchamp, Nicolas, 79, 192, 195, 200
Biet, Jean, see Beauchamp, Jean
Biet fils, Nicolas, 193
Billaut, Adam (poet), 65
Boesset (King's Superintendent of Music), 114
Boileau, 203
Boiron, André, see Baron
Boisrobert, 80, 88, 147
Boisvert, 190
Boisvert, Mlle, 196
Bojart, Armande, 83
Boncourt, 196
Bossuet, 24
  controversy with Caffaro, 38–9, 41
Bourgeois, Catherine, 187
Boursault, 35, 145
Boyer, Abbé, 82, 98, 126, 127, 145, 147
Brécourt, 23, 81, 82, 98, 146
  life of as an actor, 202–3
Brighella (Italian actor), 52
Buffequin, Denis (designer), 79, 80, 81, 82, 127

Cadmus et Hermione (grand opera), 119
Caffaro, 24
  controversy with Bossuet, 38–9, 41

Campistron, 98, 99
Catholic Church, mystery plays staged by, 14
Champeron
  dealings with the Comédie-Française, 93, 95
  dealings with the Paris Opera, 115–19
Champmeslé, 70, 72, 82, 140, 202
Champmeslé, Mlle, 69–71, 82, 98, 104, 122, 204
  death of, 71
  entering the Hotel Guénégaud company, 69, 95
  relationship with Racine, 70–1
Chapoton, 79
Chapuzeau, Samuel, 37–8, 66, 72, 88, 122, 129, 136, 139, 148, 162, 182, 201
  describing provincial theatre, 156–8
Châteauneuf, Pierre, 197, 198
Chevalier, 36, 81, 146
Chevillet, Charles, see Champmeslé
Christina, Queen of Sweden, patron to Philandre, 183–4
Chryséide et Arimant (Mairet), 54
Church
  attitude towards actors in seventeenth century, 13–26, 166
  influence on the theatre of, 13–26, 166
Cinna, 86
Circé (Chapoton), 79
Circé (T. Corneille), 94, 95, 144
Clavel, 170
Cléopâtre (Benserade), 62
Cleopâtre (Mairet), 147
Clerselier, Denis, see Nanteuil
Clitandre (Corneille), 74
Cocu Imaginaire (Molière), 37, 147
Coirat (Belleroche), 196
Comédie des Comédiens, 31
Comédie des Tuileries, 60
Comédie Française, 83, 97–104, 145
  building of, 103–4
  Etoile tennis courts as site for, 103
  first performance at Hôtel Guénégand by, 98
  inauguration of, 59

La Grange as administrator of, 99

Mlle Champmeslé at, 70

performances of, 121

Raymond Poisson at, 72

royal monopolies over, 60

supervision by the Dauphine in, 17

Comici Confederati, in the Hôtel de Bourgogne, 106

Company of the Holy Sacrement, in campaign against the theatre, 34

Condé, Grand, as patron to Molière, 179

Confrères de la Passion, 56, 61, 73

in conflict with the Royal Company, 57–9

influence on the theatre of, 45–55

Convive de Pierre, 109

Corneille, Pierre, 16, 28, 31, 33, 40, 60, 62, 64, 65, 73, 75, 76, 80, 81, 82, 83, 88, 98, 122, 124, 126, 127, 143, 144, 155–6, 184, 200, 206

influence on the theatre of, 30

success of, 77

writing for Montdory, 74

writing for the Royal Company, 61, 79

Corneille, Thomas, 66, 79, 80, 84, 88, 94, 144, 145

Corneille's heroic theatre, influence on female public of, 30

Costume

splendour of in the Parisian theatre, 129

use of in French theatre, 128, 130

Coups de l'amour et de la fortune (Boisrobert), 147

Critique de l'école des femmes (Molière), 30

Dancourt, 146

Dassoucy, 178

D'Aubignac, Abbé, 33–4, 37, 123

Dauvilliers, 99, 200

De Beauchamp, Mlle, 195

De Beauchamp, Nicolas, *see* Biet-Beauchamp, Nicolas

De Belin, Comte, as protector of the Théâtre du Marais, 74

De Bourbon, Henri-Jules, as patron of the theatre, 187

De Condé, Prince, 189

patron to the theatre, 183, 187–188

De Conti, Prince, patron to Molière, 177

De Fatouville, Nolant (writer), 110

De Gorla, Giacomo, 191

De Gorla, Marquise-Thérèse, *see* Du Parc, Mlle

De Guise, Duc, patron of art, 190

Deierkauf-Holsboer, Mme, 78

De la Chappe, Jeanne, 66, 200

De la Fratte, Mlle, 196

De Lan, François, 192

De Lan, Hugues, 190, 193

De Lan, Marguerite, 193

De la Source, Mlle, 191

De la Tessonnerie, Gillet, 79

De Modène, Comte, patron of art, 190

De Molin, Tirso, 193

De Mollier, Louis, 82

D'Ennebaut, 82

D'Ennebaut, Françoise Mathieu, 200

D'Eperon, Duc, patron to Molière, 177

De Rieu, Michel, 187

De Roserat, Jean, 191

De St Sorlin, Desmarets, 33

De Sévigné, Charles, 70

De Sévigné, Mme, 70–1, 204

Desfontaine, Nicolas, 84

Desgilberts, Guillaume, *see* Montdory

Desmares, Marie, *see* Champmeslé, Mlle

Desmarets, 197

Des Oeillets, Mlle, 67, 70, 81, 82, 122

financial position of, 145

De Soulas, Josias, *see* Floridor

Des Réaux, Tallemand, 62, 76

D'Estriché, 83

Des Urlis, Catherine, 81, 93

Des Urlis, Etienette, 202

De Tonnere, 71

De Viau, Théophile, 16, 54, 59
De Villiers, 72, 146
De Visé, Donneau, 35, 72, 82, 88, 90, 94, 127–8, 145, 147, 172
first dramatic critic, 65
Dom Juan (Molière), 20, 36, 39, 69, 88, 126, 127
Dom Juan (new version by T. Cornielle), 94, 145
Don Juan (Tirso de Molina), 193
D'Orbay, François, architect of the Comédie-Française, 100–4
Dorimond, Louis, 146, 172, 192, 193, 196, 204
D'Orléans, Gaston, as patron of the theatre, 190
D'Ouville, 78
Dramatic literature, growth of in the seventeenth century, 27
Dramatic technique, first study of, 34
Drouin, Nicolas, 192
Du Croissy, 62
Dufresny, 110
Du Landas, Joseph, see Dupin
Dumont, Marie, 193
love affair of, 204–5
Du Parc, 81, 85
Du Parc, Mlle, 67–9, 81, 122, 162, 191, 200, 202, 304
death of (1668), 69
relationship with Molière, 68
relationship with Racine, 69
Dupin, Joseph, 192
Du Pin, Louise Jacob, 23
Dupin, Louise Joseph, 200
Dupin, Mlle, 22, 202
Du Raincy, 196, 197
Du Rieu, Michel, 185
Du Ryer, 16, 59, 79, 84
Dutch court, theatre banned in, 195

Ecolier de Salamanque (Scarron), 72
Esope à la cour (Bousault), 145
Esope à la ville (Bousault), 145
Etiennette, Hubert, 81

Farce
end of classical in the Théâtre de Bourgogne, 59
performed in the seventeenth century, 28

revival of in Paris, 86
Favart, 111
Festin de Pierre ou l'Athée foudroyé (Tirso de Molina), 193
Fête de Vénus (Boyer), 82
Finta Pazza (Italian opera by Sacrati), 79, 108, 126
Fiorelli, Tiberio, see Scaramuccio
Fléchelle, see Gaultier-Garguilles
Floridor, 17, 63, 77, 78, 180, 181, 200, 202
as one of the great seventeenth-century actors, 67
as successor to Bellerose, 64
career of, 64–5
favoured by Louis XIV, 66–7
financial position of, 146
joining the Royal Company (1647), 60, 78–9
Floridor, Charles, 197–8
Francion (Charles Sorel), 108
Free companies (without a protector), 160–74

Gacon, 39
Galanteries du duc d'Ossone (Mairet), 30
Ganasse, Albert, 106
Gassot, Nicole, 200
Gassot, Philibert, see Du Croissy
Gaultier-Garguilles, 28, 48, 53, 179
death of, 59
Gelosi, Italian company in Paris, 106
Georges Dandin (Molière), 89
Germanicus (Boursault), 83
Gherardi, historian of the Italian theatre, 105
Gilbert, 88
Gougenot, 31, 147
Goyot, Mlle, 83
Gros-Guillaume, 28, 30, 53, 179
company of, 46–55, 57, 64
death of (1634), 59
success in Paris of, 50
Gros-René, 67
Guérin, Charles, 197
See also L'Espérance
Guérin, Marguerite, 197
Guérin, Robert, 182, 184, 185
company of, 73
See also Gros-Guillaume
Guérin, Victoire, 200

Guéru, Hugues, *see* Gaultier-Garguilles

Hardy, Alexandre (poet), 47, 49, 53, 60, 179
  struggle for recognition of, 142
  writing for the Royal Company, 59, 61
Hautefeuille, 191
Hauteroche, 72, 146
  as one of the great seventeenth-century actors, 67
Héraclitus, 79
Hervé, Marie, 200
Histoire due Théatre due Marais (Mme Deierkauf-Holsboer), 78
Hôtel D'Argent, 49
  Robert Guérin's company in, 57
Hôtel de Bourgogne, 18, 30, 31, 36, 48, 49, 54, 64, 86, 87, 94
  actors at, 27, 28
  amalgamated with Hôtel Guénégaud, 97–8
  comedy writers at, 71
  company of, 28, 35
  influence on the theatre of, 45–55
  modernization of, 61
  period of glory of, 64
  Royal Company at, 56–72
  specializing in literary drama, 59–60
  taken over by Italian company, 72
  See also Royal Company
Hôtel Guénégaud, 22
  amalgamated with Hôtel de Bourgogne, 97–8
  King's Company at, 92–6
  Palais-Royal company moved into, 93

Illustre Théâtre, 84, 158, 190, 192
  struggles of, 85
Impromptu du l'Hôtel de Condé (Montfleury *fils*), 147
Iphigénie (Racine), 94, 148
Italian Comedy
  expelled by Louis XIV, 111
  importance of in the French theatre, 105–12
  maintained by the king, 110

Jacob, Zacharie, *see* Montfleury
Jodelet, 59, 60, 64, 74, 77, 81, 90
  financial position of, 145
  ordered to act in the Royal Company, 75
  working for Molière, 78
Jodelet (d'Ouville), 78
Jolimont, 196
Judith (Boyer), 145

King's Comedians, 54
King of England's company, 195
King's Company
  at the Hôtel Guénégaud, 92–6
  at the Palais-Royal, 84–91
  at the Théâtre due Marais, 73–83

La Brie, 86
La Calprenède, 30
La Comédie des Comédiens, 147
La Comtesse d'Escarbagnas (Molière), 88
La Couture, 190
La Critique de l'école des femmes (Molière), 35, 69, 88
La Descente d'Orphée aux Enfers (Chapoton), 79, 82
La Devineresse (T. Corneille and de Visé), 95, 145
La Fausse Prude, scandal of, 110–111
La Fête de Vénus (Boyer), 127
La Fille Vice-Roi (Nanteuil), 169
La Fleur, *see* Gross-Guillaume and Guérin, Robert
La Fleur, Mme, 64
La Galerie du Palais (Corneille), 74
La Grange, 87, 202
  as administrator of the Comédie-Française, 99
  manager at the Palais-Royal, 92
La Grange-Chancel, 98
La Maison des Jeux (Charles Sorel), 128
L'Amante invisible (Nanteuil), 169
La Mesnardière, 123
La Mort d'Adonis (Perrin), 114
La Mort d'Asdrubal (Montfleury), 66
La Mort de César (Scudéry), 76

La Mort de Mithridate (La Calprenède), 30
L'Amour médecin (Molière), 88, 90
L'Amour Sentinelle (Naneuil), 168
La Naissance d'Hercule (Boyer), 126
La Pastorale comique (Molière), 90
La Place royale (Corneille), 74
L'Apologie de Guillot-Gorju (popular farce 1634), 30
Laporte, 49, 187
La Princesse d'Elide (Molière), 90
La Railleur (Mareschal), 76
La Roque, 75, 79, 81, 83, 145
  as manager of the Marais Company, 80
La Serre, 66
La Source, 193, 194, 195, 196, 197, 198
La Suite du Menteur, 78
La Suivante (Corneille), 74
La Thorillière, 81, 82, 200
La Toison d'Or (Corneille), 81, 82, 127
La Tuilerie, 72, 146, 200
Le Veuve (Corneille), 74
La Voisin, 202
Le Bourgois Gentilhomme (Molière), 83, 89, 90, 113, 172
Le Cid (Corneille), 16, 20, 122, 124, 155-6
  attempt to censor, 30
  overwhelming success of, 76-7
  quarrel over, 33
Le Cocu Imaginaire (Molière), 86, 144
L'Ecole des femmes (Molière), 35, 36, 87, 88, 147
Le Comte de Roquefeuille, ou le Docteur extravagant (Nanteuil), 168
Le conte, Valleran, 27, 46-55, 50, 51, 57, 62, 77, 157, 201
Lecouvreur, Adrienne, 23
Le Dépit amoureux (Molière), 86
Le Docteur amoureux (Molière), 86
Le Febvre, Mathieu, *see* Laporte
Le Festin de Pierre (Dorimond), 172
Le Folle querelle (Subligny), 147

Le Grand, 146
Le Grand divertiseement de Versailles (Molière), 89
Legrand, Henri, *see* Turlupin
Leibintz, 39
Lelio, 111
Le Malade imaginaire (Molière), 19, 89, 91, 92, 94
Le Mariage de Bacchus et d'Ariane (De Visé), 82, 127, 128
Le Mariage Forcé, 69
Le Médecin malgré lui, 104
Le Mercure galant (Donneau de Visé), 82, 93, 94, 95
Le Messier, Pierre, *see* Bellerose
Le Misanthrope (Molière), 20, 69, 88, 90, 92
Le Noir, Charles, 54, 57, 60, 73
  costumes of, 129
  death of, 77
  financial position of, 145
  ordered to perform in the Royal Company, 75
Le Noir, Charlotte, 200
Le Noir, Mlle, 64
Le Noir, Mme, 54, 60, 74
  ordered to perform in the Royal Company, 75
Le Poète basque et Le Baron de la Crasse (Raymond Poisson), 72
Le Riche, Toussaint, *see* Hautefeuille
Le Roy, Catherine, 200
Le Sac de Carthage (la Serre), 66
Le Sage, 72
Les Amants magnifiques (Molière), 90
Les Amours de Diane et d'Endymion, 116
Les Amours de Jupiter et de Sémélé (Abbé Boyer), 82, 127
Les Amours de Vénus et d'Adonis (Donneau de Visé), 82, 127
Les Amours du Soleil, 82
Les Comédiens de Mademoiselle, 192
Les Facheux (Molière), 88, 89, 144
Les femmes savantes (Molière), 33, 88
Les Fêtes de l'Amour et de Bacchus, 119

Les Fourberies de Scypin (Molière), 88
Le Sicilien (Molière), 90
L'Espérance, 167
  See also Guérin, Charles
Les Plaisirs de l'Île Enchantée (Molière), 89, 90
Le Précieuses Ridicules (Molière), 59, 86, 88, 90, 131, 144, 147
L'Espy, 60, 74, 81
  financial position of, 145
  ordered to act in the Royal Company, 75
  return to Théâtre Marais of, 77
  working for Molière, 86
Les Véritables Précieuses (Somaize), 86, 147
L'Etourdi (Molière), 86
Le Triomphe de l'Amour, 117
Le Trompeur puni (m. de Scudéry), 75
L'Heritier imaginaire (Nanteuil), 169
L'Illusion Comique (Corneille), 31, 76
L'Impromptu de l'Hôtel de Condé (Montfleury-*fils*), 36, 188
L'Impromptu de Versailles (Molière), 31, 35, 63, 65, 67, 69, 88, 121, 131, 147, 188
Locatelli, Domenico, see Trivelin
Loiseau, Gilberte, 190
Longchamp, 187, 188, 200
Louis XIV, as patron of the theatre, 186, 193
Lulli, 17, 18, 83, 97, 113, 206
  acquiring monopoly of opera, 117–18
  difficulties with Molière, 89
  given the Palais-Royal, 92
  granted directorship of the Royal Academy of Music, 118
  success of 119–20

Mademoiselle d'Orléans, 192
  company of, 192, 193, 194, 196, 198
Magon, 84
Mairet, 16, 28, 29, 30, 53, 54, 59, 64, 76, 124, 155

Maison des Jeux (Charles Sorel), 60
Mantua company, in Paris (1623), 108
Marais, the, see Théâtre du Marais
Marc Antoine (Mairet), 76
Marcoureau, Antoine, 191
Marcoureau, Pierre, see Beaulieu
Mareschal, 76
Marianne (Tristan l'Hermite), 28, 76
Marivaux, 111
Martinelli, Tristano, 106–7
Mattée, Jean, see Philandre
Maximes et Réflexions sur la Comédie (Bossuet), 24
Médée (Corneille), 76, 124
Medici, Marie de, 106–7
Mélicerte (Molière), 90
Mélite (Pierre Corneille), 73, 74
Mellet, Claudine, 187
Mères Coquettes (Donneau de Visé), 147
Mères Coquettes (Quinault), 147
Meunier, Angélique, 180
Millot, Anne, 192
Millot, Philippe, 192, 193, 195, 196
Mirame (Desmarets), 16, 28, 60, 122, 126
Molière, 16, 18, 24, 30, 31, 33, 35, 37, 39, 40, 59, 62, 63, 65, 67, 71, 72, 81, 82, 98, 113, 118, 121, 126, 147, 158, 188, 189, 199, 200, 202, 204, 205, 206
  abandoned by the king, 83
  as actor and playwright, 146
  as cause of rivalry in the theatre, 35–6
  at Nantes (1649), 162
  at Pézénas (1653), 162
  creating ballet-comedy, 89
  death of, 19–20, 83, 91, 92, 119
  difficulties with Lulli, 89
  financial position of, 140, 145–6
  forming the *Illustre Théâtre*, 84
  gift of mimicry of, 132–4
  given the old Palais-Royal, 87
  imprisonment of, 85
  literary fight of, 87
  marriage of, 90
  patrons of, 177
  payment received for plays by, 144

Molière (*cont.*)
  provincial career of, 84–5, 178–9
  relationship with Mlle du Parc,
    68
  relations with the Italian theatre,
    106
  reviving farce in Paris, 86, 88
  rivalry of with other companies,
    89
  status as an actor of, 17
  touring company of, 155
  use of theatrical costumes by, 129
Monchaingre, Jean, *see* Philandre
Monsieur de Pourceaugnac
  (Molière), 88, 90
Montdory, 28, 29, 48, 50, 123
  as best tragedian in Paris, 76
  as founder member of the Royal
    Company, 74
  as member of the Prince of
    Orange's company, 73
  financial position of, 145
  founding the Théâtre du Mar-
    ais, 74
  retirement of, 77
  trained by le Conte, 157
Montfleury, 66, 146, 200
  as one of the great seventeenth-
    century actors, 67
  mocked by Molière, 67
Montfleury *fils*, 72, 146, 147, 188
Mort de Crispe (Tristan), 84
Mort de Pompée (Corneille), 184
Mort de Sénèque (Tristan), 84
Mousson, Françoise, 196
Mystery plays, 14, 56

Naissance d'Hercule (Rotrou), 79
Nanteuil, 146, 167, 168, 169, 170,
  171, 197
  biography of, 167–74
  career of, 158, 173
  forming various companies, 167–
    173
Nicole, 35
Nicomède (Corneille), 66

Oedipe (Corneille), 65
Opera
  birth of, 113–20
  introduction of Italian, 16
  monopoly of granted to Lulli,
    97, 113

royal monopolies over, 60
Orfeo (Italian opera by Rossi), 79,
  126

Page disgracié (Tristan l'Hermite),
  201
Palais Cardinal, 60
  theatre built in (1630), 16
Palais-Royal theatre, 19, 28, 35, 59,
  71, 81, 121, 189
  amalgamated with Théâtre du
    Marais, 93, 97
  Italian opera at, 79
  King's company at the, 84–91
  Louis XIV at patron of, 89
  merger with Théâtre Marais, 83
  moving into the Hôtel Guéné-
    gaud, 93
  re-opening of, 92
Paris Opera House, official creation
  of (1669), 115
Paroles de musique (Perrin), 114
Patrons, in the theatre, 175–98
Pernay, Anne, 185
Perrault, 90
Perrin, Pierre
  director of the Paris Opera,
    114
  first idea of opera conceived by,
    113
  imprisonment of, 116–17
  translator of the *Aenid*, 113
Perside (Nicolas Desfontaine), 84
Petit, Benoît, joining with Val-
  leran, 47
Petit-Jean, Pierre Ragnault, *see* La
  Roque
Phèdre et Hippolyte (Pradon), 94,
  145, 148
Phèdre (Racine), 70, 98, 104, 148
Philandre, 79, 182, 184, 205
  career of, 180–9
  death of, 189
  patrons of, 182–4
  return to provinces of, 80
Pienes et Plaisirs de l'Amour, 117
Pinel, Georges, 185
Pitel, Henri, *see* Longchamp
Plaisirs de l'île enchantée, 69
  settings for, 125
Poète sans fard (Gacon), 39
Poetique (La Mesnardière), 123
Poisson, family of actors, 200

Poisson, Raymond, 71-2, 146, 200, 202
Polyeucte, 28, 30
Pomone, 115
Portrait du peintre (Boursault), 35
Pradon, 94, 98, 145, 148
Pratique du Théâtre (1657) (Abbé d'Aubignac), 33-4, 123
Précieuses ridicules (Molière), 35
Préflery, 197
Prince de Condé's company, 79, 179
Prince of Orange
  Montdory in the company of, 73
  patron to the theatre, 182, 186
Provincial theatres, 155-9
Psyché (Molière), 113, 119, 144
Pulchérie (Corneille), 83
Pyrame et Thisbé (Théophile de Vian), 54

Quinault, 80, 98, 113, 147
  highest paid dramatist, 145

Racan, 54, 59
Racine, 16, 23, 24, 40, 65, 66, 68, 79, 88, 94, 98, 122, 144, 147-51, 200, 204, 206
  relationship with Mlle Champmeslé, 70-1
  relationship with Mlle du Parc, 69
  turning against the theatre, 100-101
Raisin, 98, 99, 146, 202, 204
Raisin, Mlle, 205
Regnard, 72, 110
Riccoboni, see Lelio
Richelieu, Cardinal de, 25, 30, 33, 126, 145
  as protector of the Théâtre du Marais, 74
  building a theatre in the Palais Cardinal (1630), 16
  influence of on seventeenth-century theatre, 54
  supporting Montdory, 75, 77
Robert Guérin-Bellerose company, see Royal Company
Robin, Philibert, 79
Rodogune (Corneille), 62, 78
Romainville, 196, 198

Roman comique (Scarron), 85, 177, 199
Rosidor, 82, 146, 168, 195, 197, 200
Rosidor, Mlle, 195
Rosimond, 23, 82, 98, 146, 202, 204
  joining the Palais-Royal, 92
Rossi, 79
Rotrou, 16, 53, 79, 143
  struggle for recognition of, 142
  writing for the Royal Company, 59, 61
Royal Academy of Dancing and Music, founded by Louis XIV, 17
Royal Academy of Music, 120
  directorship granted to Lulli, 118
  first royal patronage of, 118
Royal Company, 56-72, 74
  in conflict with the Confrères de la Passion, 57
  settled in the rue Mauconseil (1629), 59
'Royal Company of Pygmees', 111
Royal Company of the Hôtel Guénégaud, 83
Royal declaration (1641) affirming dignity of theatre, 17

Sacrati, 79
St Laurent, fairs at, 111
St Germain-des-Prés, fairs at, 111
Sarasin, 162
Scaramouche, 86
Scaramuccio, 108
Scarron, 63, 72, 78, 85, 88, 177, 199
Scévole (du Ryer), 84
Scudéry, Georges de, 16, 29, 31, 33, 59, 75, 76
Serdin, François, 187
Sertorius (Corneille), 82
Silvanire (Mairet), 124
Somaize, 86, 147
Sophobisbe (Corneille), 65
Sophonisbe (Mairet), 28, 66, 155
Sorel, Charles, 60, 108, 123, 128
Sourdéac
  dealings with the Comédie-Française, 93, 95
  dealings with the Paris Opera, 115-19
Stage design, importance of, 124-7
Subligny, 147
Sylvie et Sylvanire (Mairet), 54

Tallemant des Réaux, 51, 63, 64, 114, 123
Tartuffe (Molière), 20, 24, 36, 39, 88, 91, 93, 144, 147, 197
Taxes, paid by actors, 165
Testament de Gaultier Garguilles, 63
Theatre
  advertisement of plays for, 136
  argument for and against Molière in, 35–6
  ban of Dutch court on, 195
  behaviour of audiences in, 134–5
  commercial rivalry in, 147–51
  company of the Holy Sacrament against the, 34
  contrast in, 157
  disorder in, 134–6
  history of the Parisian, 45
  importance of stage design in the, 124–7
  influence of the church on, 166
  in the provinces, 155–9
  merger with Palais-Royal, 83
  patrons of the, 175–6
  payment for seats in, 139–41, 164
  pension schemes in, 141
  performances in, 121–37
  role of authors in, 142–5
  struggle of the, 13–26
  under strict local authority, 163–164, 196
  use of a spokesman in, 136–7
Théâtre du Marais, 28, 31, 36, 54, 59, 60, 67, 70, 72, 145, 181
  amalgamated with the Palais-Royal, 93, 97
  closure of, 93
  destroyed by fire, 78
  Floridor at, 64
  founding of, 74
  King's company at the, 73–83
  rebuilding of, 78
  receiving royal grants, 74
  re-opening of (1644), 78
  revival of, 82
  struggles of, 78, 80
  success of, 74–5
  supported by Cardinal de Richelieu, 74
Théâtre du Petit Bourbon, 86
  pulled down, 87

Théâtre français (Chappuzeau), 38
Theatrical companies
  financial arrangements of, 138–146
  organization of, 138–51
Thébaïde (Racine), 144
Tite et Bérénice (Corneille), 144
Torelli, Giacomo, 108
Torelli, Jacques, 125
Traité contre les danses et les comedies, 15
Traité de la Comédie (Nicole), 35
Traité de la Comédie selon la Tradition de l'Eglise (Molière), 37
Trepeau, Rachel, first French actress, 53–5
Tristan L'Hermite, 28, 63, 76, 84, 201
Trivelin, 108
Turlupin, 28, 52, 53, 179
  death of (1637), 59

Ulysee dans l'îlede Circè (Boyer), 79, 126

Vallée, Marie, 82, 93
Valleran le Conte Company, 46–55
  joining with Benoît Petit, 47
Valliot, Mlle ('La Valliotte'), 64
Varlet, see Verneuil
Vautrel, François, 50, 179
Verneuil, 82
Vigarini, Charles, 125
Villabé, 187
Villiers, 73, 74
  joined the Hôtel de Bourgogne, 60
  managing the Marais company, 77
  transferred to the Royal Company, 77
Villiers, Mme, 60, 74
Virginie (Mairet), 29
Visionnaires (Desmarets de St Sorlin), 33

Zélinde ou la Vengeance des Marquis (Donneau de Visé), 35